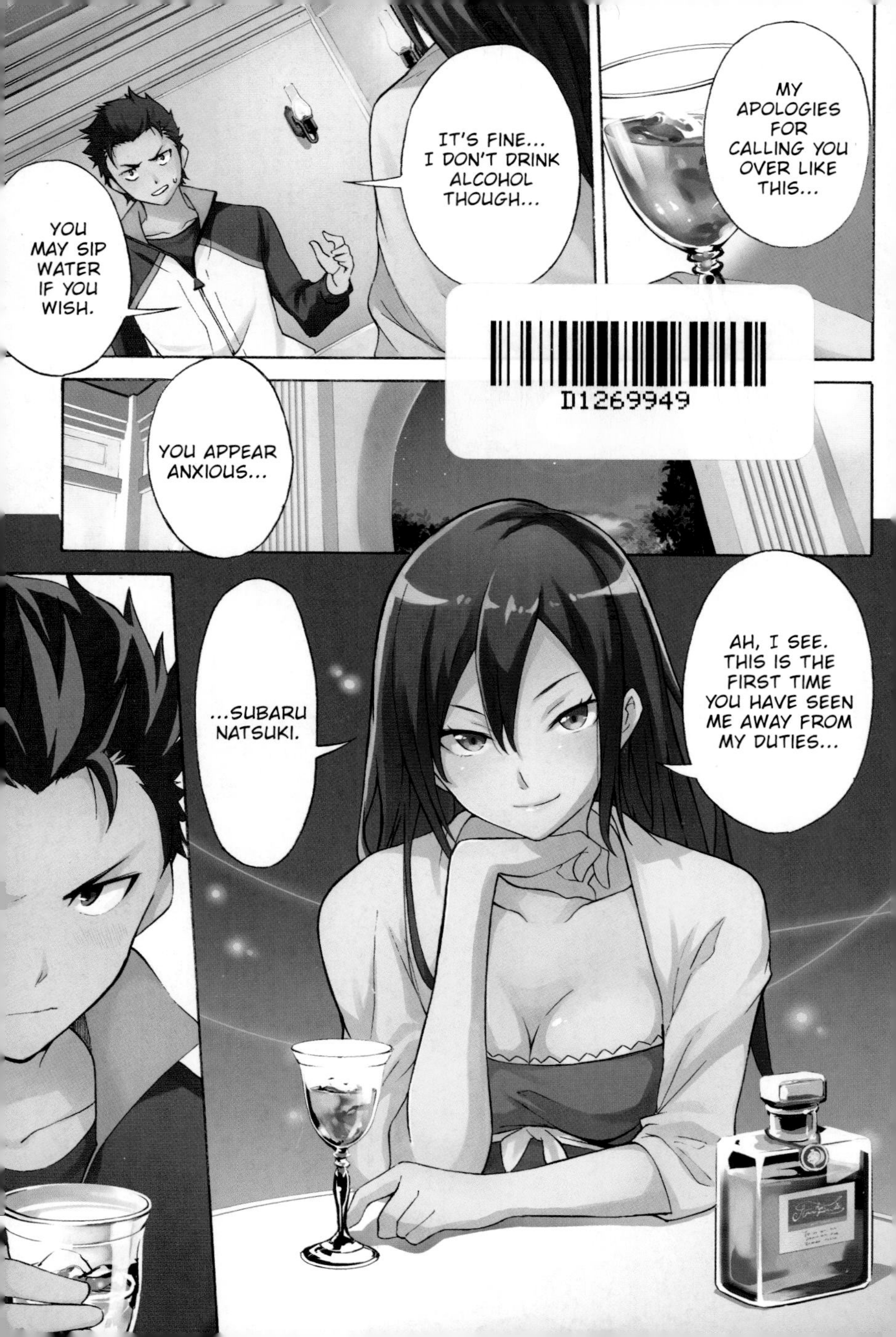
MY APOLOGIES FOR CALLING YOU OVER LIKE THIS...
IT'S FINE... I DON'T DRINK ALCOHOL THOUGH...
YOU MAY SIP WATER IF YOU WISH.
YOU APPEAR ANXIOUS...
AH, I SEE. THIS IS THE FIRST TIME YOU HAVE SEEN ME AWAY FROM MY DUTIES...
...SUBARU NATSUKI.

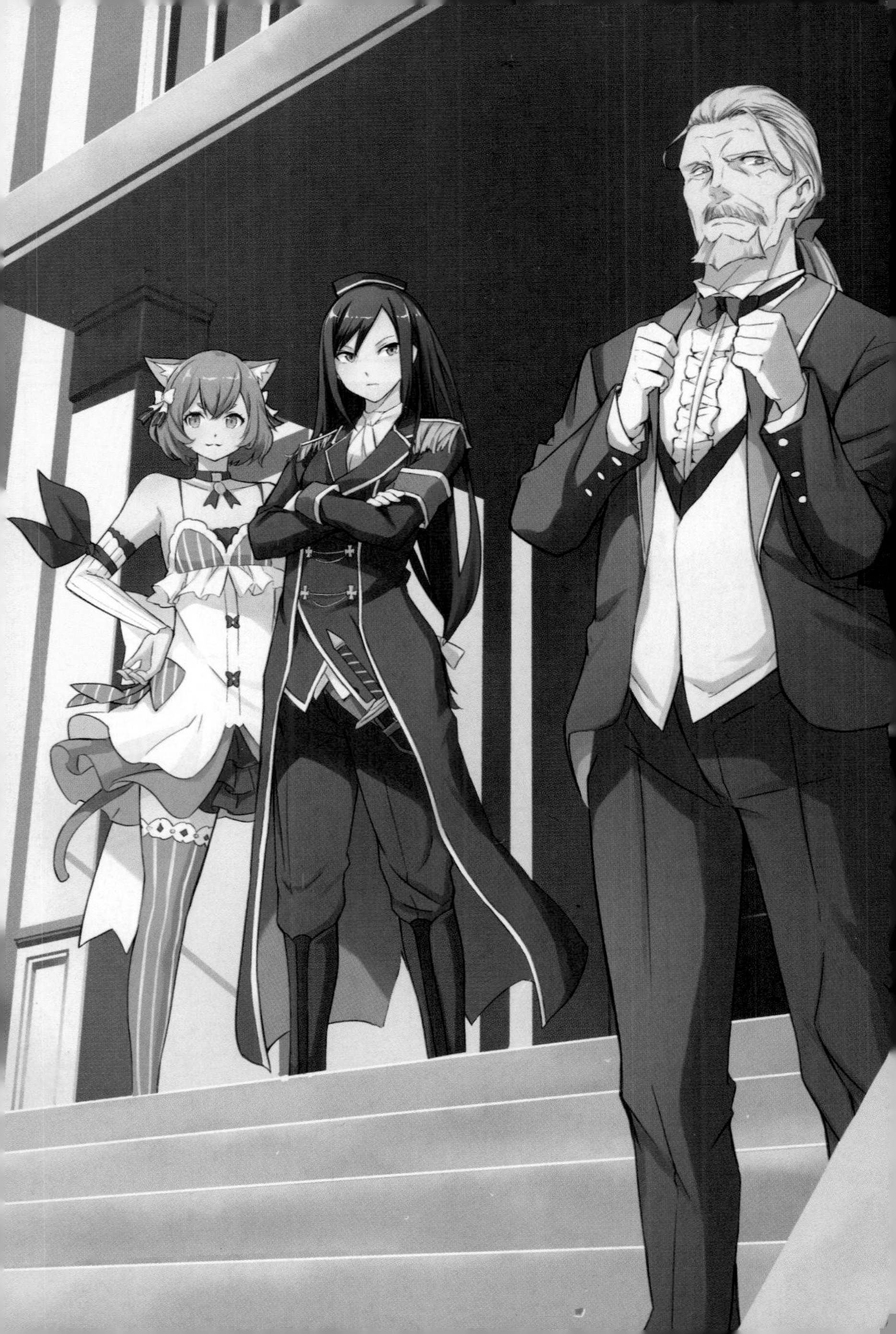

Episode 11

A Situation in Motion

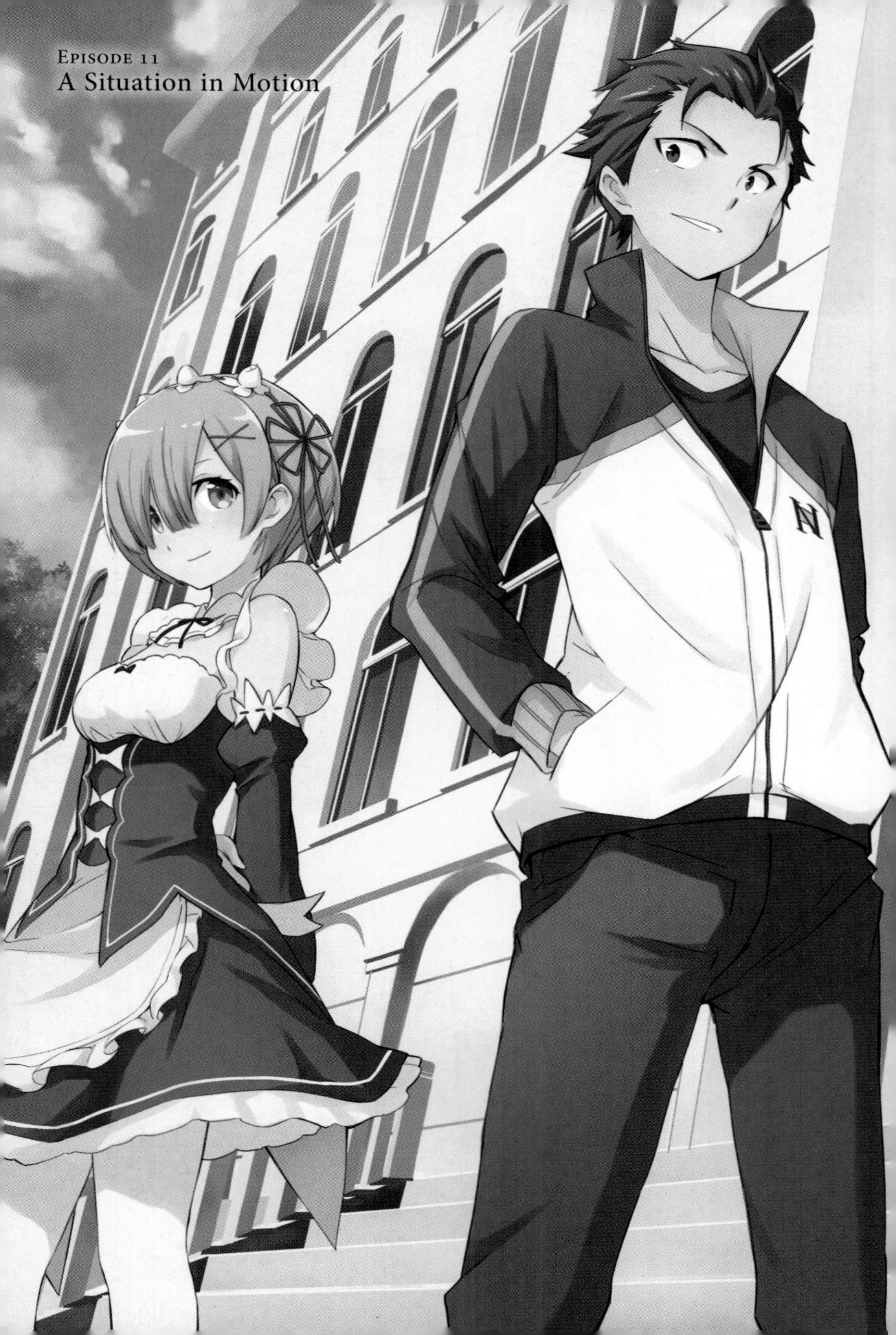

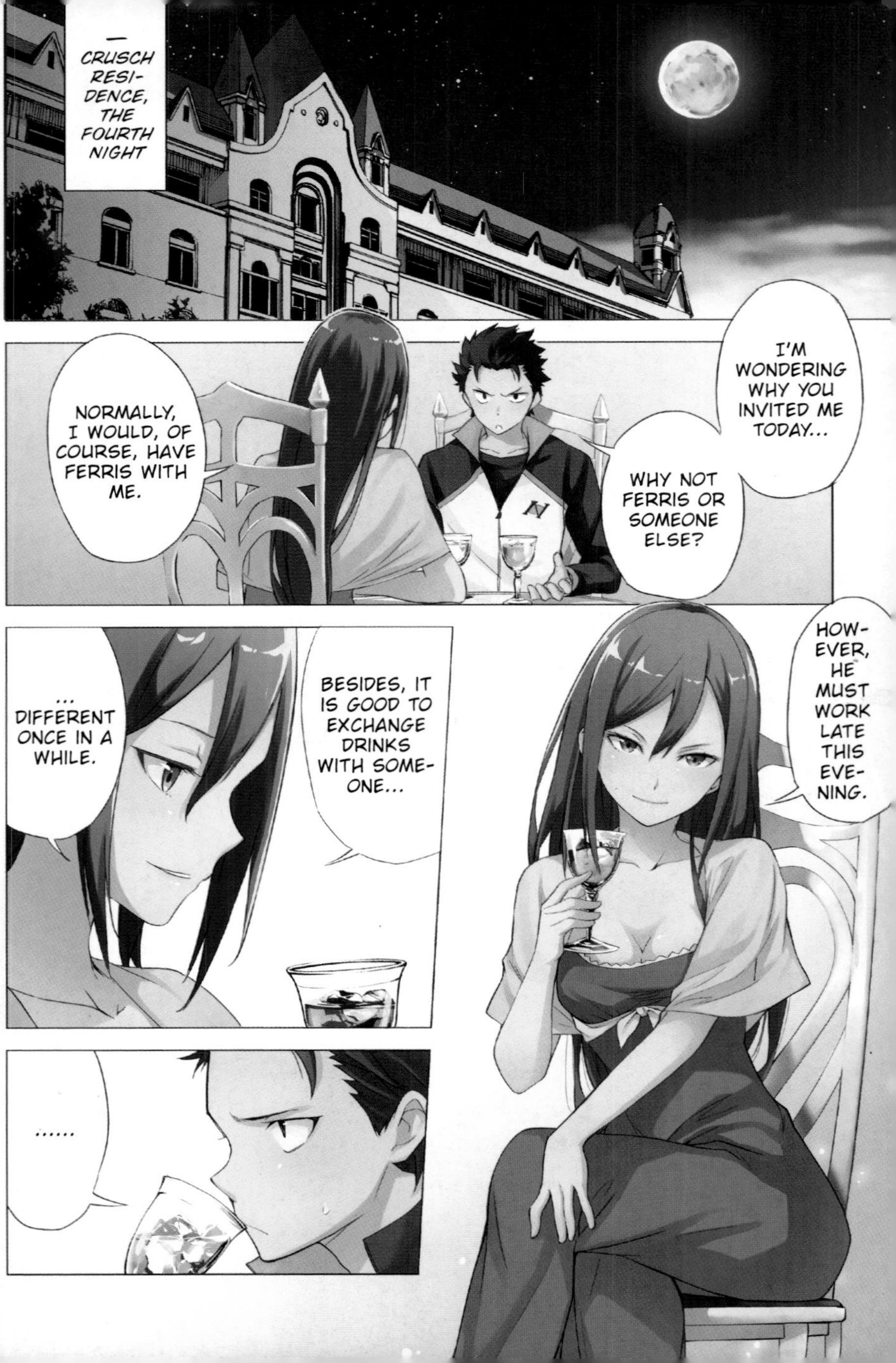
—CRUSCH RESIDENCE, THE FOURTH NIGHT
I'M WONDERING WHY YOU INVITED ME TODAY...
WHY NOT FERRIS OR SOMEONE ELSE?
NORMALLY, I WOULD, OF COURSE, HAVE FERRIS WITH ME.
HOWEVER, HE MUST WORK LATE THIS EVENING.
BESIDES, IT IS GOOD TO EXCHANGE DRINKS WITH SOMEONE...
...DIFFERENT ONCE IN A WHILE.
......

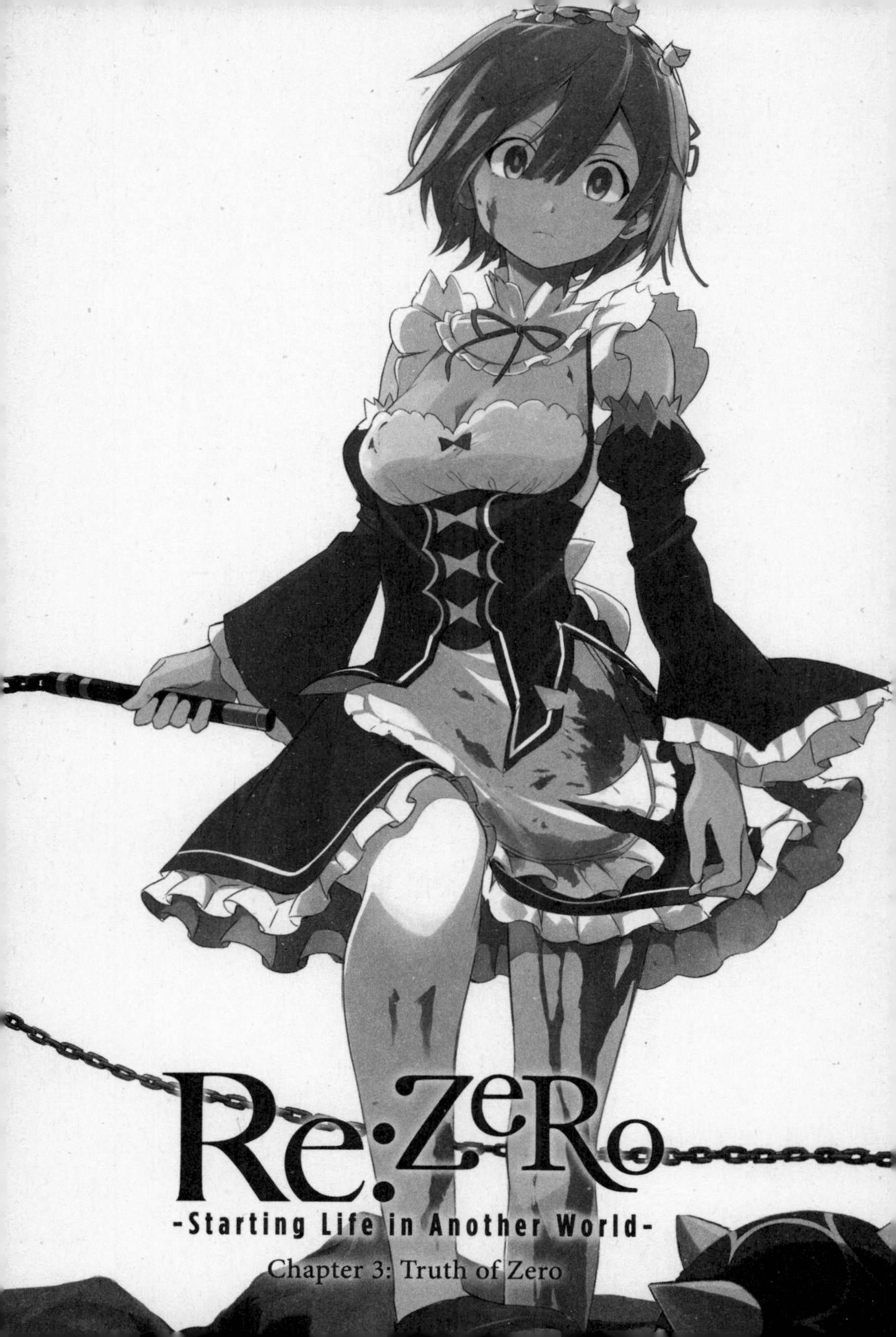
Re:ZeRo
-Starting Life in Another World-
Chapter 3: Truth of Zero

Re:ZERO -Starting Life in Another World-

Chapter 3: Truth of Zero

The only ability Subaru Natsuki gets when he's summoned to
another world is time travel via his own death. But to save her,
he'll die as many times as it takes.

Contents

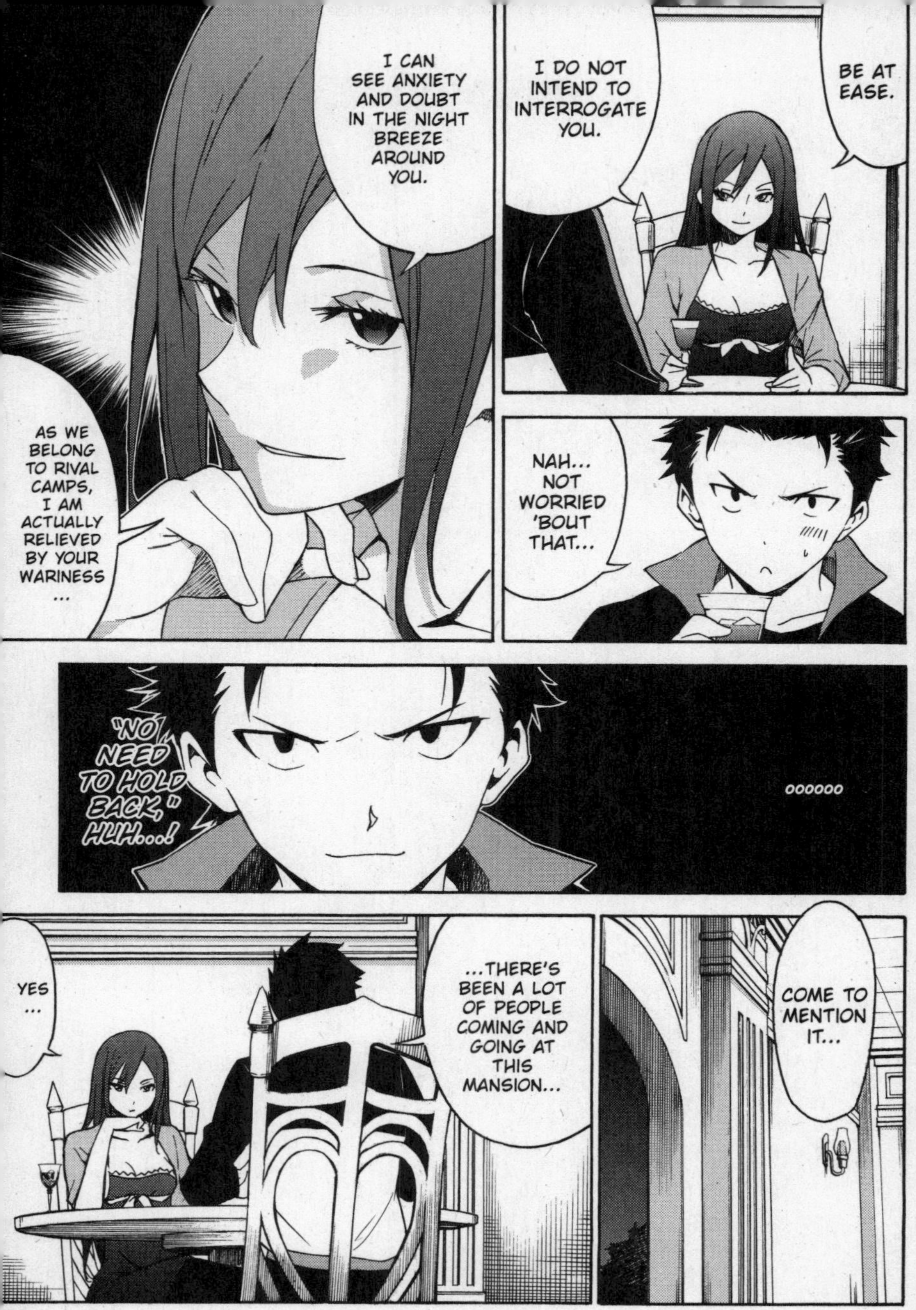
BE AT EASE.
I DO NOT INTEND TO INTERROGATE YOU.
NAH... NOT WORRIED 'BOUT THAT...
I CAN SEE ANXIETY AND DOUBT IN THE NIGHT BREEZE AROUND YOU.
AS WE BELONG TO RIVAL CAMPS, I AM ACTUALLY RELIEVED BY YOUR WARINESS...
oooooo
"NO NEED TO HOLD BACK," HUH...!
COME TO MENTION IT...
...THERE'S BEEN A LOT OF PEOPLE COMING AND GOING AT THIS MANSION...
YES...

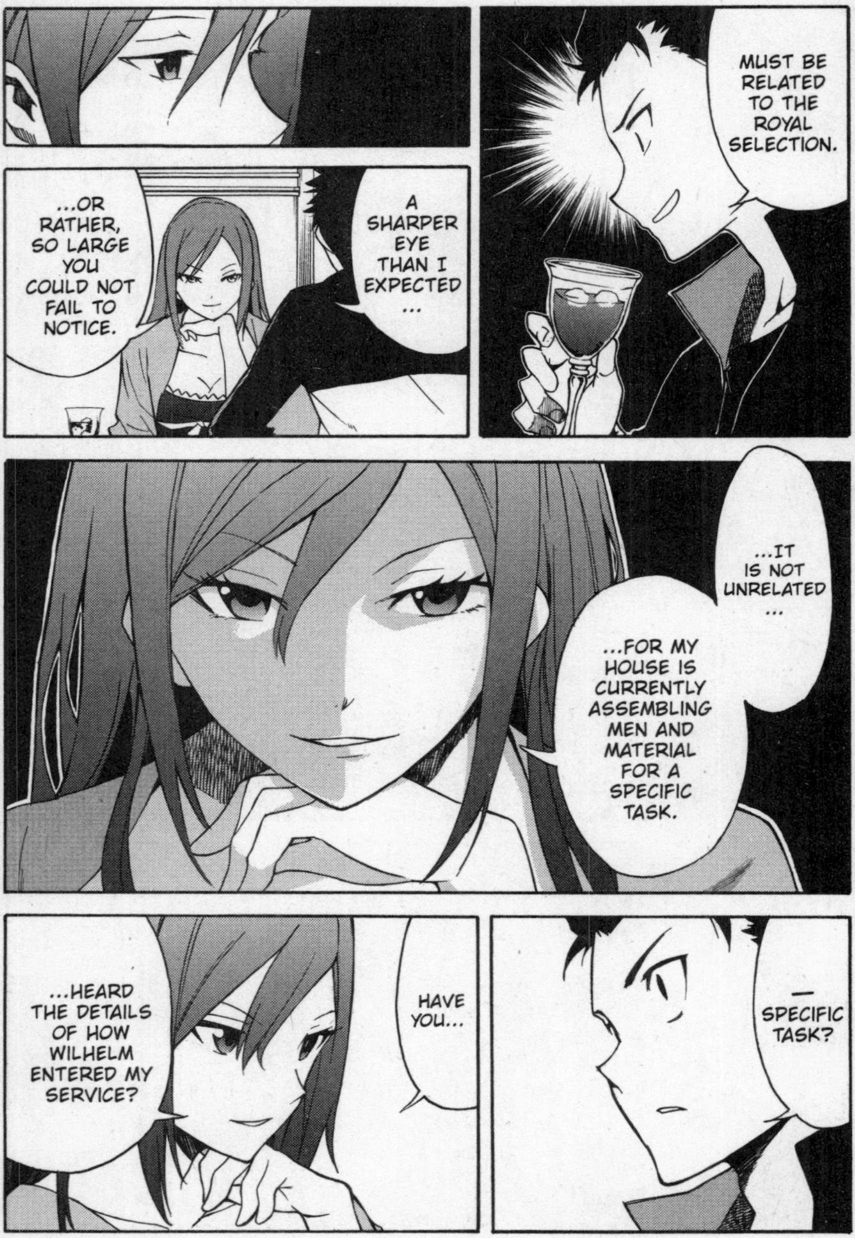
MUST BE RELATED TO THE ROYAL SELECTION.
A SHARPER EYE THAN I EXPECTED...
...OR RATHER, SO LARGE YOU COULD NOT FAIL TO NOTICE.
...IT IS NOT UNRELATED...
...FOR MY HOUSE IS CURRENTLY ASSEMBLING MEN AND MATERIAL FOR A SPECIFIC TASK.
—SPECIFIC TASK?
HAVE YOU...
...HEARD THE DETAILS OF HOW WILHELM ENTERED MY SERVICE?

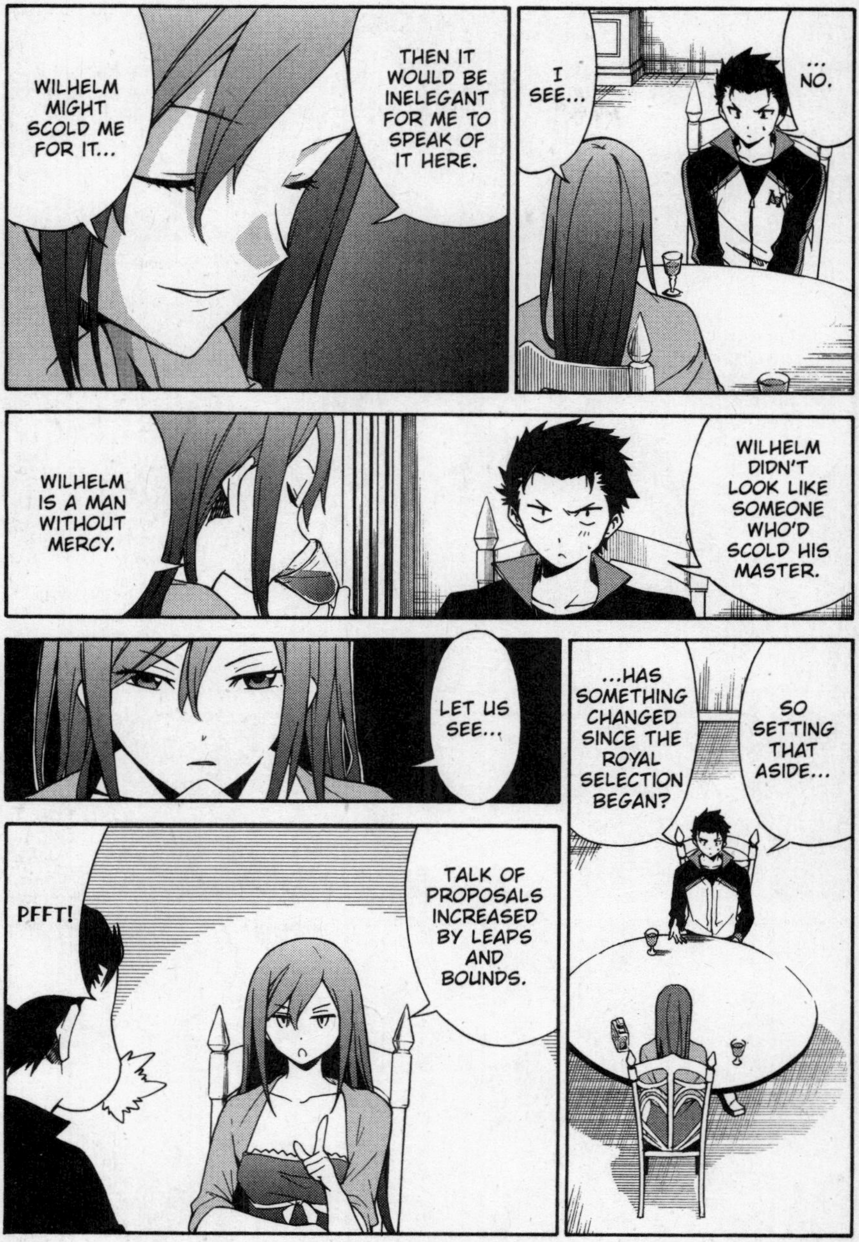
...NO.
I SEE...
THEN IT WOULD BE INELEGANT FOR ME TO SPEAK OF IT HERE.
WILHELM MIGHT SCOLD ME FOR IT...
WILHELM DIDN'T LOOK LIKE SOMEONE WHO'D SCOLD HIS MASTER.
WILHELM IS A MAN WITHOUT MERCY.
SO SETTING THAT ASIDE...
...HAS SOMETHING CHANGED SINCE THE ROYAL SELECTION BEGAN?
LET US SEE...
TALK OF PROPOSALS INCREASED BY LEAPS AND BOUNDS.
PFFT!

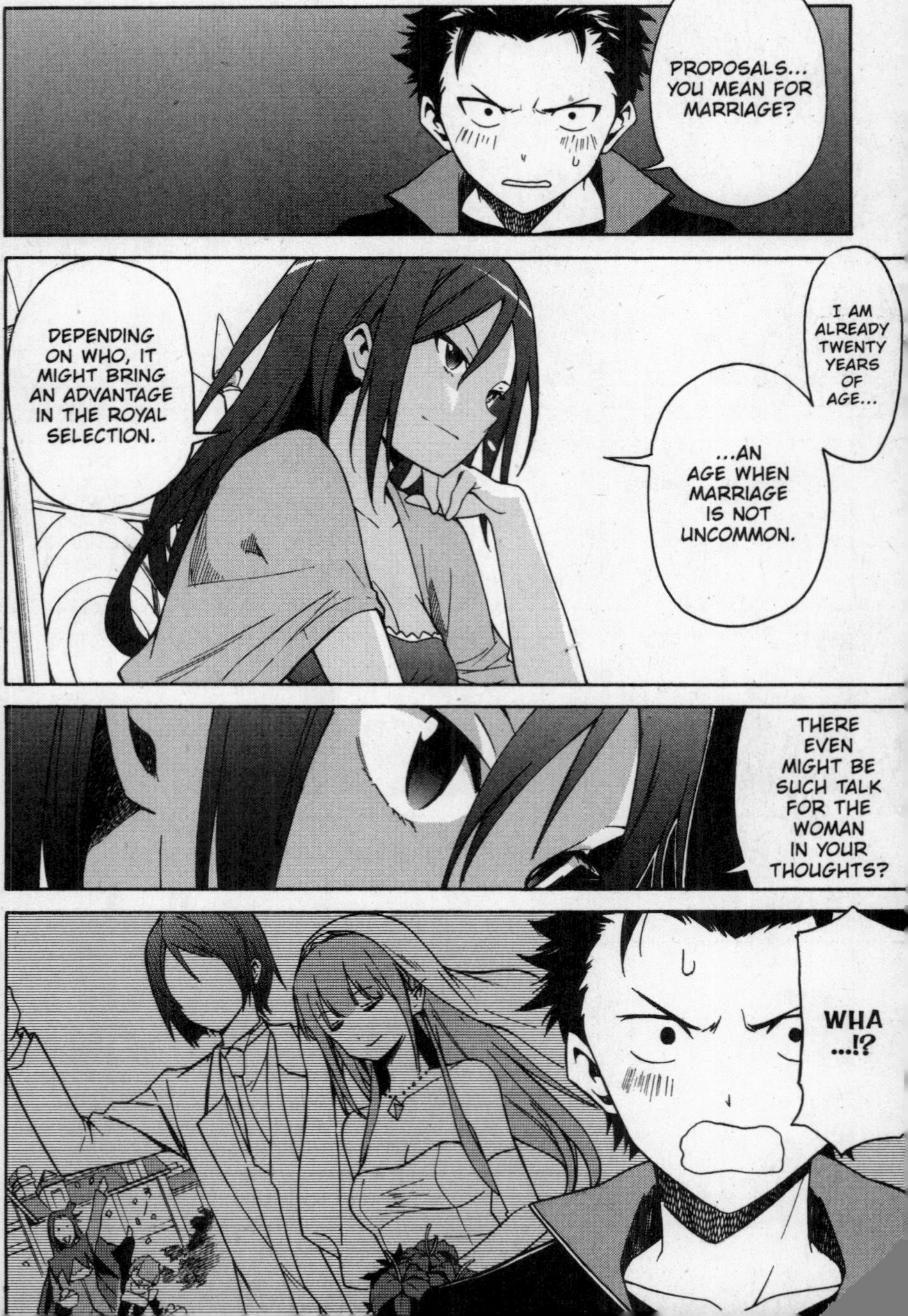
PROPOSALS... YOU MEAN FOR MARRIAGE?
I AM ALREADY TWENTY YEARS OF AGE...
...AN AGE WHEN MARRIAGE IS NOT UNCOMMON.
DEPENDING ON WHO, IT MIGHT BRING AN ADVANTAGE IN THE ROYAL SELECTION.
THERE EVEN MIGHT BE SUCH TALK FOR THE WOMAN IN YOUR THOUGHTS?
WHA ...!?

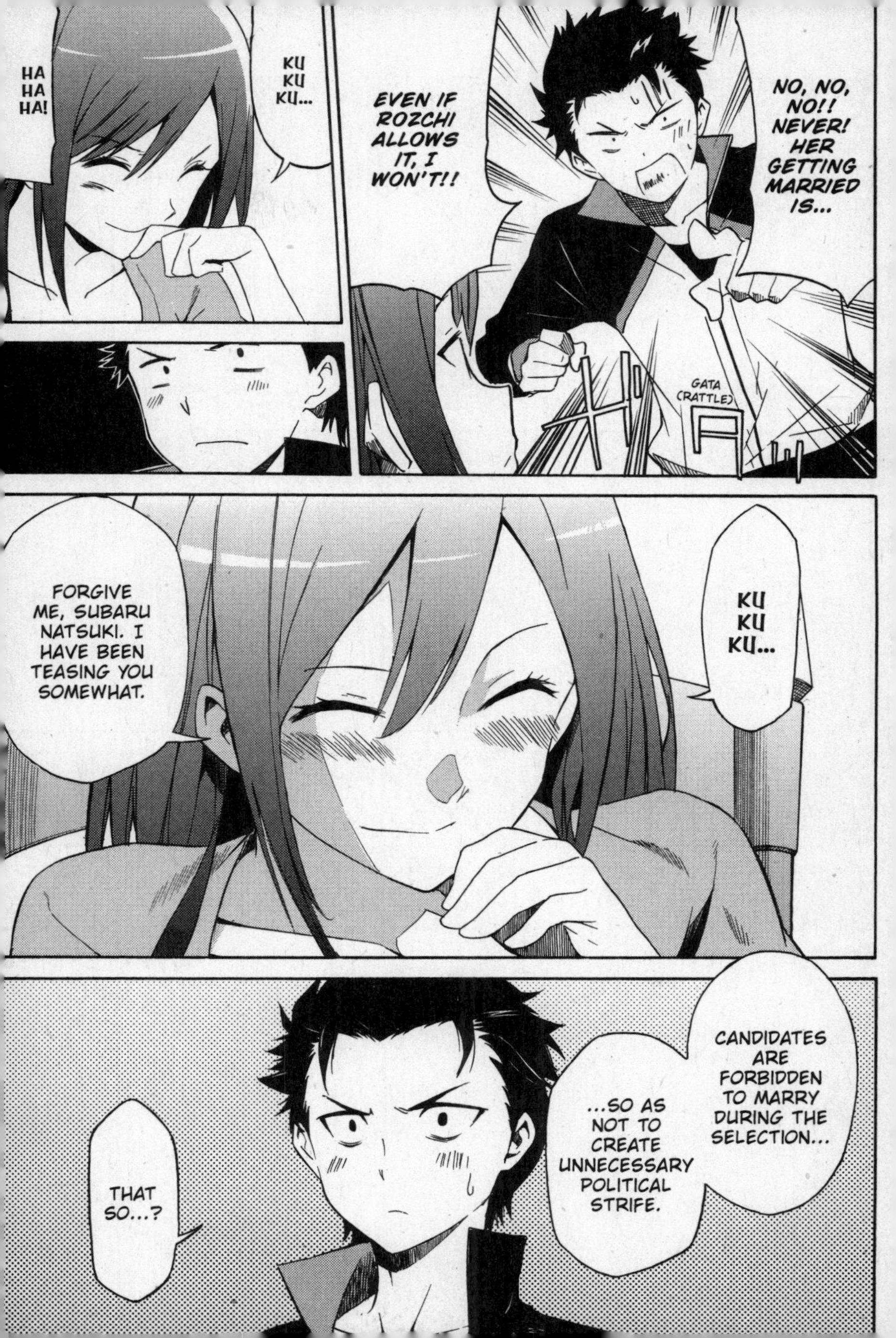

NO, NO, NO!! NEVER! HER GETTING MARRIED IS...
EVEN IF ROZCHI ALLOWS IT, I WON'T!!
GATA (RATTLE)
KU KU KU...
HA HA HA!
KU KU KU...
FORGIVE ME, SUBARU NATSUKI. I HAVE BEEN TEASING YOU SOMEWHAT.
CANDIDATES ARE FORBIDDEN TO MARRY DURING THE SELECTION...
...SO AS NOT TO CREATE UNNECESSARY POLITICAL STRIFE.
THAT SO...?

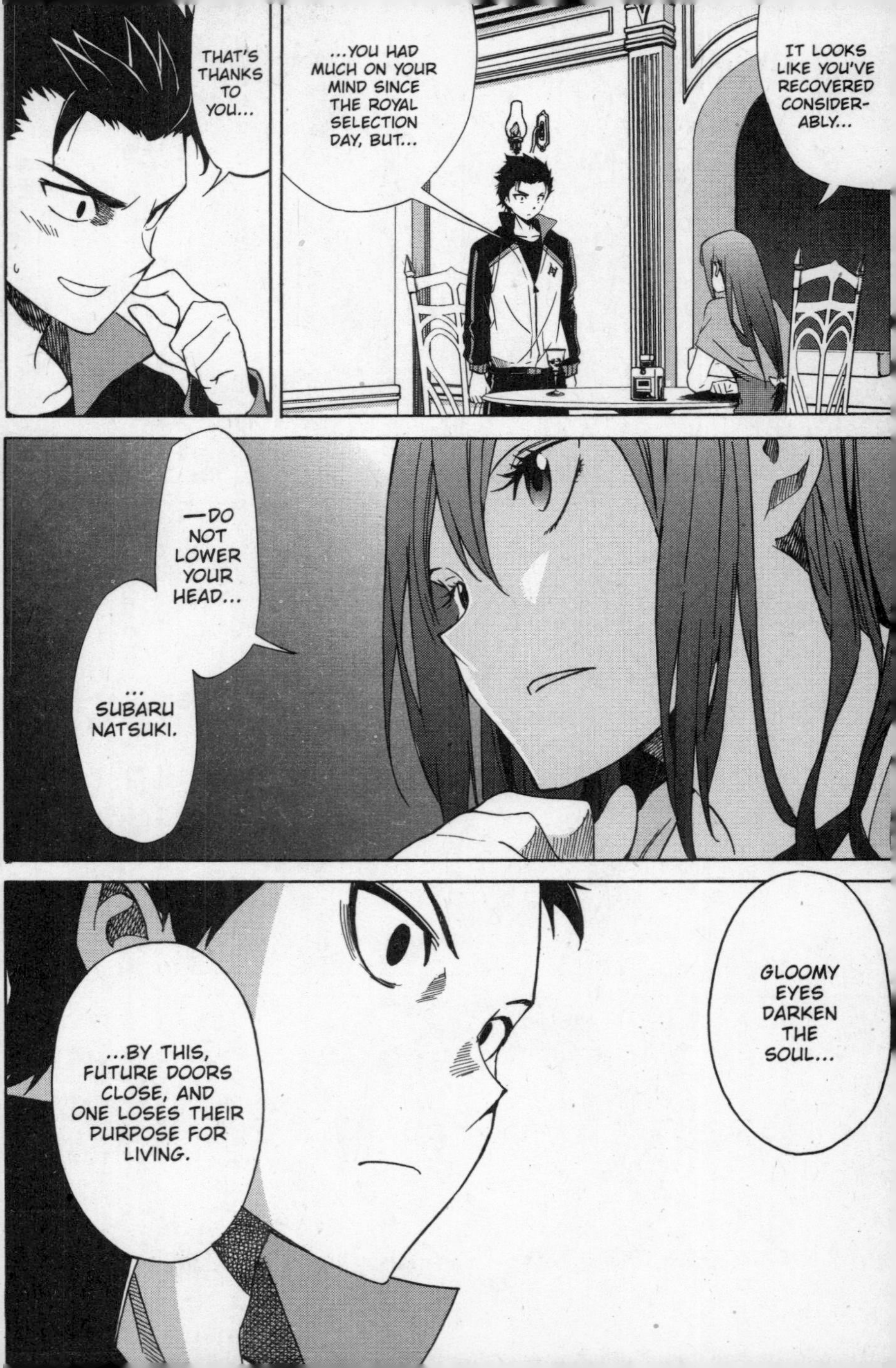
IT LOOKS LIKE YOU'VE RECOVERED CONSIDER-ABLY...
...YOU HAD MUCH ON YOUR MIND SINCE THE ROYAL SELECTION DAY, BUT...
THAT'S THANKS TO YOU...
—DO NOT LOWER YOUR HEAD...
... SUBARU NATSUKI.
GLOOMY EYES DARKEN THE SOUL...
...BY THIS, FUTURE DOORS CLOSE, AND ONE LOSES THEIR PURPOSE FOR LIVING.

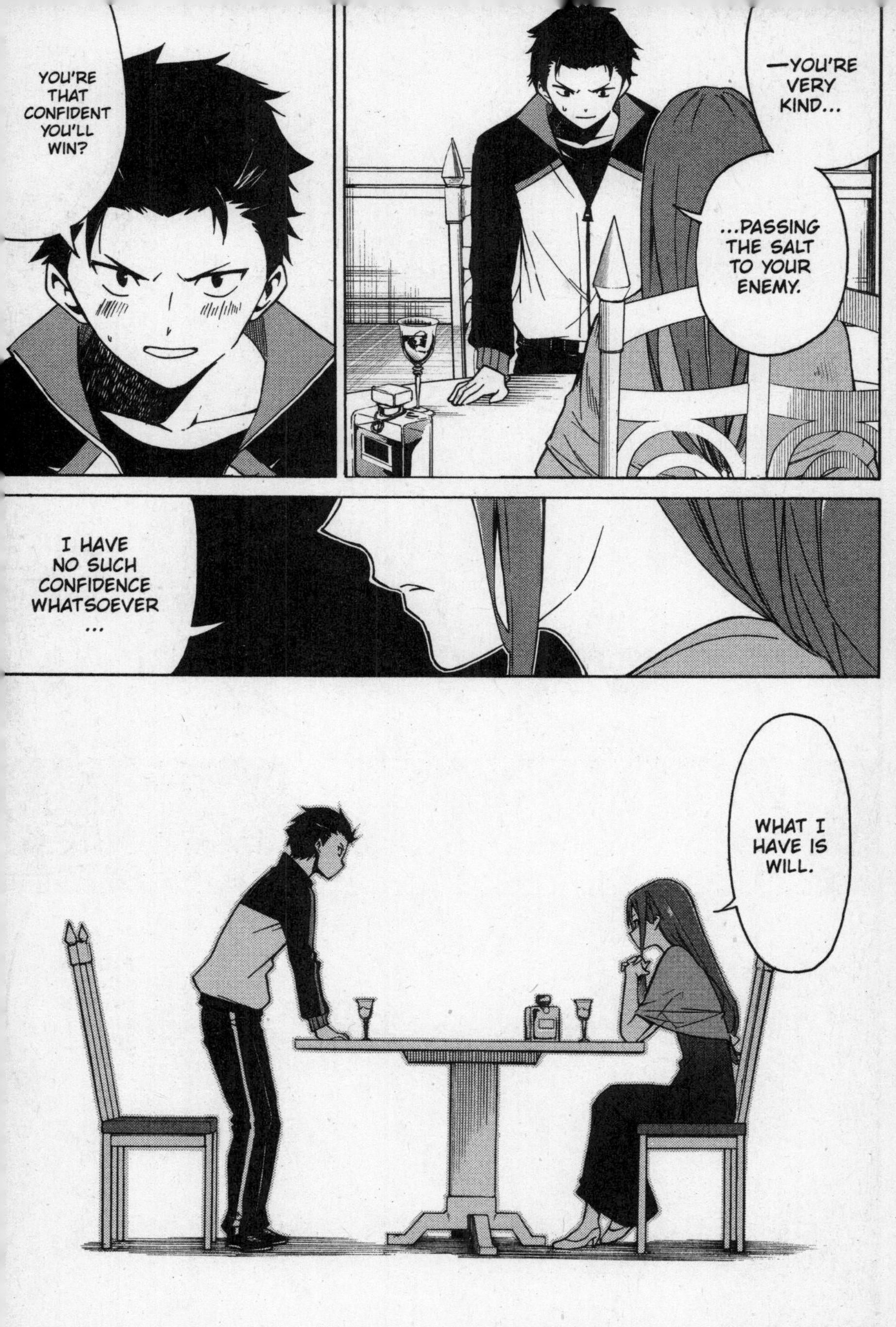
—YOU'RE VERY KIND...
...PASSING THE SALT TO YOUR ENEMY.
YOU'RE THAT CONFIDENT YOU'LL WIN?
I HAVE NO SUCH CONFIDENCE WHATSOEVER...
WHAT I HAVE IS WILL.

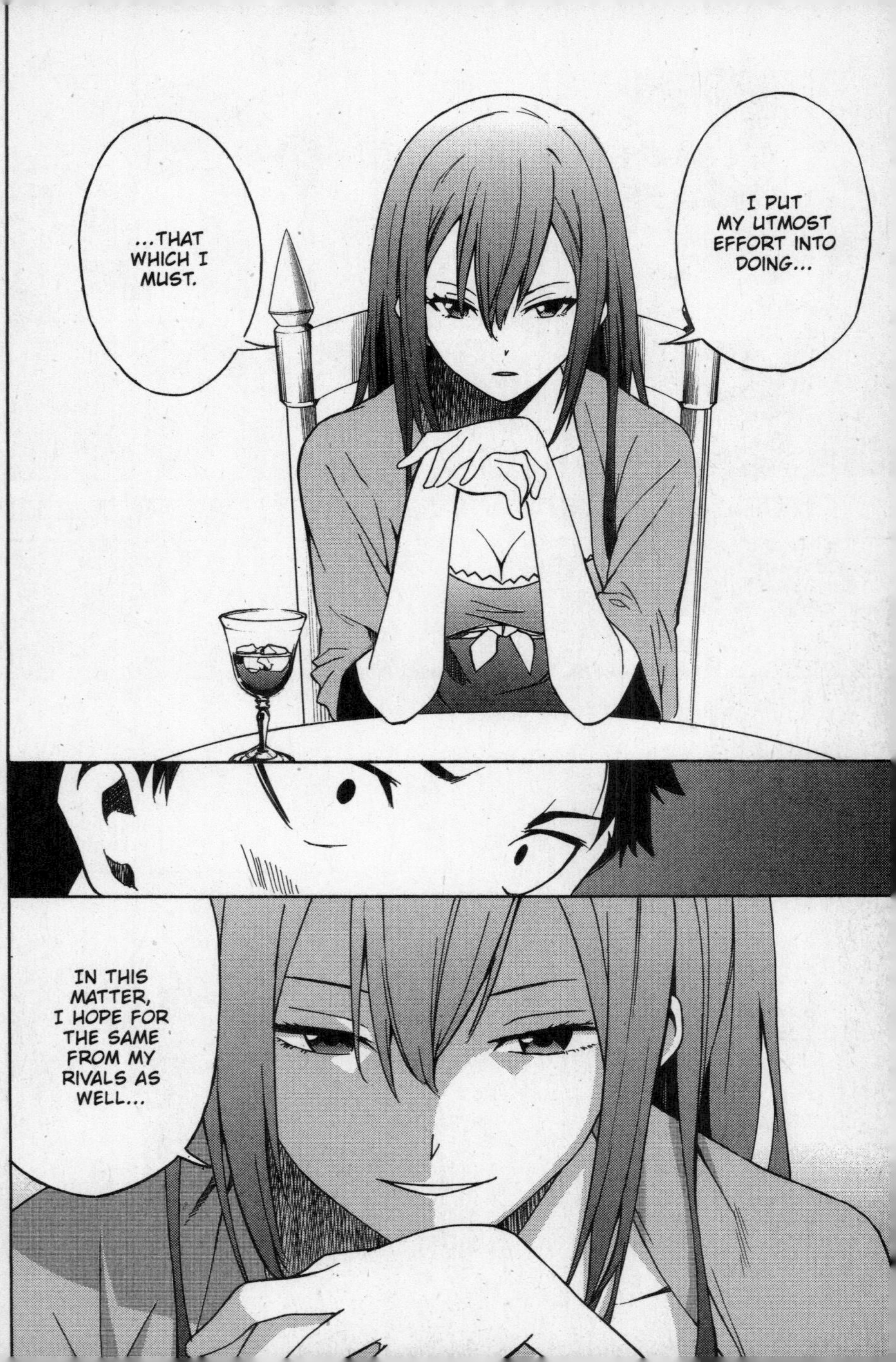
I PUT MY UTMOST EFFORT INTO DOING...
...THAT WHICH I MUST.
IN THIS MATTER, I HOPE FOR THE SAME FROM MY RIVALS AS WELL...

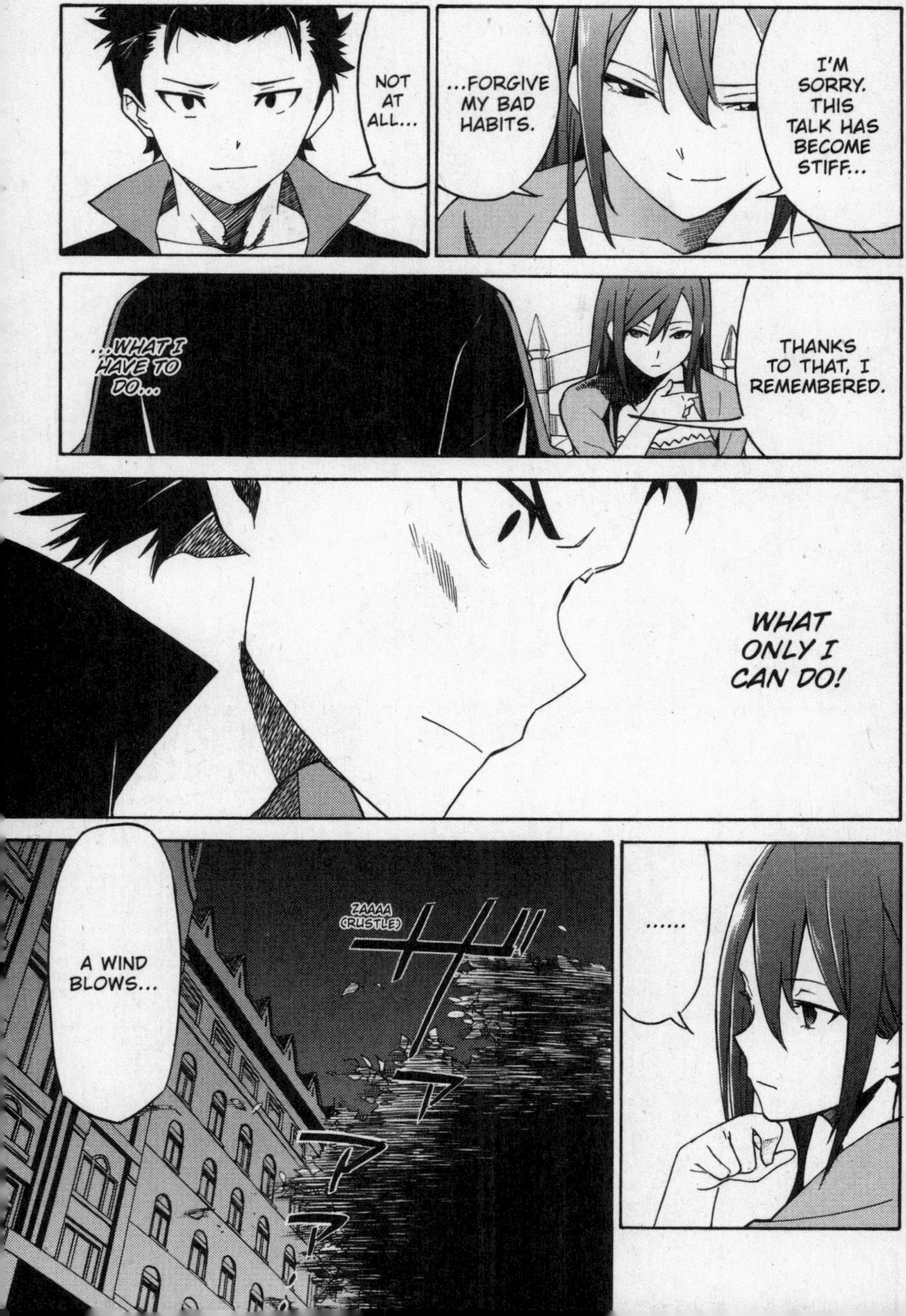
I'M SORRY. THIS TALK HAS BECOME STIFF...
...FORGIVE MY BAD HABITS.
NOT AT ALL...
THANKS TO THAT, I REMEMBERED.
...WHAT I HAVE TO DO...
WHAT ONLY I CAN DO!
......
ZAAAA (RUSTLE)
A WIND BLOWS...

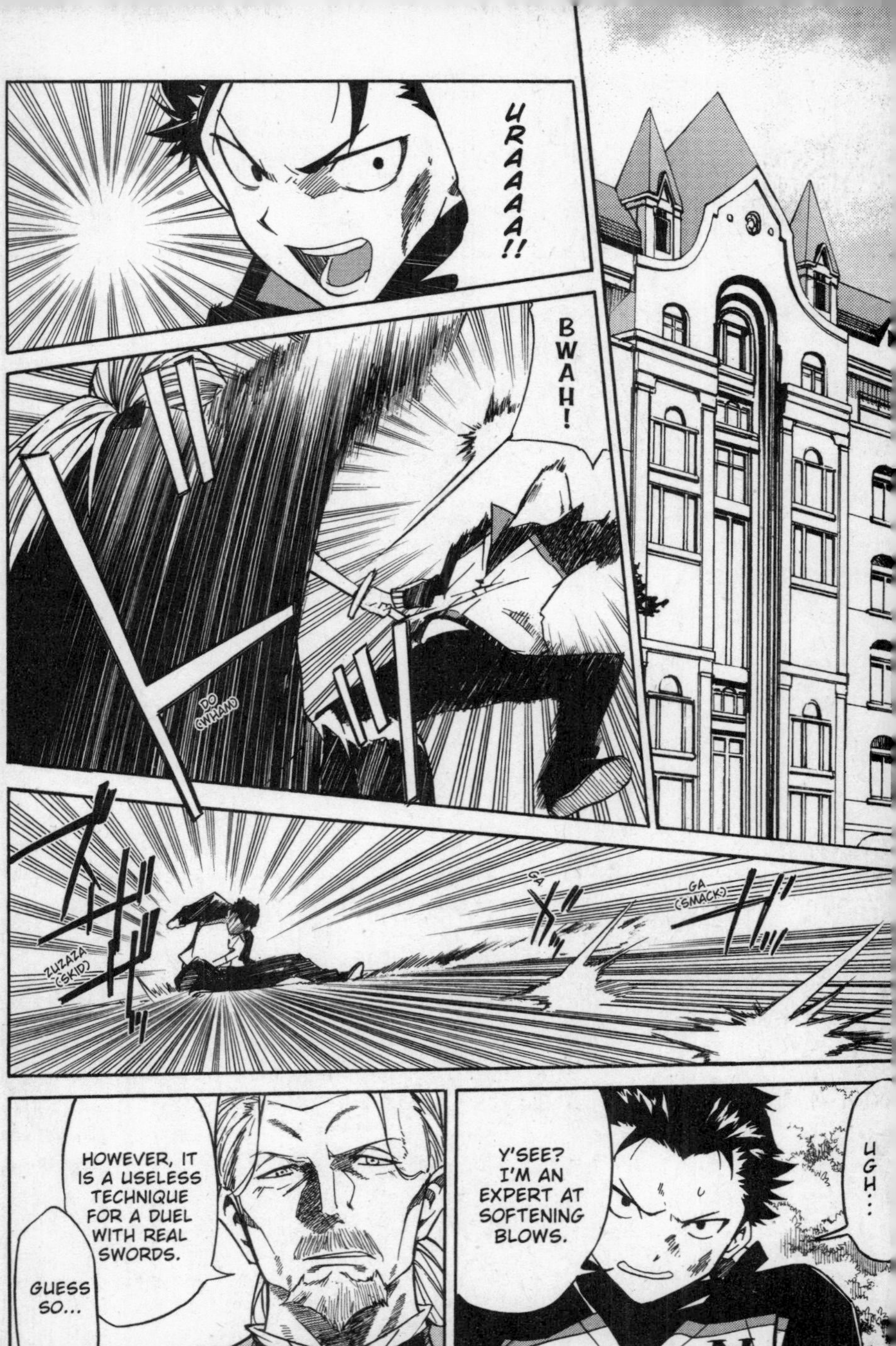
URAAAAA!!
BWAH!
DO (WHAM)
GA (SMACK)
GA
ZUZAZA (SKID)
UGH...
Y'SEE? I'M AN EXPERT AT SOFTENING BLOWS.
HOWEVER, IT IS A USELESS TECHNIQUE FOR A DUEL WITH REAL SWORDS.
GUESS SO...

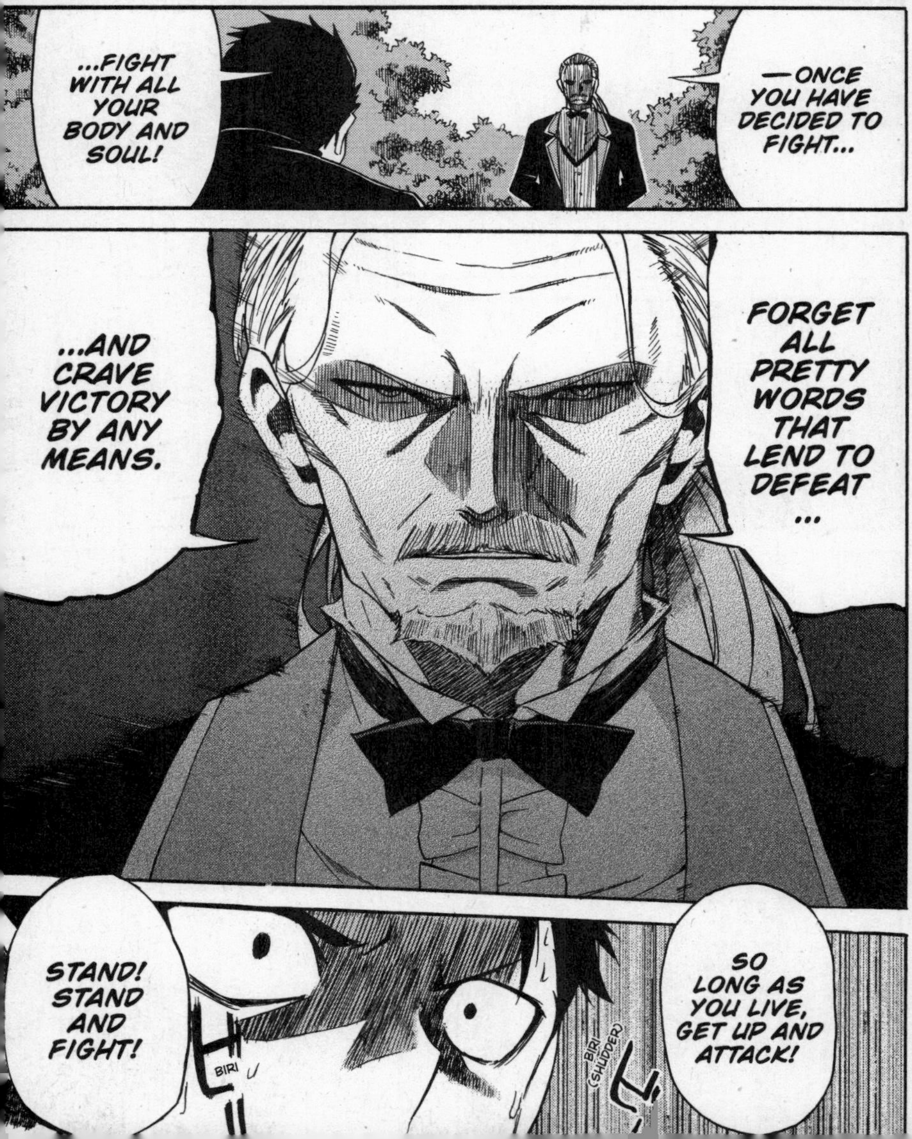
—ONCE YOU HAVE DECIDED TO FIGHT...
...FIGHT WITH ALL YOUR BODY AND SOUL!
FORGET ALL PRETTY WORDS THAT LEND TO DEFEAT ...
...AND CRAVE VICTORY BY ANY MEANS.
SO LONG AS YOU LIVE, GET UP AND ATTACK!
STAND! STAND AND FIGHT!
BIRI (SHUDDER)
BIRI

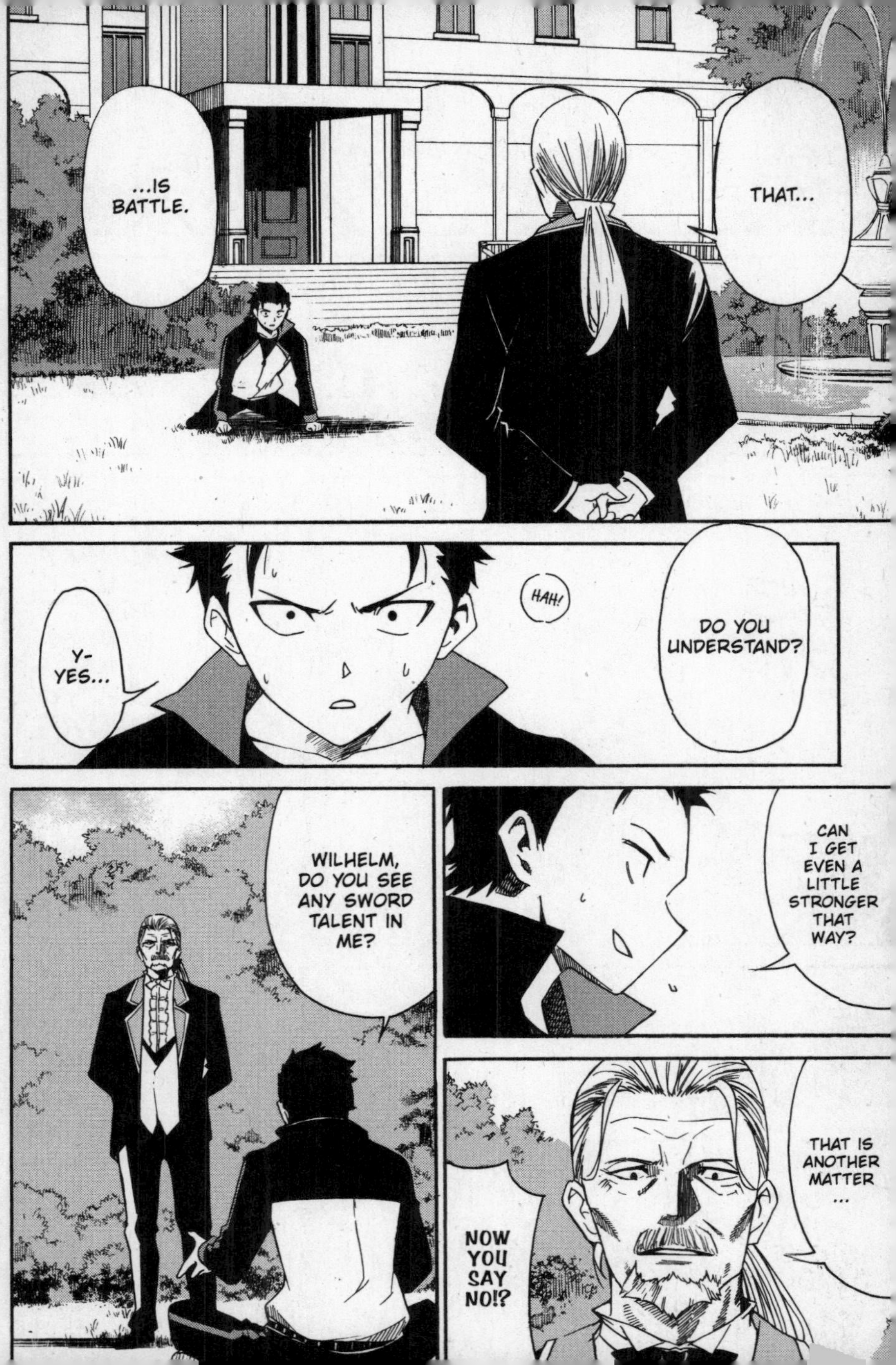
THAT...
...IS BATTLE.
DO YOU UNDERSTAND?
HAH!
Y- YES...
CAN I GET EVEN A LITTLE STRONGER THAT WAY?
THAT IS ANOTHER MATTER ...
NOW YOU SAY NO!?
WILHELM, DO YOU SEE ANY SWORD TALENT IN ME?

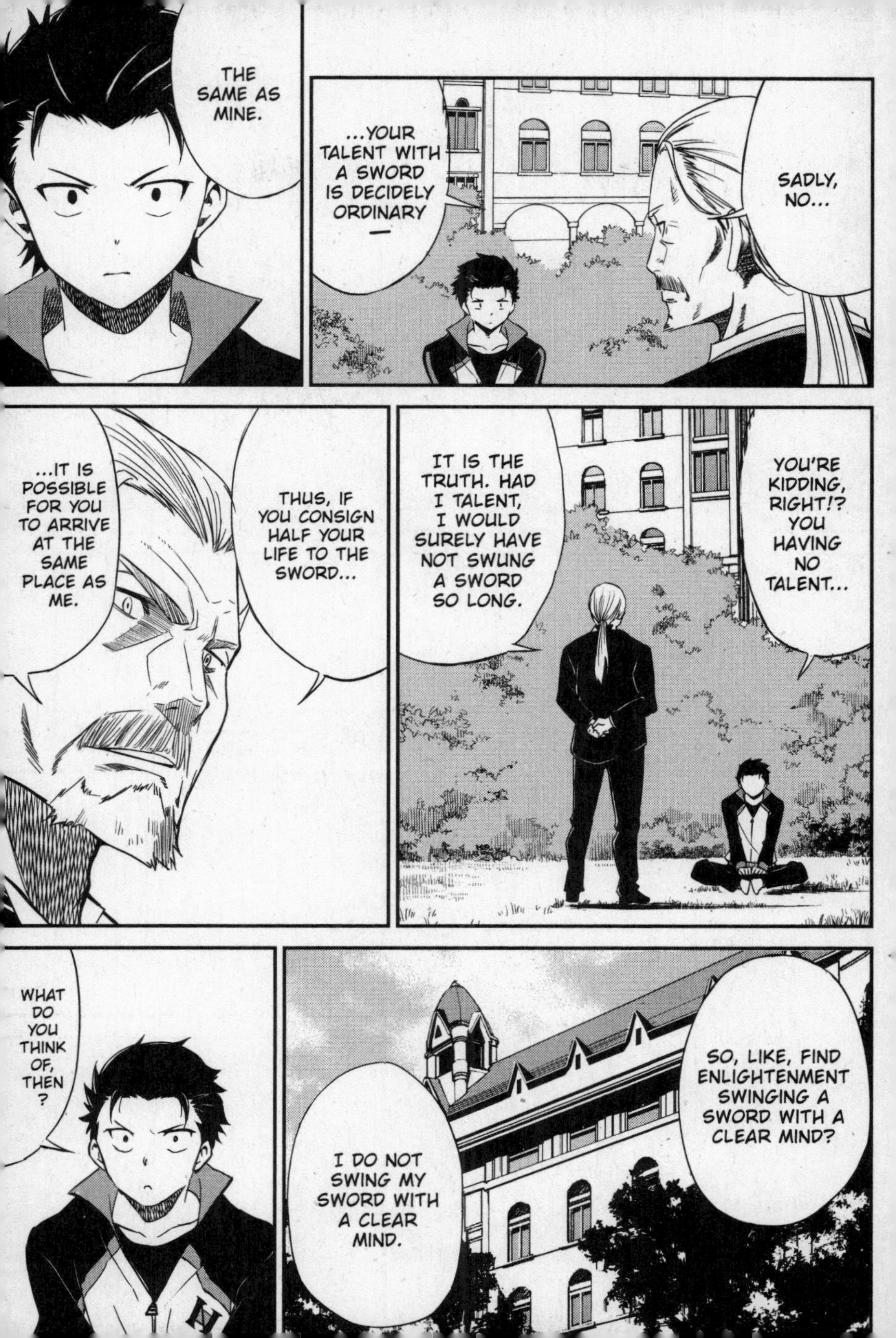
SADLY, NO...
...YOUR TALENT WITH A SWORD IS DECIDELY ORDINARY —
THE SAME AS MINE.
YOU'RE KIDDING, RIGHT!? YOU HAVING NO TALENT...
IT IS THE TRUTH. HAD I TALENT, I WOULD SURELY HAVE NOT SWUNG A SWORD SO LONG.
THUS, IF YOU CONSIGN HALF YOUR LIFE TO THE SWORD...
...IT IS POSSIBLE FOR YOU TO ARRIVE AT THE SAME PLACE AS ME.
SO, LIKE, FIND ENLIGHTENMENT SWINGING A SWORD WITH A CLEAR MIND?
I DO NOT SWING MY SWORD WITH A CLEAR MIND.
WHAT DO YOU THINK OF, THEN?

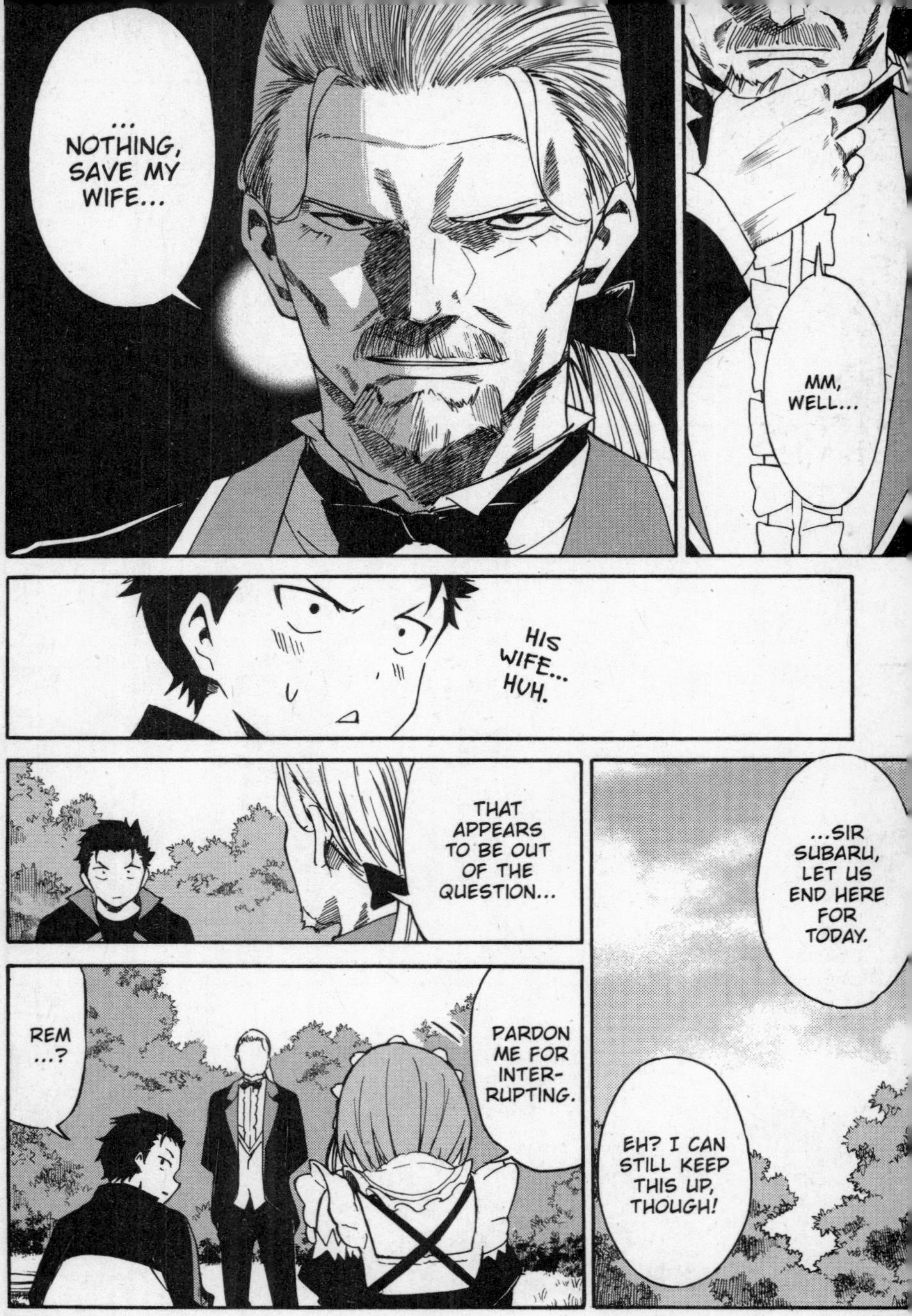
MM, WELL...
... NOTHING, SAVE MY WIFE...
HIS WIFE... HUH.
...SIR SUBARU, LET US END HERE FOR TODAY.
EH? I CAN STILL KEEP THIS UP, THOUGH!
THAT APPEARS TO BE OUT OF THE QUESTION...
PARDON ME FOR INTERRUPTING.
REM ...?

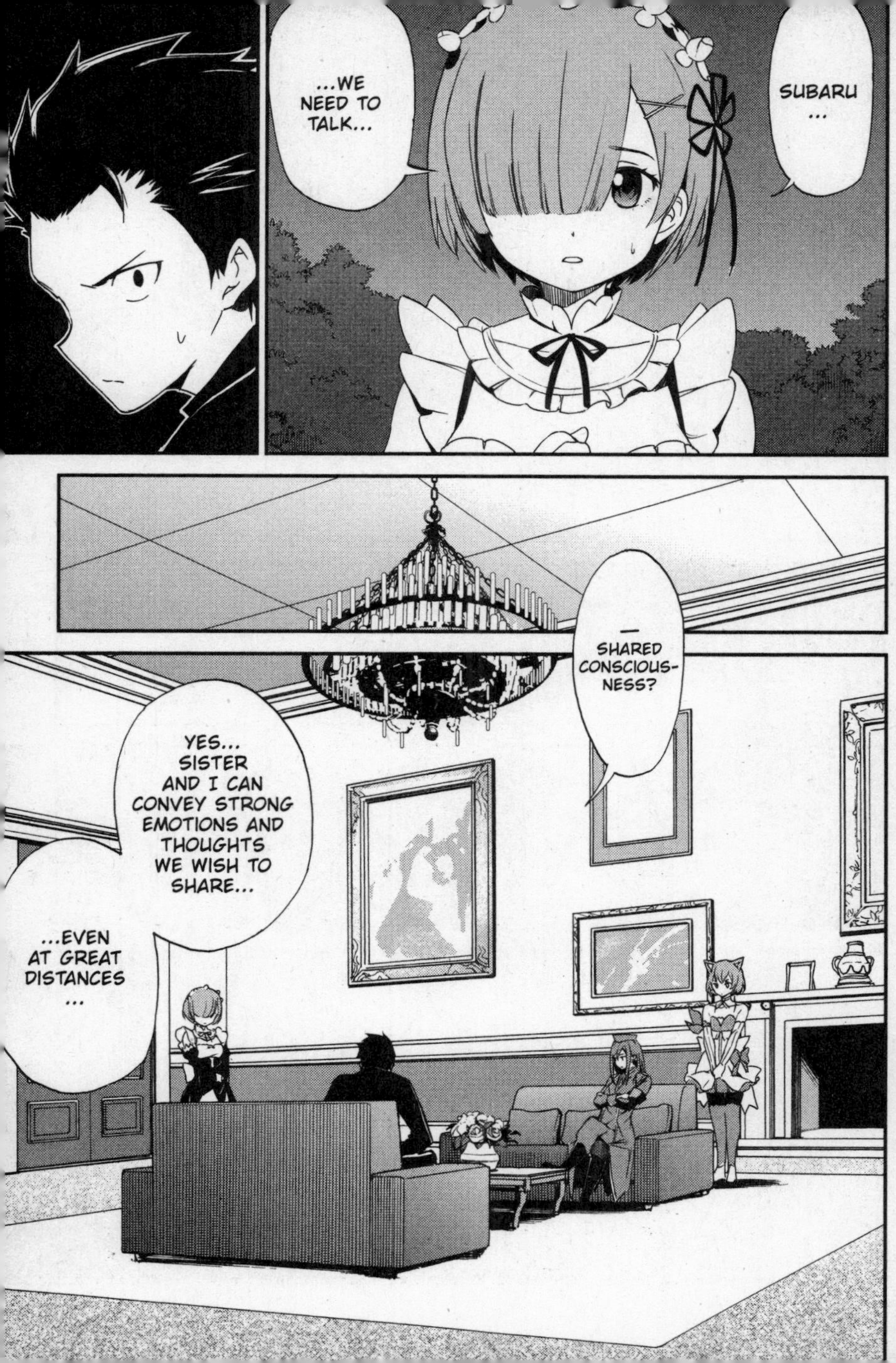
SUBARU...
...WE NEED TO TALK...
—SHARED CONSCIOUSNESS?
YES... SISTER AND I CAN CONVEY STRONG EMOTIONS AND THOUGHTS WE WISH TO SHARE...
...EVEN AT GREAT DISTANCES...

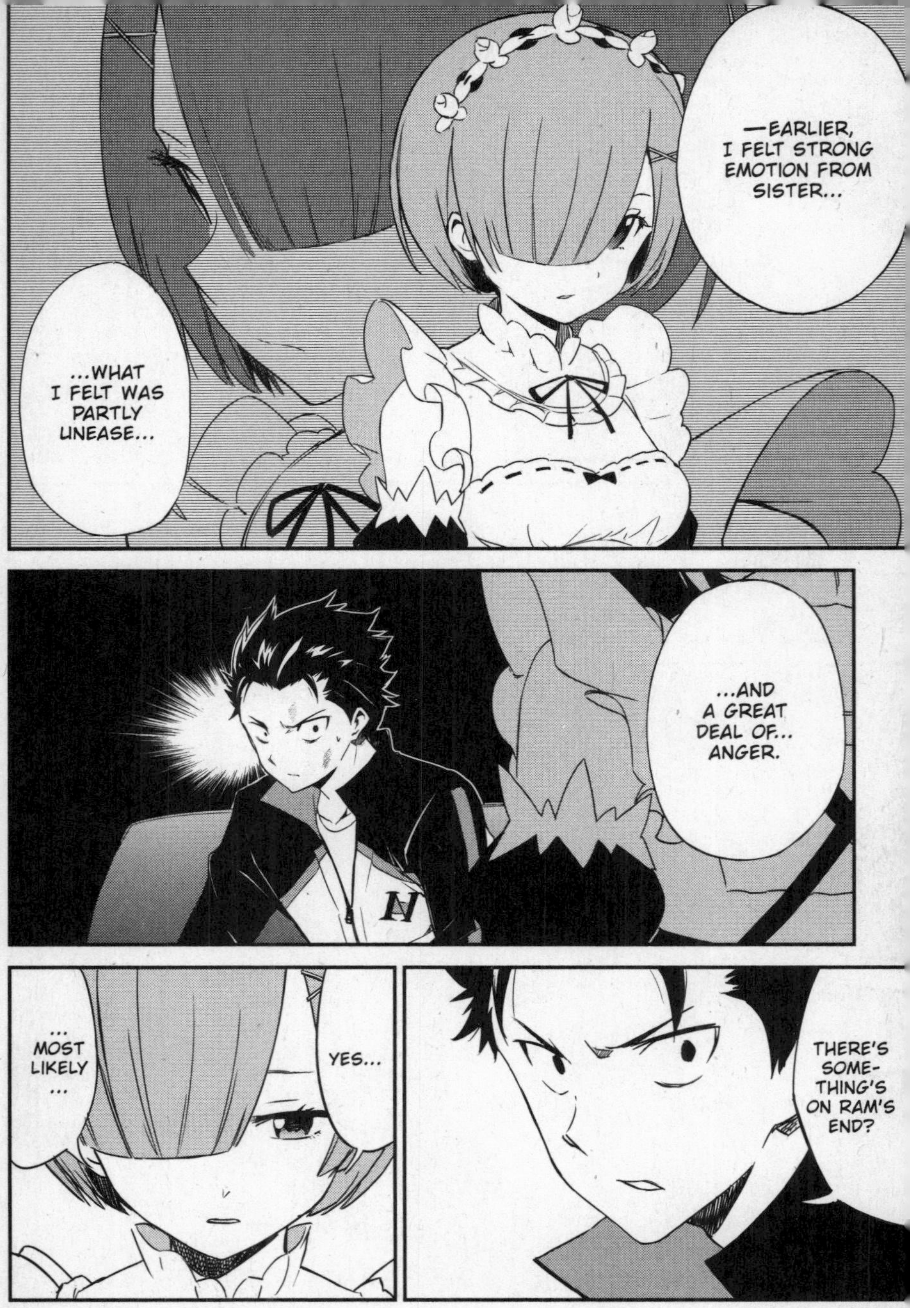
—EARLIER, I FELT STRONG EMOTION FROM SISTER...
...WHAT I FELT WAS PARTLY UNEASE...
...AND A GREAT DEAL OF... ANGER.
THERE'S SOME-THING'S ON RAM'S END?
YES...
...MOST LIKELY...

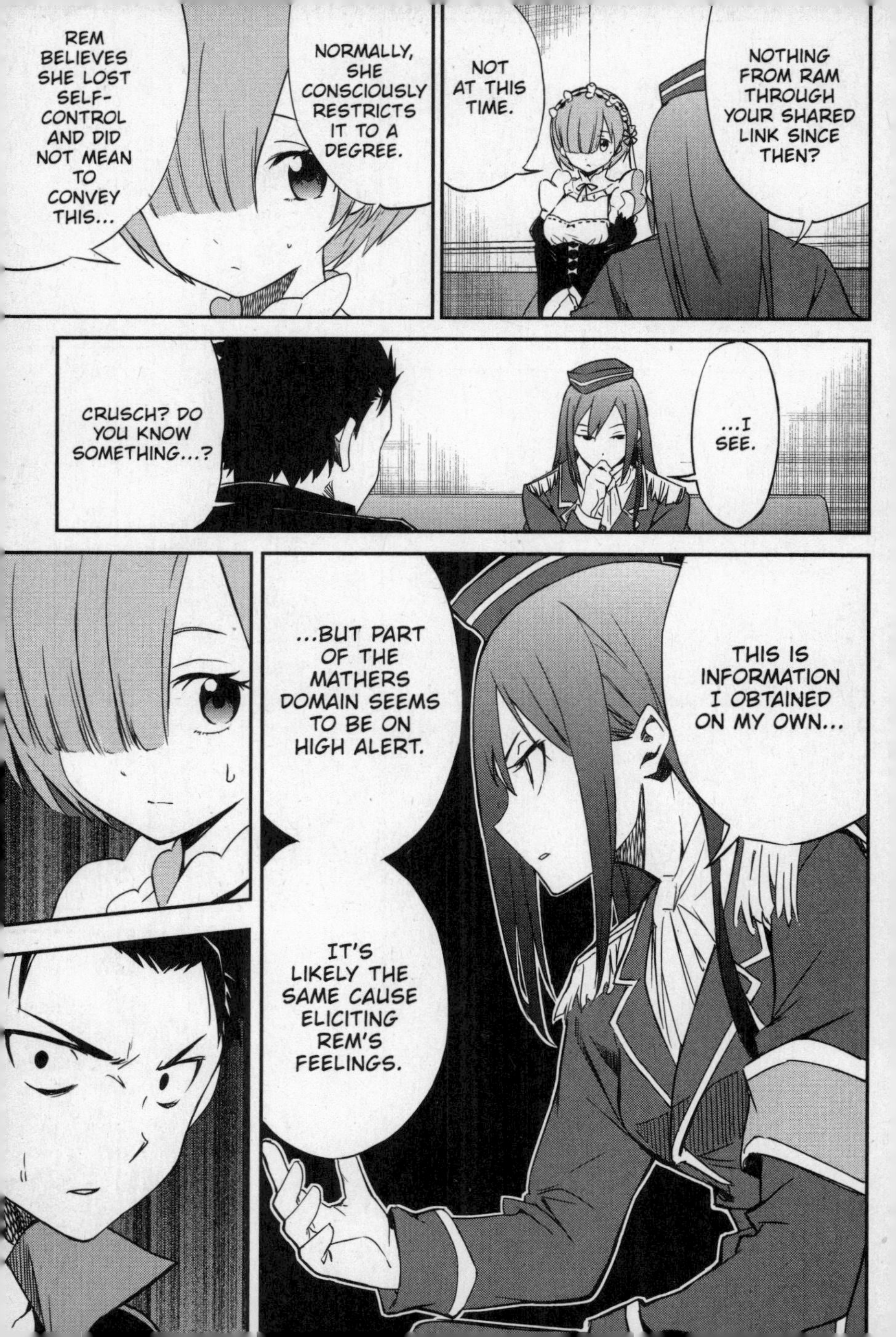
NOTHING FROM RAM THROUGH YOUR SHARED LINK SINCE THEN?
NOT AT THIS TIME.
NORMALLY, SHE CONSCIOUSLY RESTRICTS IT TO A DEGREE.
REM BELIEVES SHE LOST SELF-CONTROL AND DID NOT MEAN TO CONVEY THIS...
...I SEE.
CRUSCH? DO YOU KNOW SOMETHING...?
THIS IS INFORMATION I OBTAINED ON MY OWN...
...BUT PART OF THE MATHERS DOMAIN SEEMS TO BE ON HIGH ALERT.
IT'S LIKELY THE SAME CAUSE ELICITING REM'S FEELINGS.

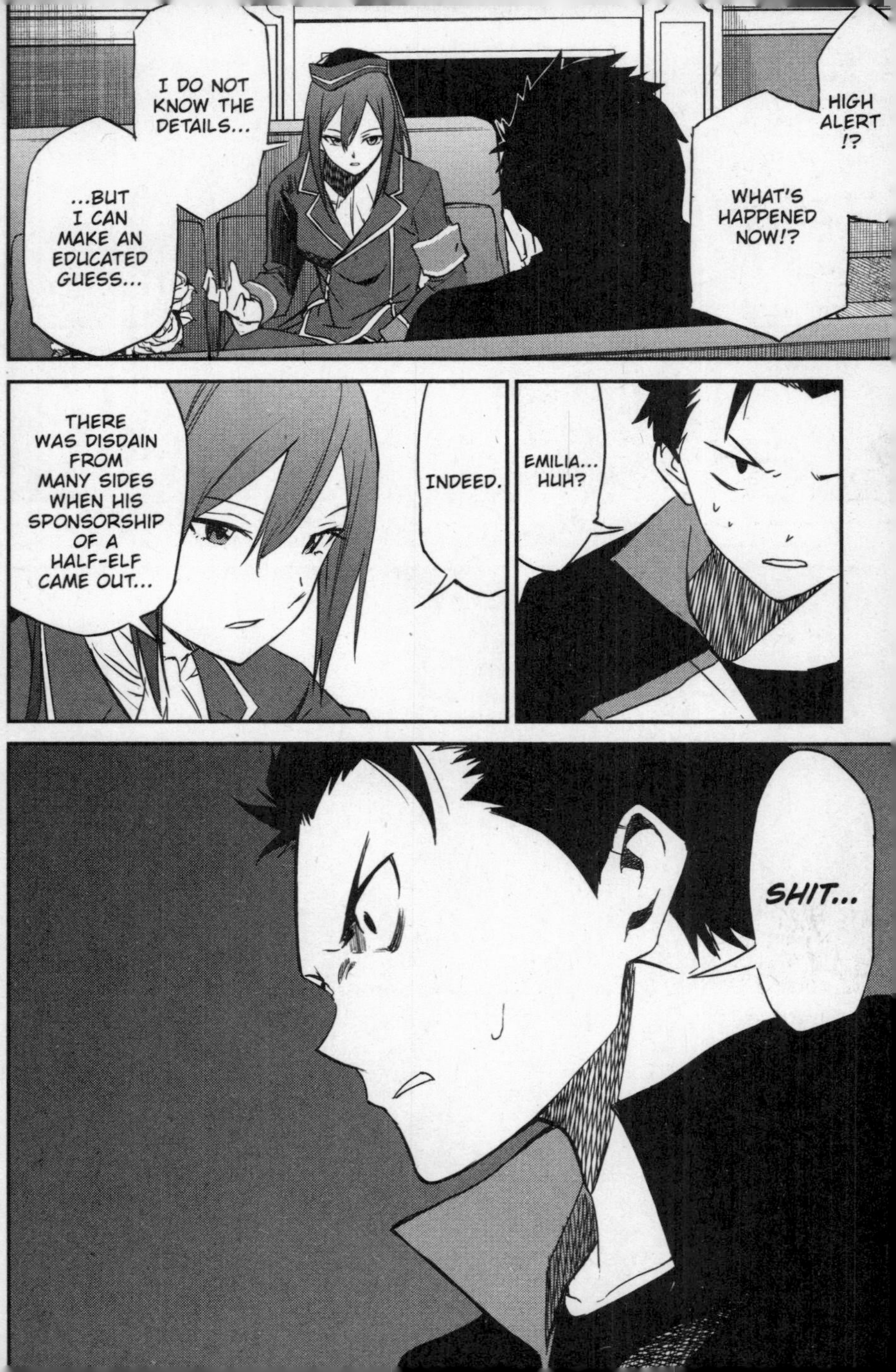
HIGH ALERT!?
WHAT'S HAPPENED NOW!?
I DO NOT KNOW THE DETAILS...
...BUT I CAN MAKE AN EDUCATED GUESS...
EMILIA... HUH?
INDEED.
THERE WAS DISDAIN FROM MANY SIDES WHEN HIS SPONSORSHIP OF A HALF-ELF CAME OUT...
SHIT...

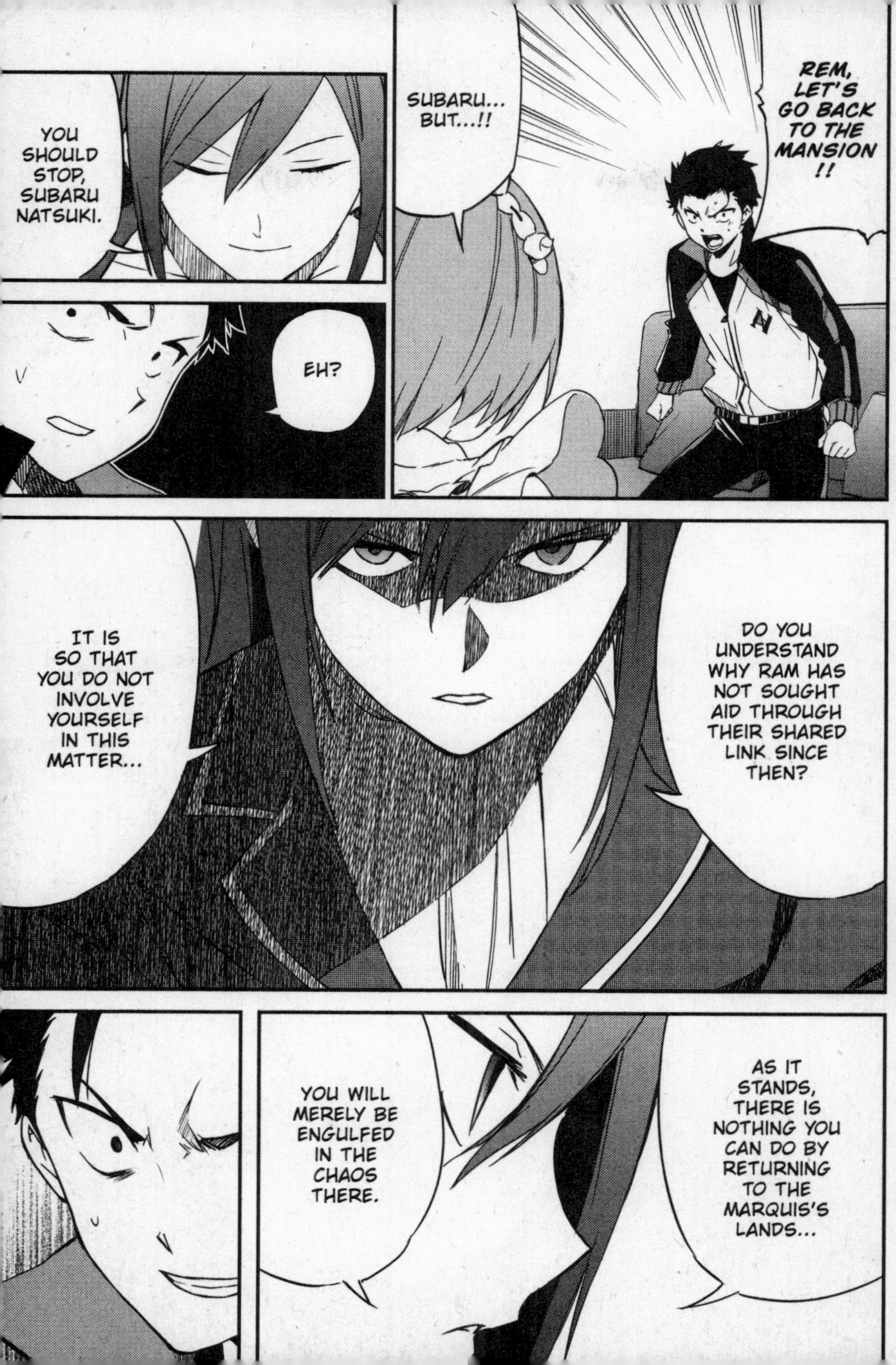
REM, LET'S GO BACK TO THE MANSION!!
SUBARU... BUT...!!
YOU SHOULD STOP, SUBARU NATSUKI.
EH?
DO YOU UNDERSTAND WHY RAM HAS NOT SOUGHT AID THROUGH THEIR SHARED LINK SINCE THEN?
IT IS SO THAT YOU DO NOT INVOLVE YOURSELF IN THIS MATTER...
AS IT STANDS, THERE IS NOTHING YOU CAN DO BY RETURNING TO THE MARQUIS'S LANDS...
YOU WILL MERELY BE ENGULFED IN THE CHAOS THERE.

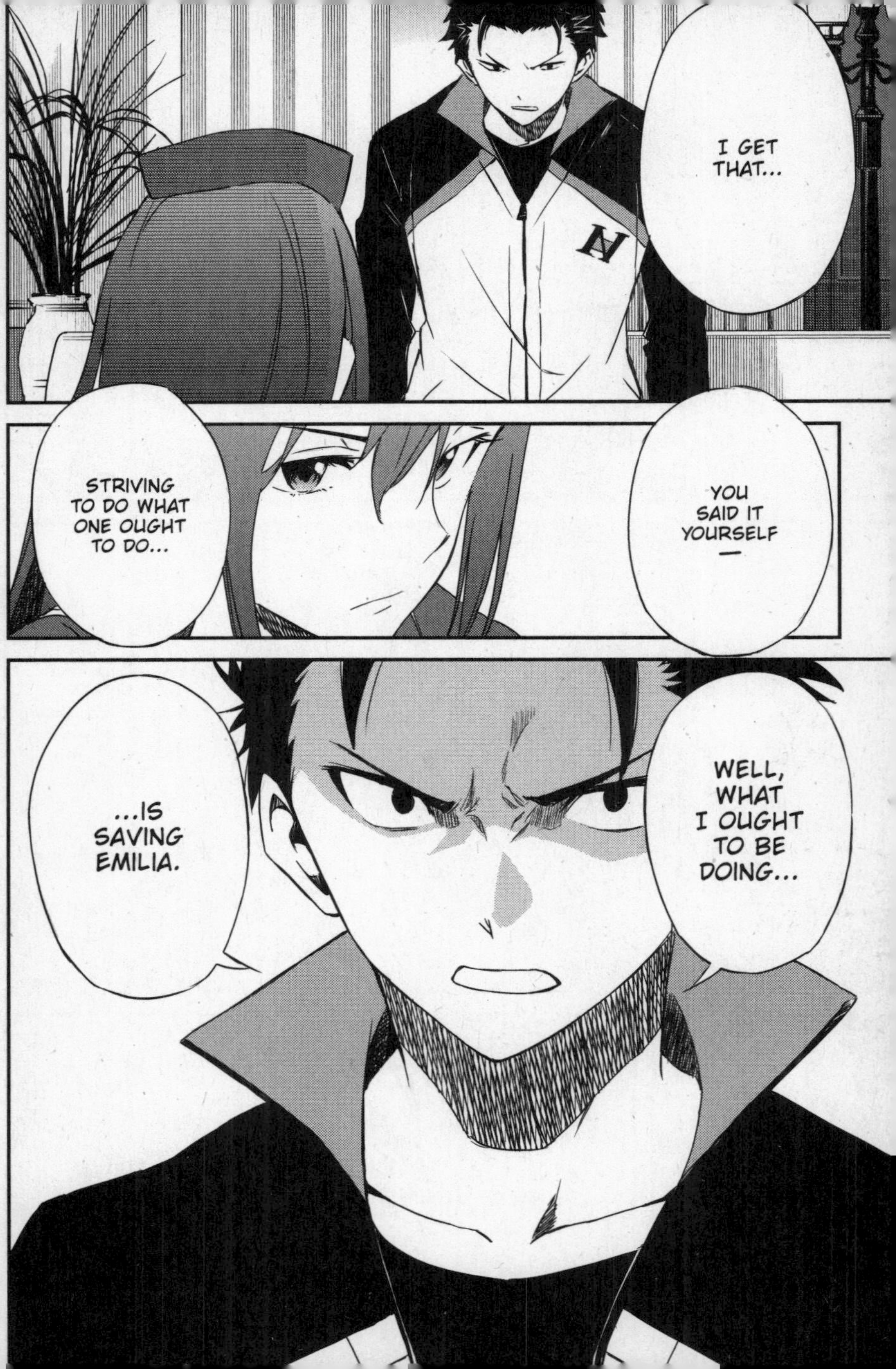
I GET THAT...
YOU SAID IT YOURSELF —
STRIVING TO DO WHAT ONE OUGHT TO DO...
WELL, WHAT I OUGHT TO BE DOING...
...IS SAVING EMILIA.

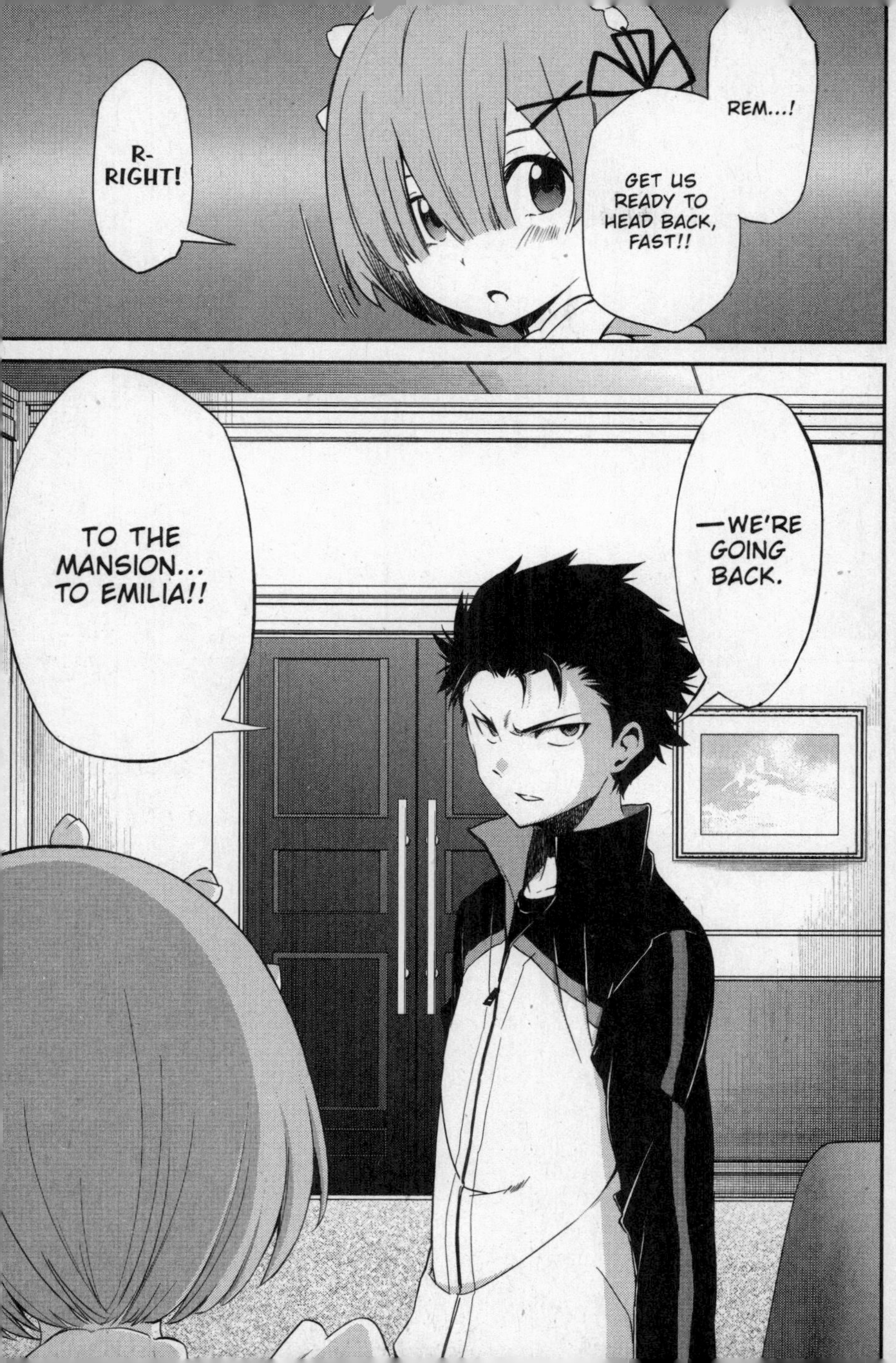
REM...!
GET US READY TO HEAD BACK, FAST!!
R-RIGHT!
—WE'RE GOING BACK.
TO THE MANSION... TO EMILIA!!

The only ability Subaru Natsuki gets
when he's summoned to another world
is time travel via his own death. But
to save her, he'll die as many times as
it takes.

Truth of Zero

Re:ZERO -Starting Life in Another World-

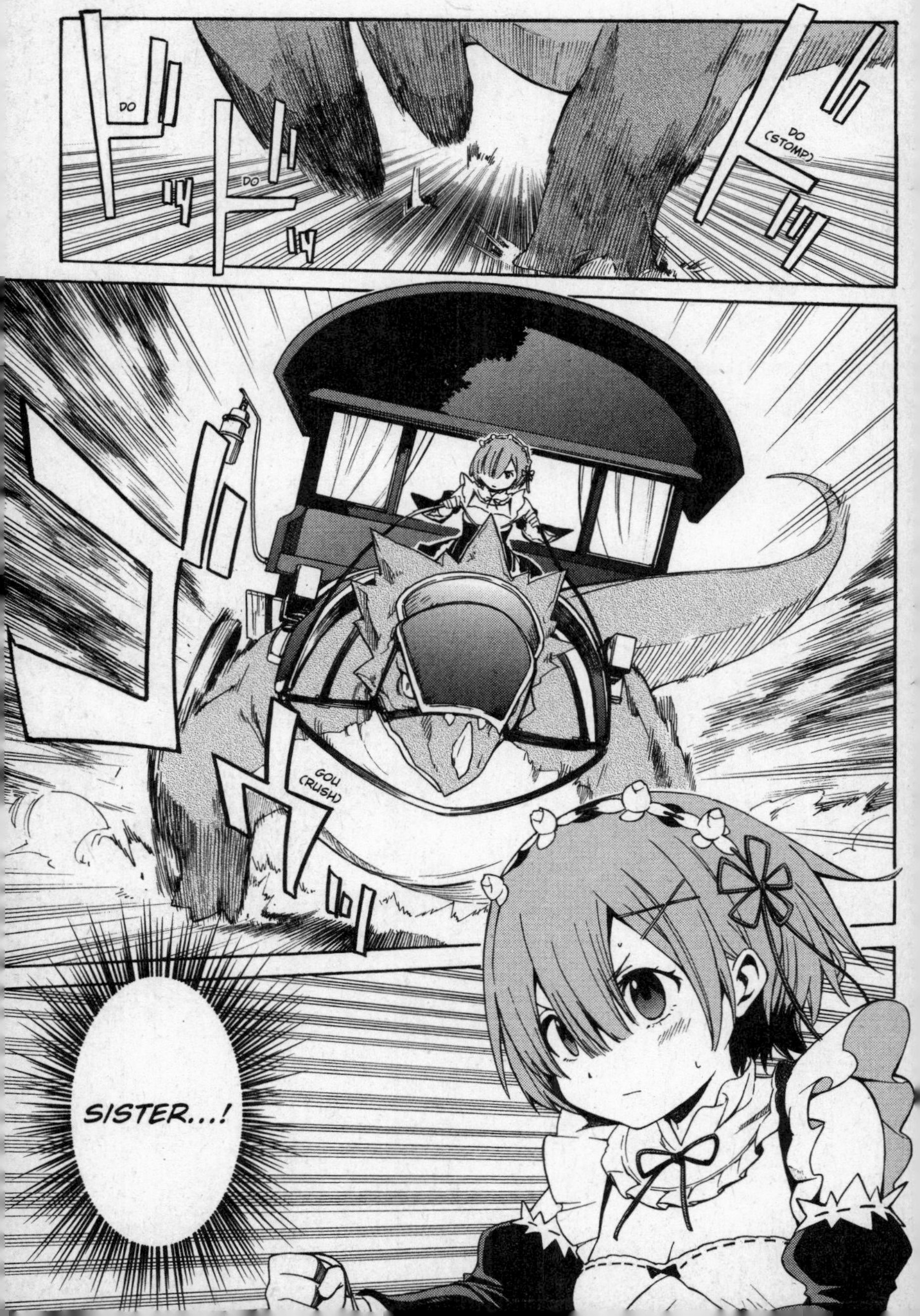
DO (STOMP)
DO
DO
GOU (RUSH)
SISTER...!

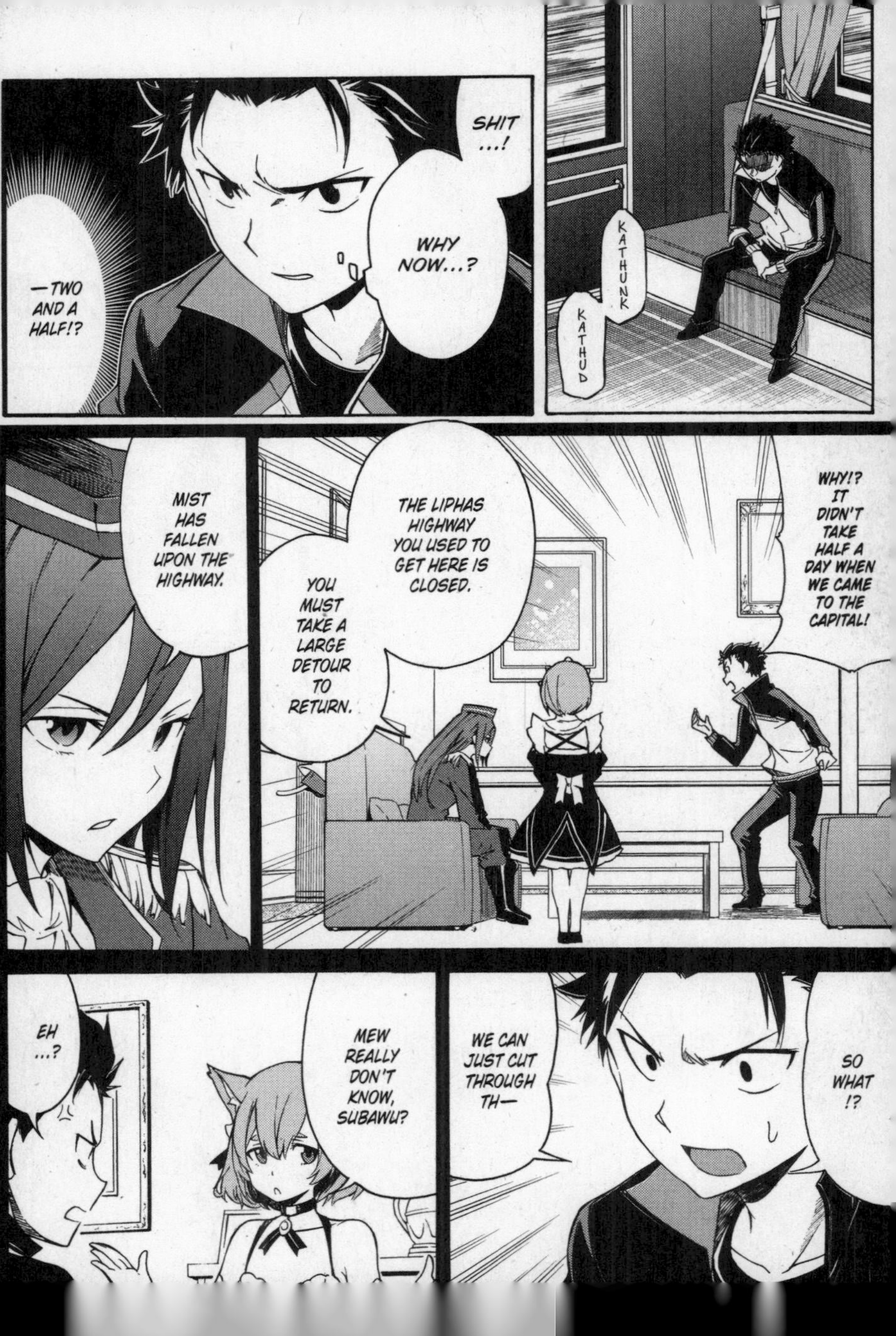
KATHUNK
KATHUD
SHIT ...!
WHY NOW...?
—TWO AND A HALF!?
WHY!? IT DIDN'T TAKE HALF A DAY WHEN WE CAME TO THE CAPITAL!
THE LIPHAS HIGHWAY YOU USED TO GET HERE IS CLOSED.
YOU MUST TAKE A LARGE DETOUR TO RETURN.
MIST HAS FALLEN UPON THE HIGHWAY.
SO WHAT!?
WE CAN JUST CUT THROUGH TH—
MEW REALLY DON'T KNOW, SUBAWU?
EH ...?

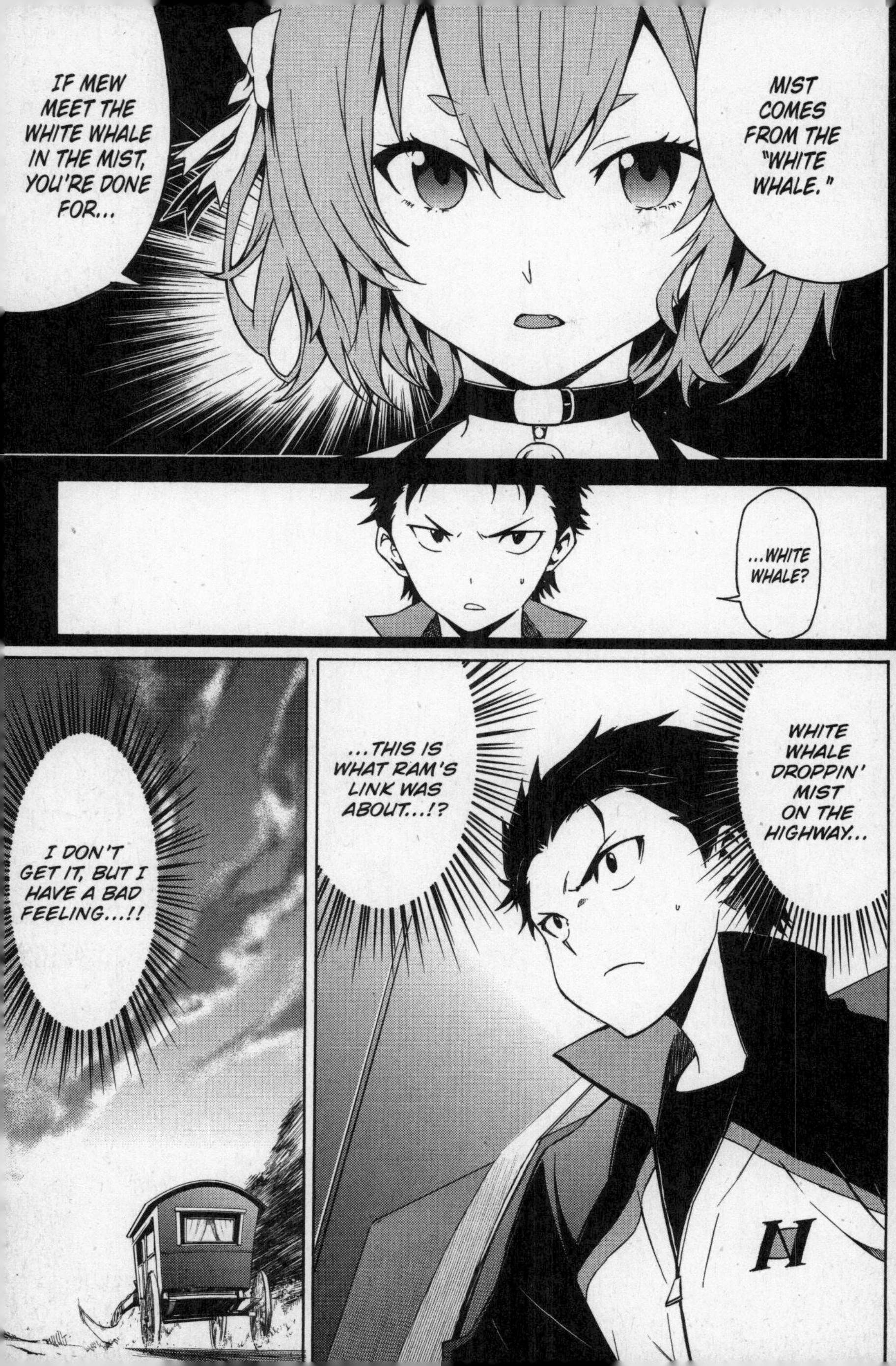
MIST COMES FROM THE "WHITE WHALE."
IF MEW MEET THE WHITE WHALE IN THE MIST, YOU'RE DONE FOR...
...WHITE WHALE?
WHITE WHALE DROPPIN' MIST ON THE HIGHWAY...
...THIS IS WHAT RAM'S LINK WAS ABOUT...!?
I DON'T GET IT, BUT I HAVE A BAD FEELING...!!

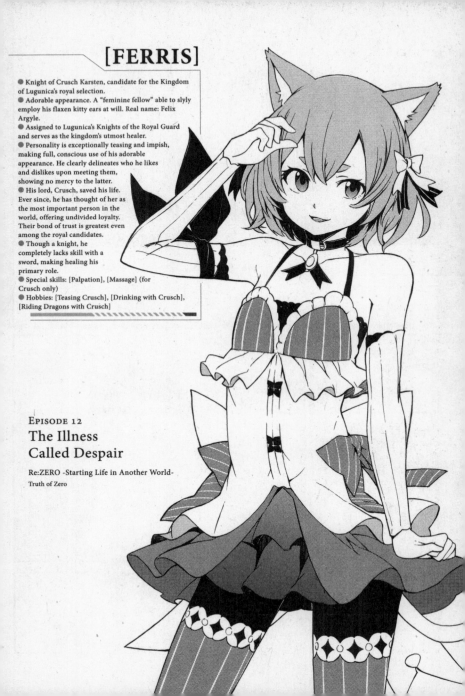

[FERRIS]

- Knight of Crusch Karsten, candidate for the Kingdom of Lugunica's royal selection.
- Adorable appearance. A "feminine fellow" able to slyly employ his flaxen kitty ears at will. Real name: Felix Argyle.
- Assigned to Lugunica's Knights of the Royal Guard and serves as the kingdom's utmost healer.
- Personality is exceptionally teasing and impish, making full, conscious use of his adorable appearance. He clearly delineates who he likes and dislikes upon meeting them, showing no mercy to the latter.
- His lord, Crusch, saved his life. Ever since, he has thought of her as the most important person in the world, offering undivided loyalty. Their bond of trust is greatest even among the royal candidates.
- Though a knight, he completely lacks skill with a sword, making healing his primary role.
- Special skills: [Palpation], [Massage] (for Crusch only)
- Hobbies: [Teasing Crusch], [Drinking with Crusch], [Riding Dragons with Crusch]

EPISODE 12

The Illness
Called Despair

Re:ZERO -Starting Life in Another World-
Truth of Zero

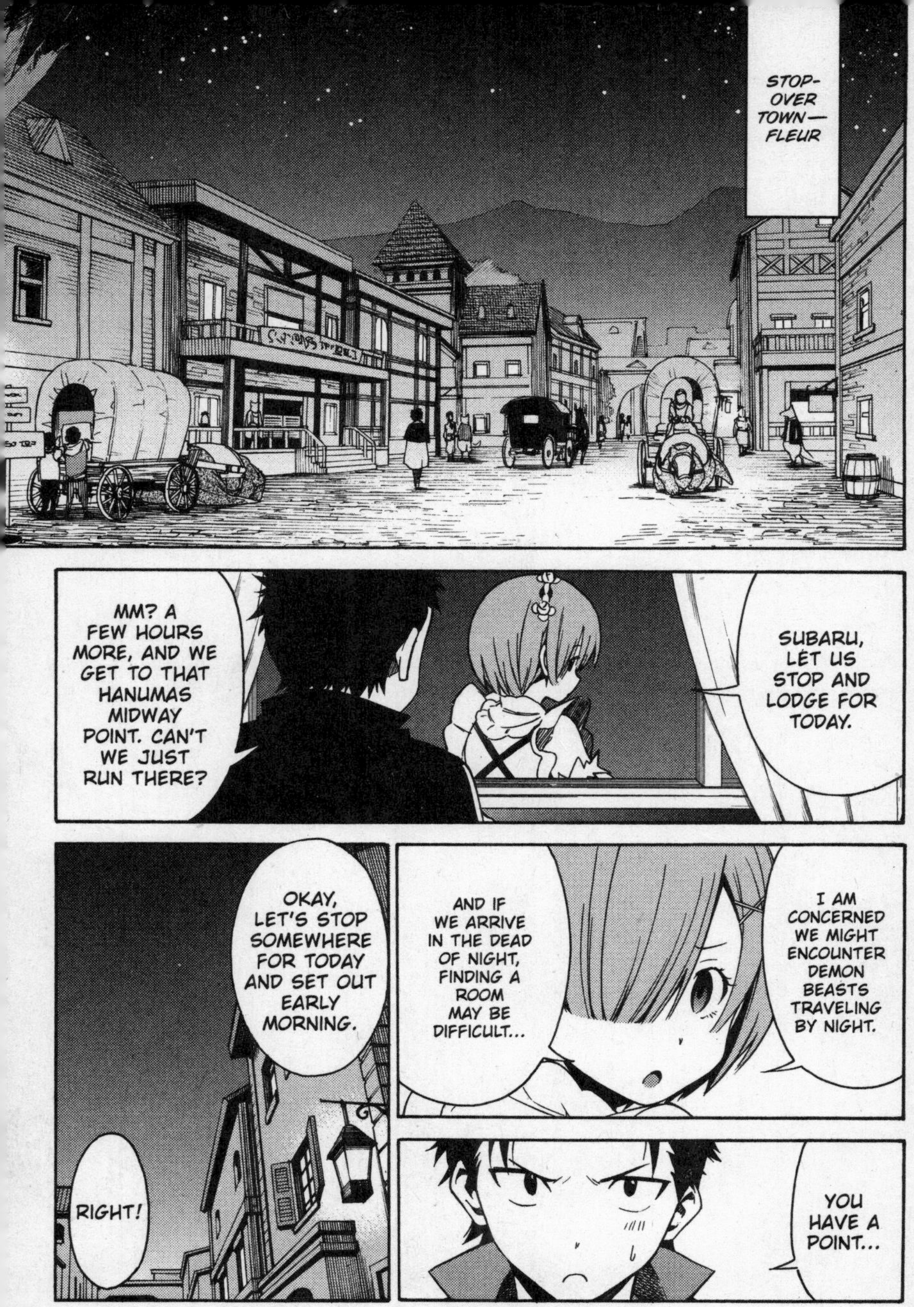
STOP-OVER TOWN—FLEUR
SUBARU, LET US STOP AND LODGE FOR TODAY.
MM? A FEW HOURS MORE, AND WE GET TO THAT HANUMAS MIDWAY POINT. CAN'T WE JUST RUN THERE?
I AM CONCERNED WE MIGHT ENCOUNTER DEMON BEASTS TRAVELING BY NIGHT.
AND IF WE ARRIVE IN THE DEAD OF NIGHT, FINDING A ROOM MAY BE DIFFICULT...
YOU HAVE A POINT...
OKAY, LET'S STOP SOMEWHERE FOR TODAY AND SET OUT EARLY MORNING.
RIGHT!

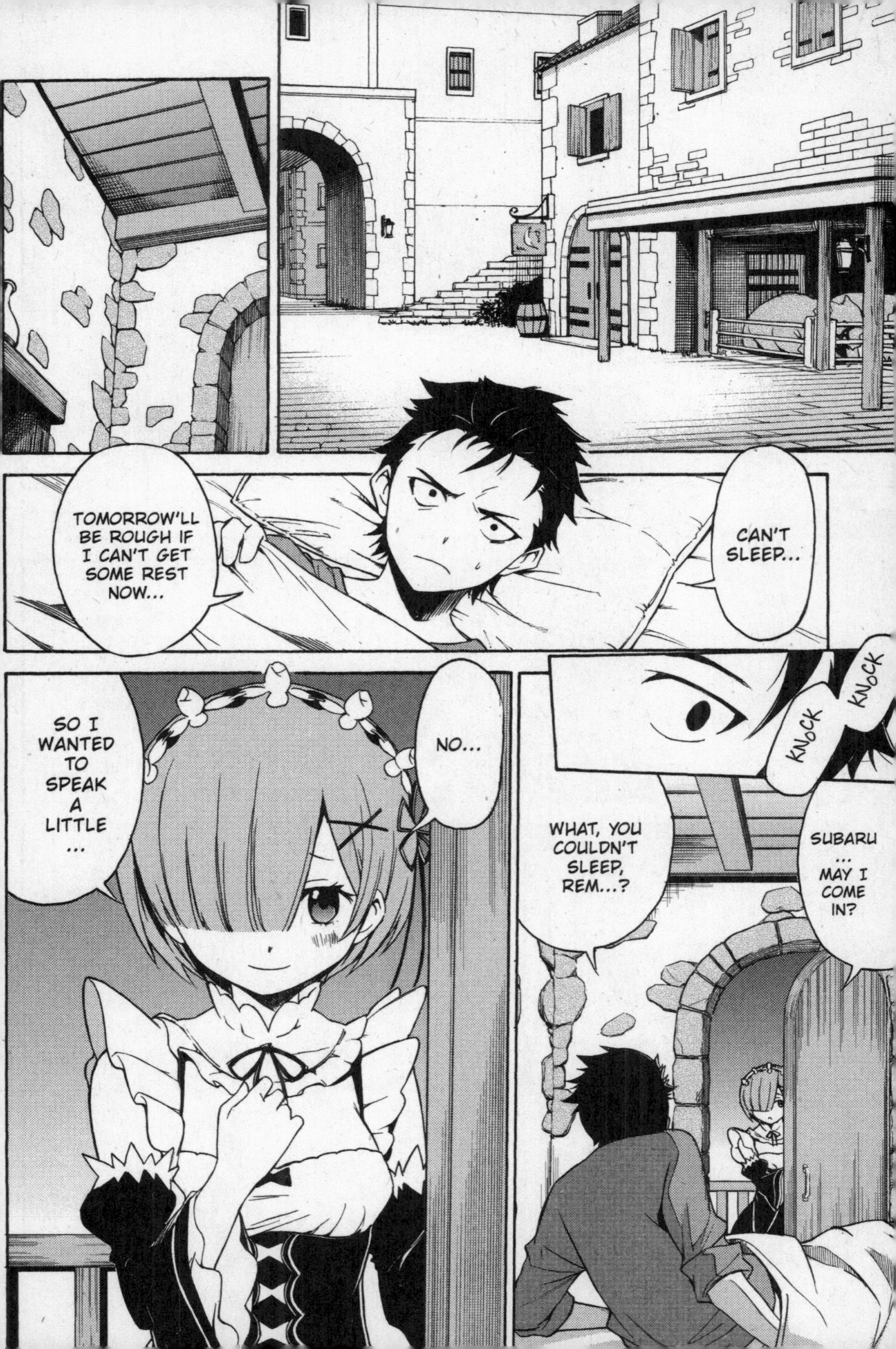
CAN'T SLEEP...
TOMORROW'LL BE ROUGH IF I CAN'T GET SOME REST NOW...
KNOCK
KNOCK
SUBARU... MAY I COME IN?
WHAT, YOU COULDN'T SLEEP, REM...?
NO...
SO I WANTED TO SPEAK A LITTLE...

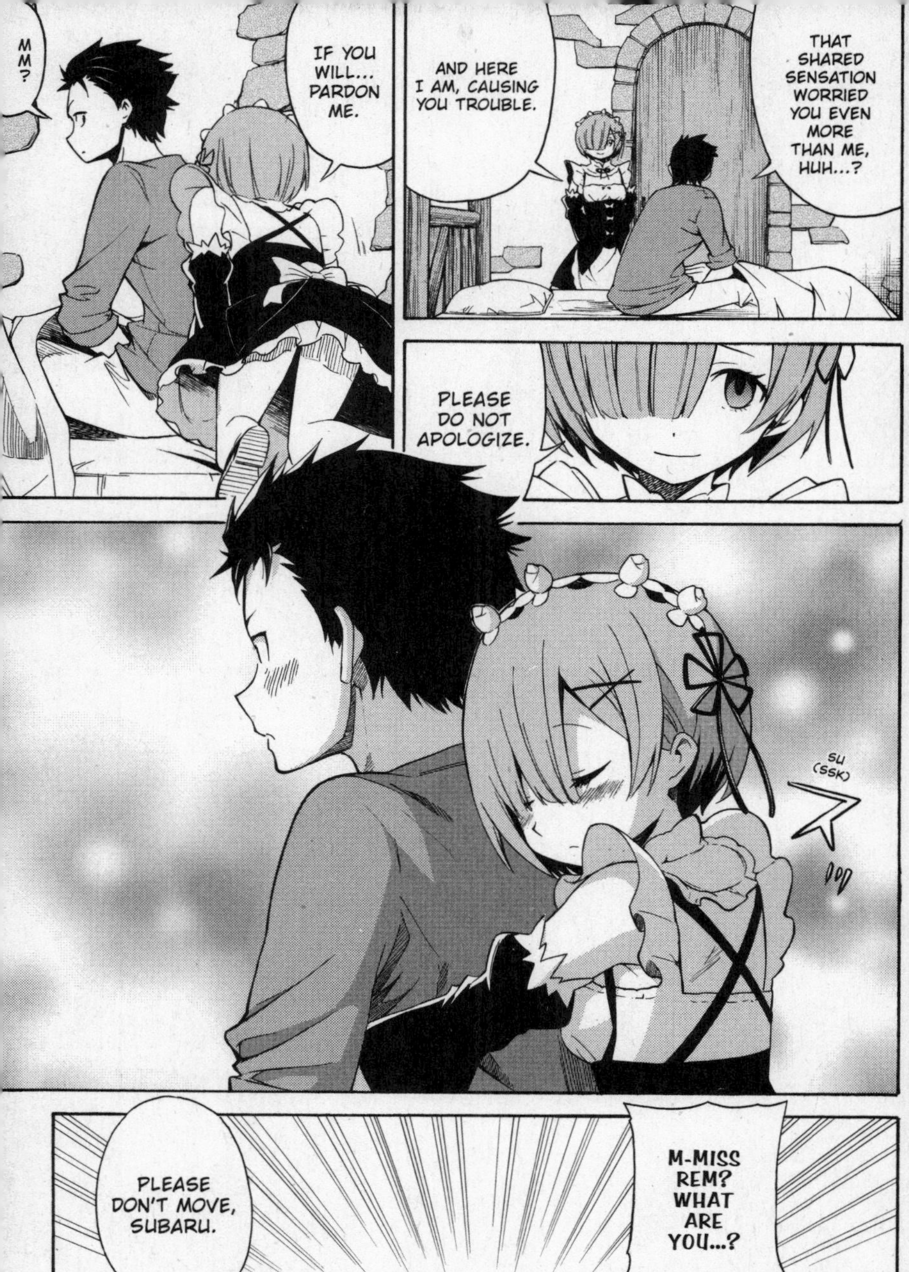

THAT SHARED SENSATION WORRIED YOU EVEN MORE THAN ME, HUH...?
AND HERE I AM, CAUSING YOU TROUBLE.
PLEASE DO NOT APOLOGIZE.
IF YOU WILL... PARDON ME.
MM?
SU (SSK)
M-MISS REM? WHAT ARE YOU...?
PLEASE DON'T MOVE, SUBARU.

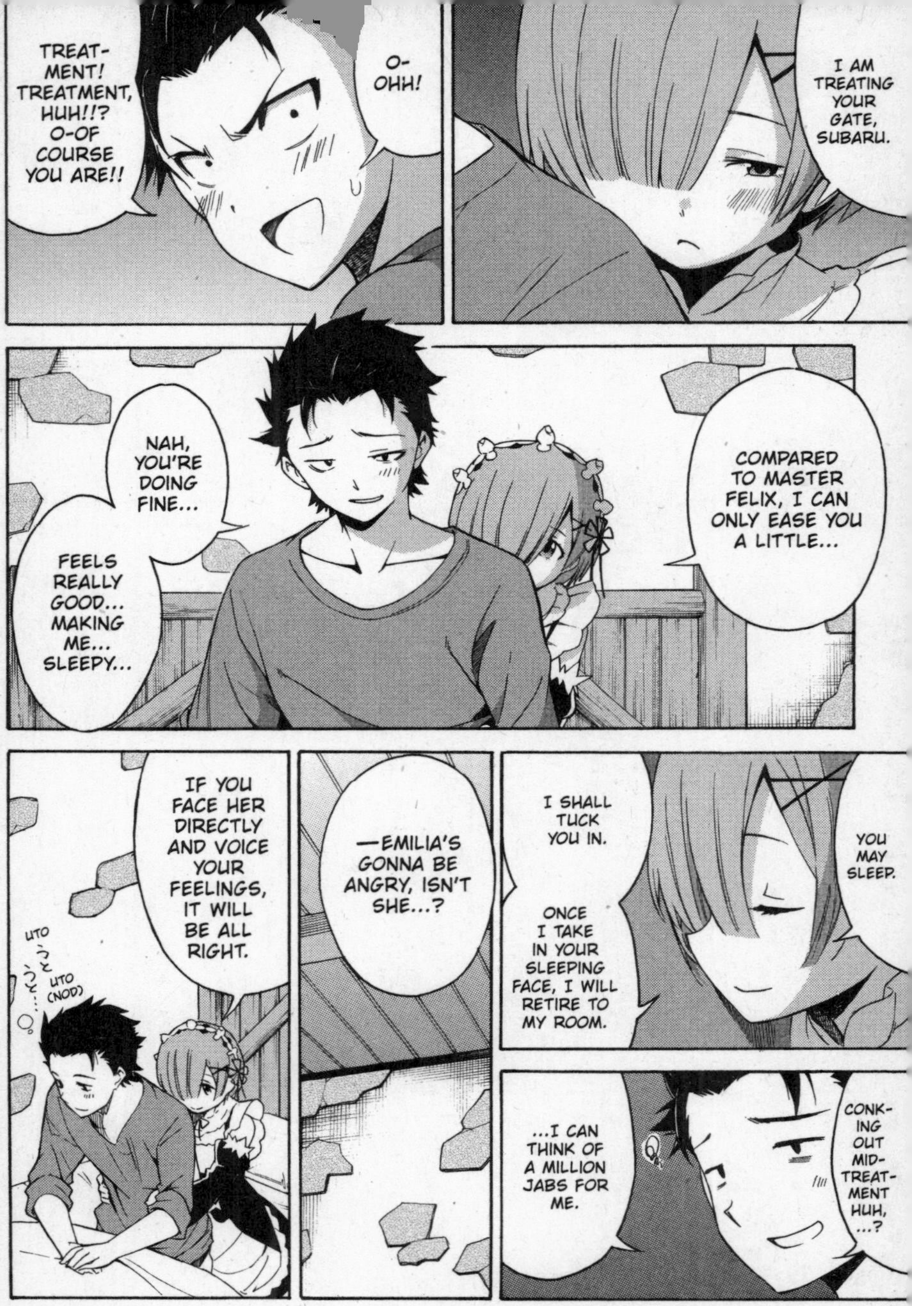
I AM TREATING YOUR GATE, SUBARU.
O-OHH!
TREATMENT! TREATMENT, HUH!!? O-OF COURSE YOU ARE!!
COMPARED TO MASTER FELIX, I CAN ONLY EASE YOU A LITTLE...
NAH, YOU'RE DOING FINE...
FEELS REALLY GOOD... MAKING ME... SLEEPY...
YOU MAY SLEEP.
I SHALL TUCK YOU IN.
ONCE I TAKE IN YOUR SLEEPING FACE, I WILL RETIRE TO MY ROOM.
CONKING OUT MID-TREATMENT HUH, ...?
...I CAN THINK OF A MILLION JABS FOR ME.
—EMILIA'S GONNA BE ANGRY, ISN'T SHE...?
IF YOU FACE HER DIRECTLY AND VOICE YOUR FEELINGS, IT WILL BE ALL RIGHT.
UTO
UTO (NOD)

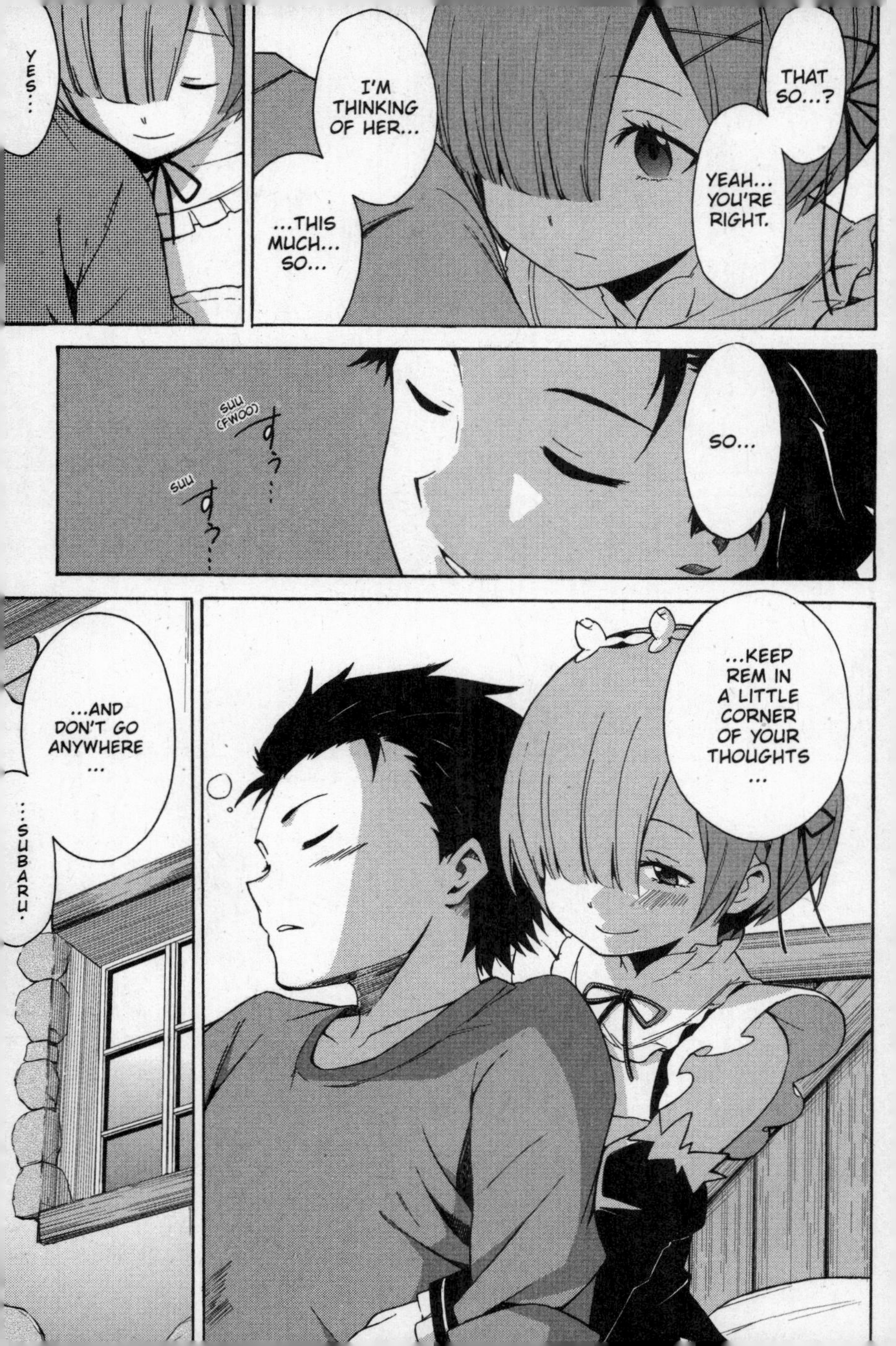
THAT SO...?
I'M THINKING OF HER...
YEAH... YOU'RE RIGHT.
...THIS MUCH... SO...
YES...
SO...
SUU (FWOO)
SUU
...KEEP REM IN A LITTLE CORNER OF YOUR THOUGHTS ...
...AND DON'T GO ANYWHERE ...
...SUBARU.

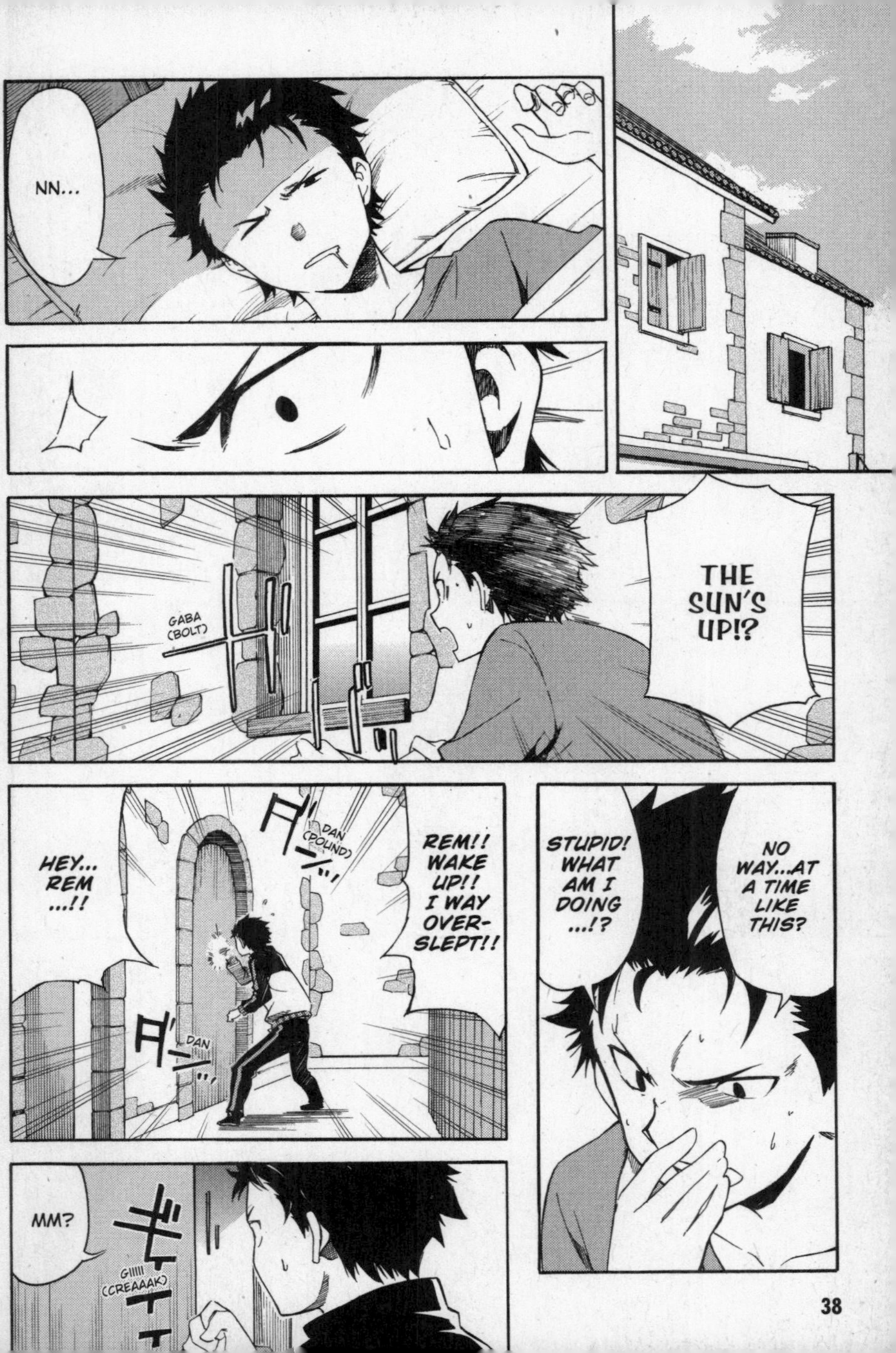
NN...
GABA (BOLT)
THE SUN'S UP!?
NO WAY...AT A TIME LIKE THIS?
STUPID! WHAT AM I DOING ...!?
REM!! WAKE UP!! I WAY OVER-SLEPT!!
DAN (POUND)
HEY... REM ...!!
DAN
MM?
GIIII (CREAAAK)

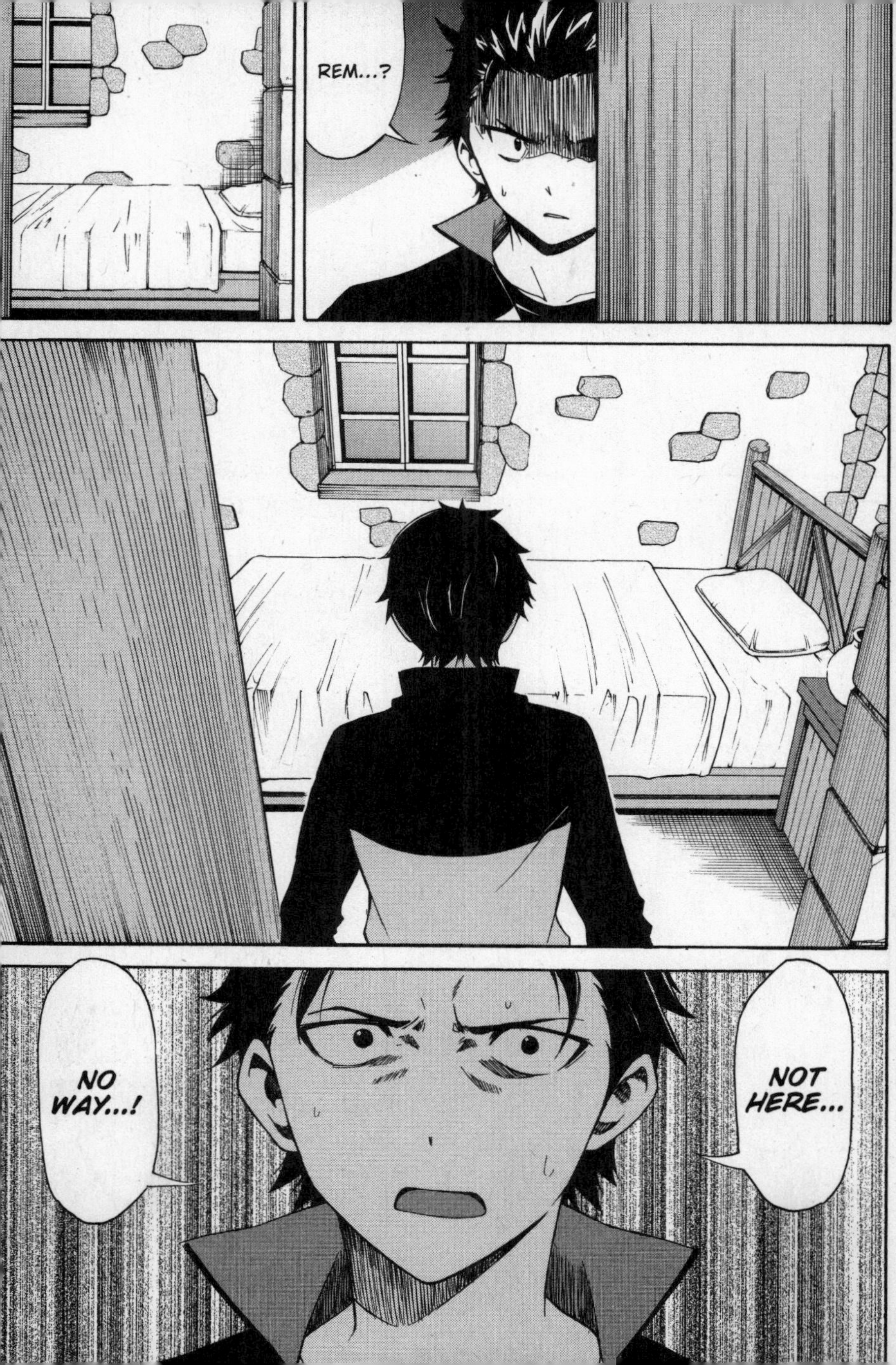
REM...?
NOT HERE...
NO WAY...!

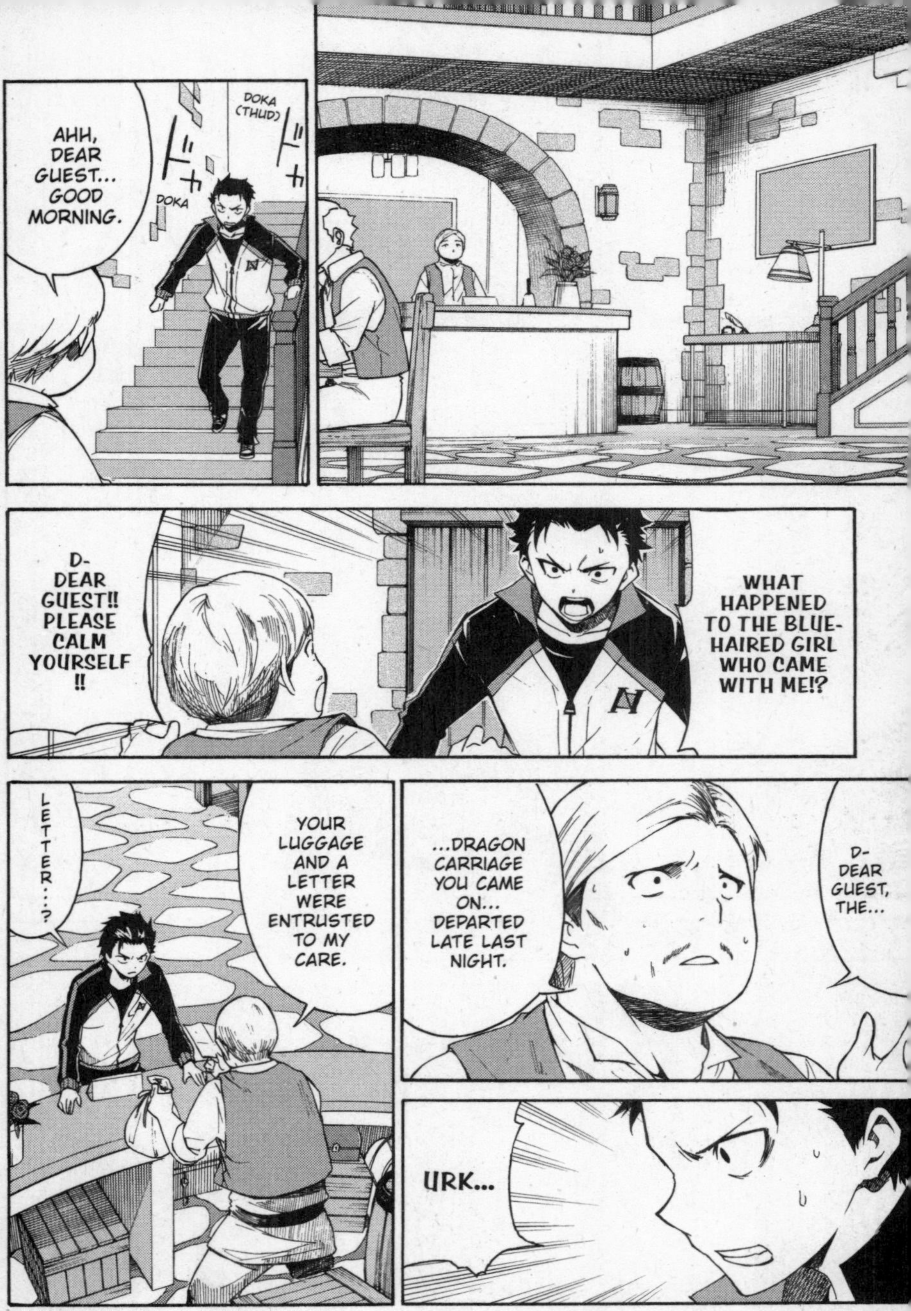

DOKA (THUD)
ドカ
ドカ
DOKA
AHH, DEAR GUEST... GOOD MORNING.
WHAT HAPPENED TO THE BLUE-HAIRED GIRL WHO CAME WITH ME!?
D-DEAR GUEST!! PLEASE CALM YOURSELF!!
D-DEAR GUEST, THE...
...DRAGON CARRIAGE YOU CAME ON... DEPARTED LATE LAST NIGHT.
URK...
YOUR LUGGAGE AND A LETTER WERE ENTRUSTED TO MY CARE.
LETTER...?

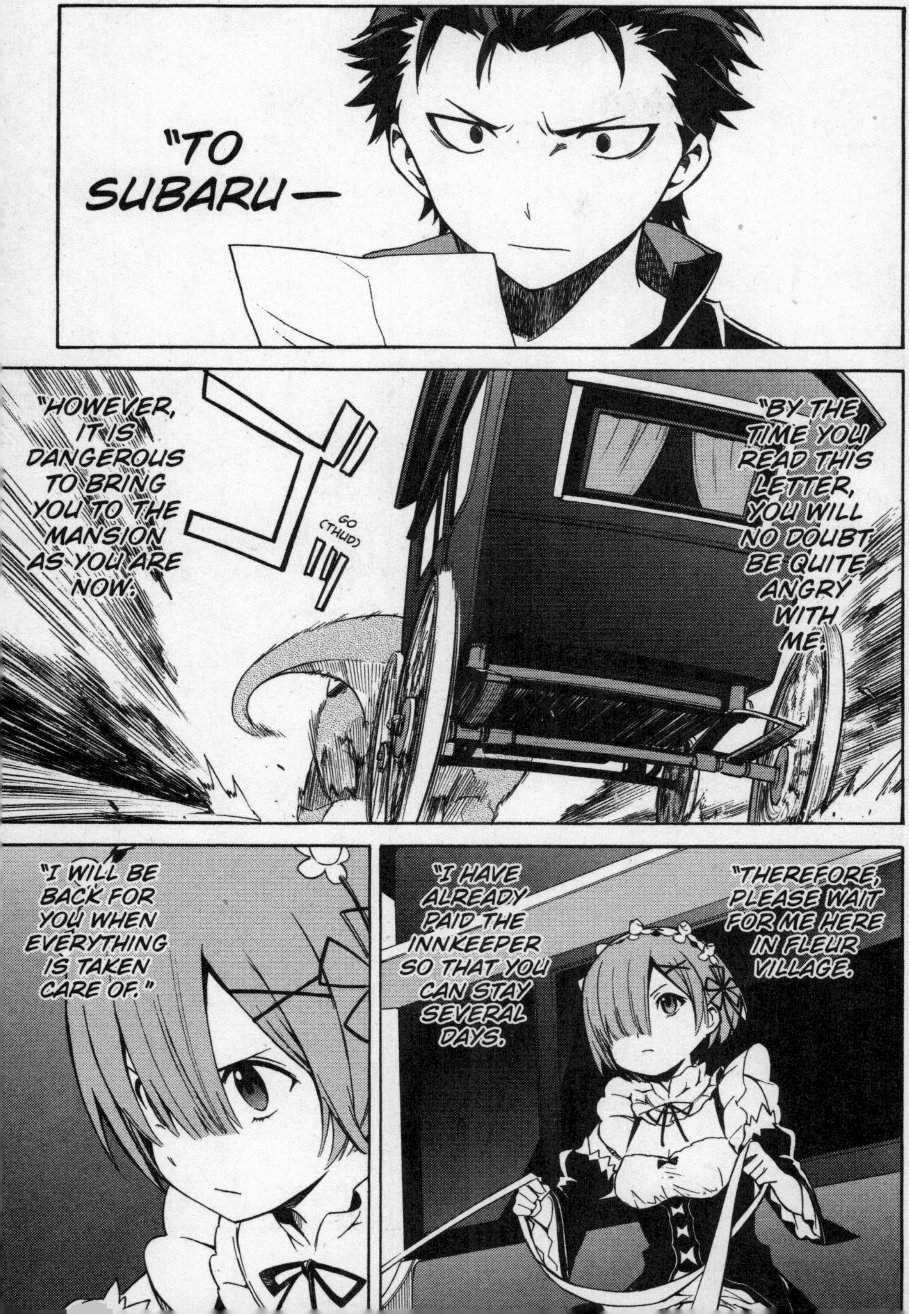
"TO SUBARU—
"BY THE TIME YOU READ THIS LETTER, YOU WILL NO DOUBT BE QUITE ANGRY WITH ME.
GO (THUD)
"HOWEVER, IT IS DANGEROUS TO BRING YOU TO THE MANSION AS YOU ARE NOW.
"THEREFORE, PLEASE WAIT FOR ME HERE IN FLEUR VILLAGE.
"I HAVE ALREADY PAID THE INNKEEPER SO THAT YOU CAN STAY SEVERAL DAYS.
"I WILL BE BACK FOR YOU WHEN EVERYTHING IS TAKEN CARE OF."

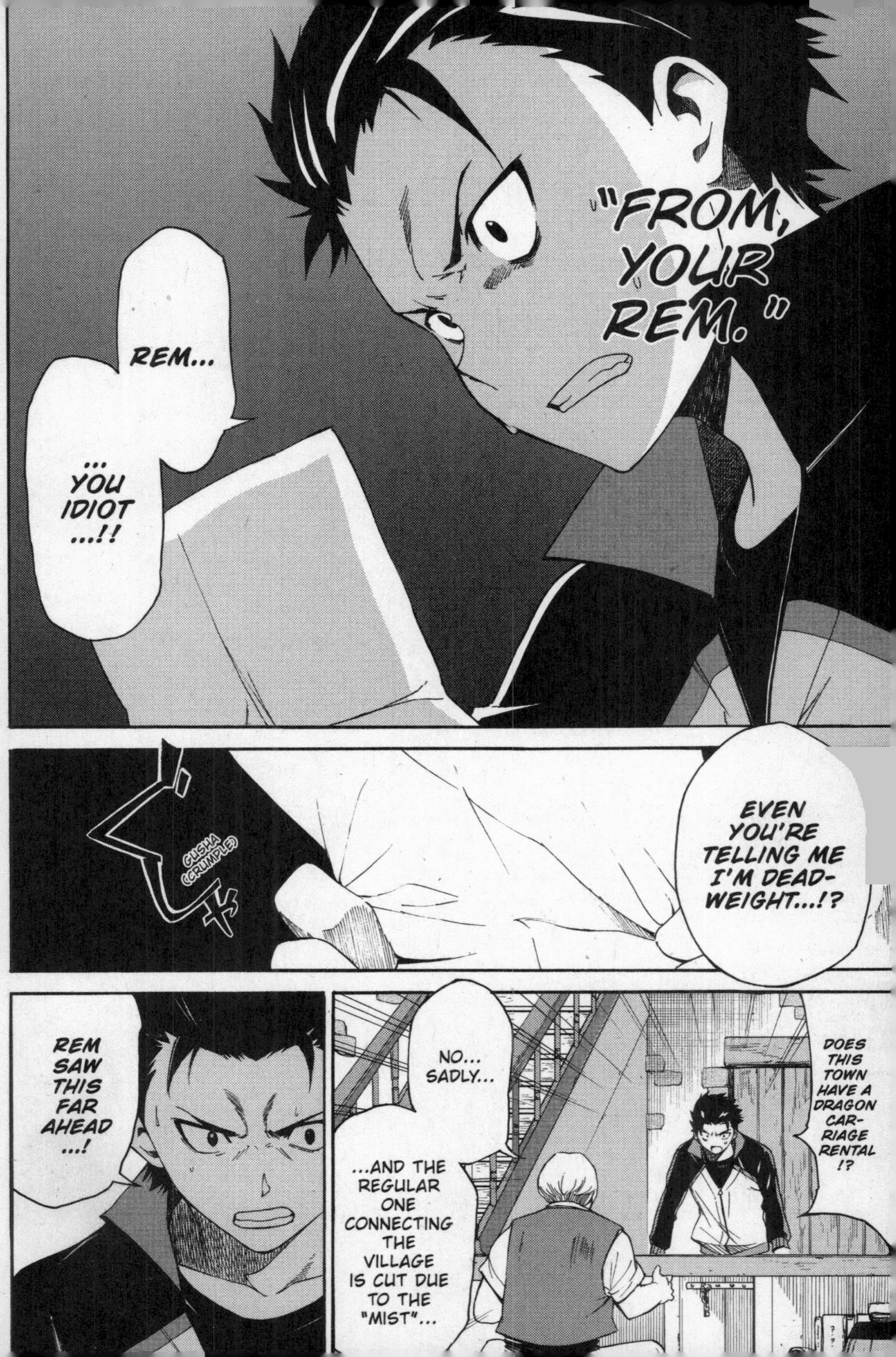
"FROM, YOUR REM."
REM...
...YOU IDIOT ...!!
EVEN YOU'RE TELLING ME I'M DEAD-WEIGHT...!?
GUSHA (CRUMPLE)
REM SAW THIS FAR AHEAD ...!
DOES THIS TOWN HAVE A DRAGON CAR-RIAGE RENTAL !?
NO... SADLY...
...AND THE REGULAR ONE CONNECTING THE VILLAGE IS CUT DUE TO THE "MIST"...

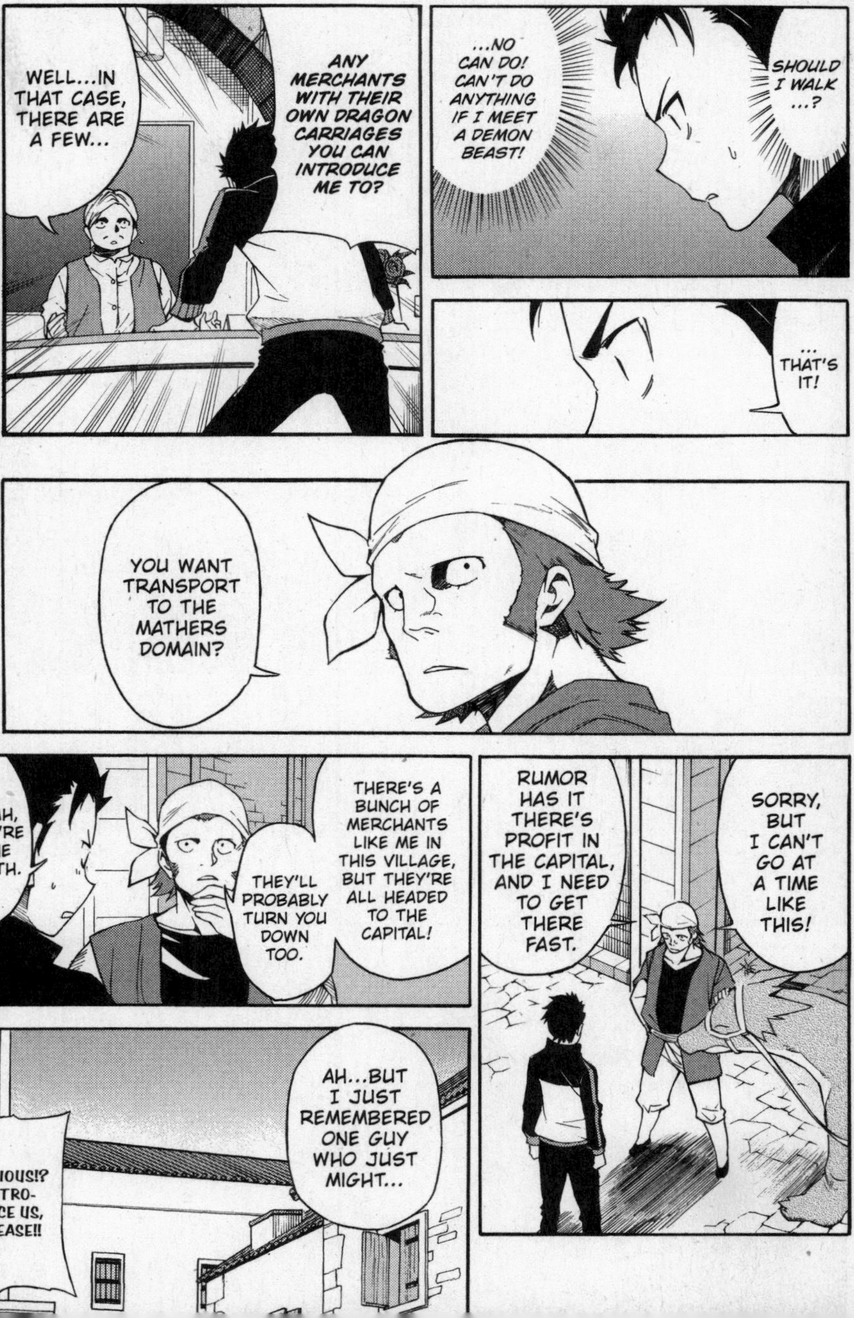
SHOULD I WALK ...?
...NO CAN DO! CAN'T DO ANYTHING IF I MEET A DEMON BEAST!
... THAT'S IT!
ANY MERCHANTS WITH THEIR OWN DRAGON CARRIAGES YOU CAN INTRODUCE ME TO?
WELL...IN THAT CASE, THERE ARE A FEW...
YOU WANT TRANSPORT TO THE MATHERS DOMAIN?
SORRY, BUT I CAN'T GO AT A TIME LIKE THIS!
RUMOR HAS IT THERE'S PROFIT IN THE CAPITAL, AND I NEED TO GET THERE FAST.
THERE'S A BUNCH OF MERCHANTS LIKE ME IN THIS VILLAGE, BUT THEY'RE ALL HEADED TO THE CAPITAL!
THEY'LL PROBABLY TURN YOU DOWN TOO.
YEAH, YOU'RE THE SIXTH.
AH...BUT I JUST REMEMBERED ONE GUY WHO JUST MIGHT...
SERIOUS!? INTRODUCE US, PLEASE!!

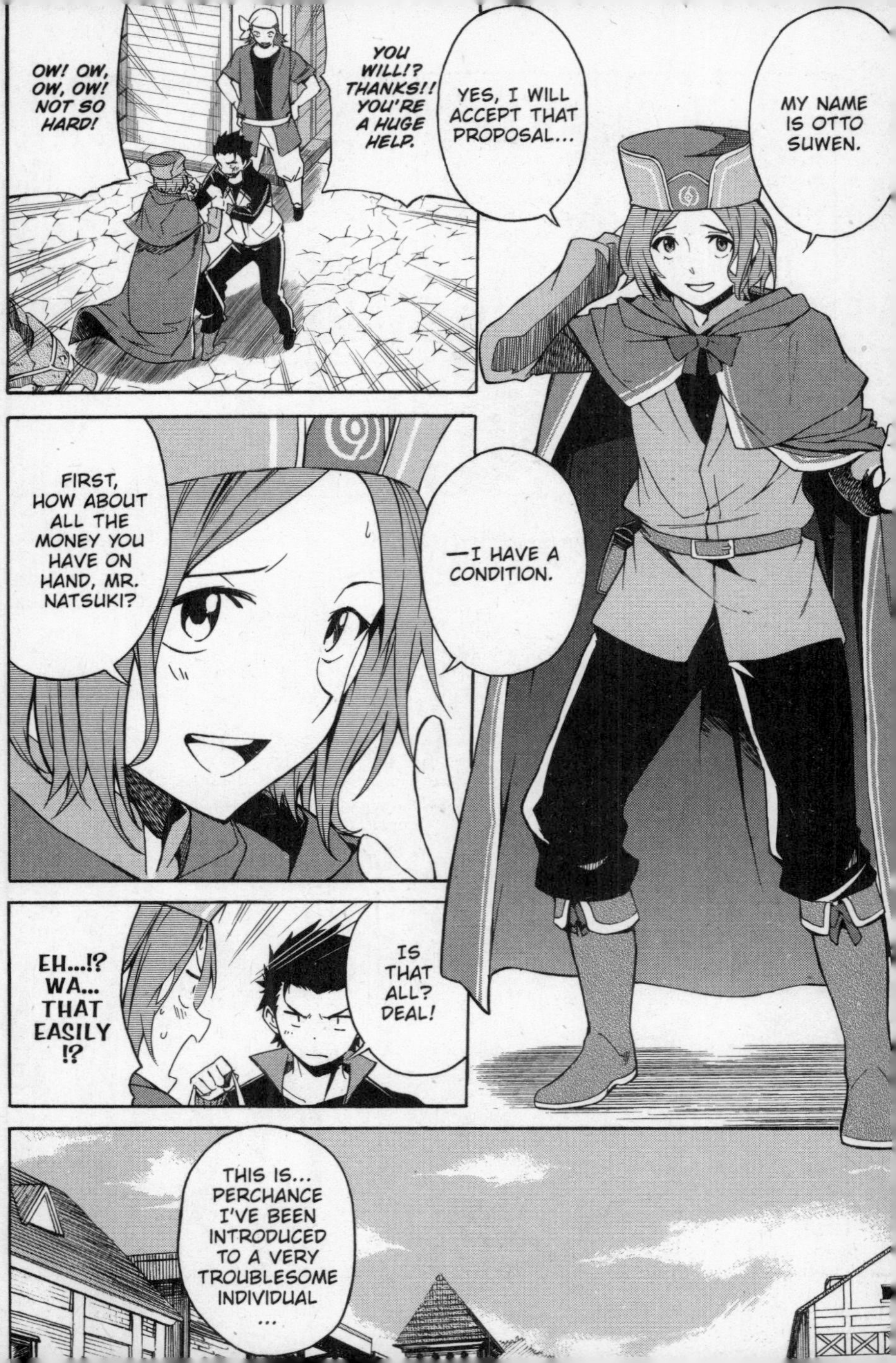

MY NAME IS OTTO SUWEN.
YES, I WILL ACCEPT THAT PROPOSAL...
—I HAVE A CONDITION.
YOU WILL!? THANKS!! YOU'RE A HUGE HELP.
OW! OW, OW, OW! NOT SO HARD!
FIRST, HOW ABOUT ALL THE MONEY YOU HAVE ON HAND, MR. NATSUKI?
IS THAT ALL? DEAL!
EH...!? WA... THAT EASILY!?
THIS IS... PERCHANCE I'VE BEEN INTRODUCED TO A VERY TROUBLESOME INDIVIDUAL...

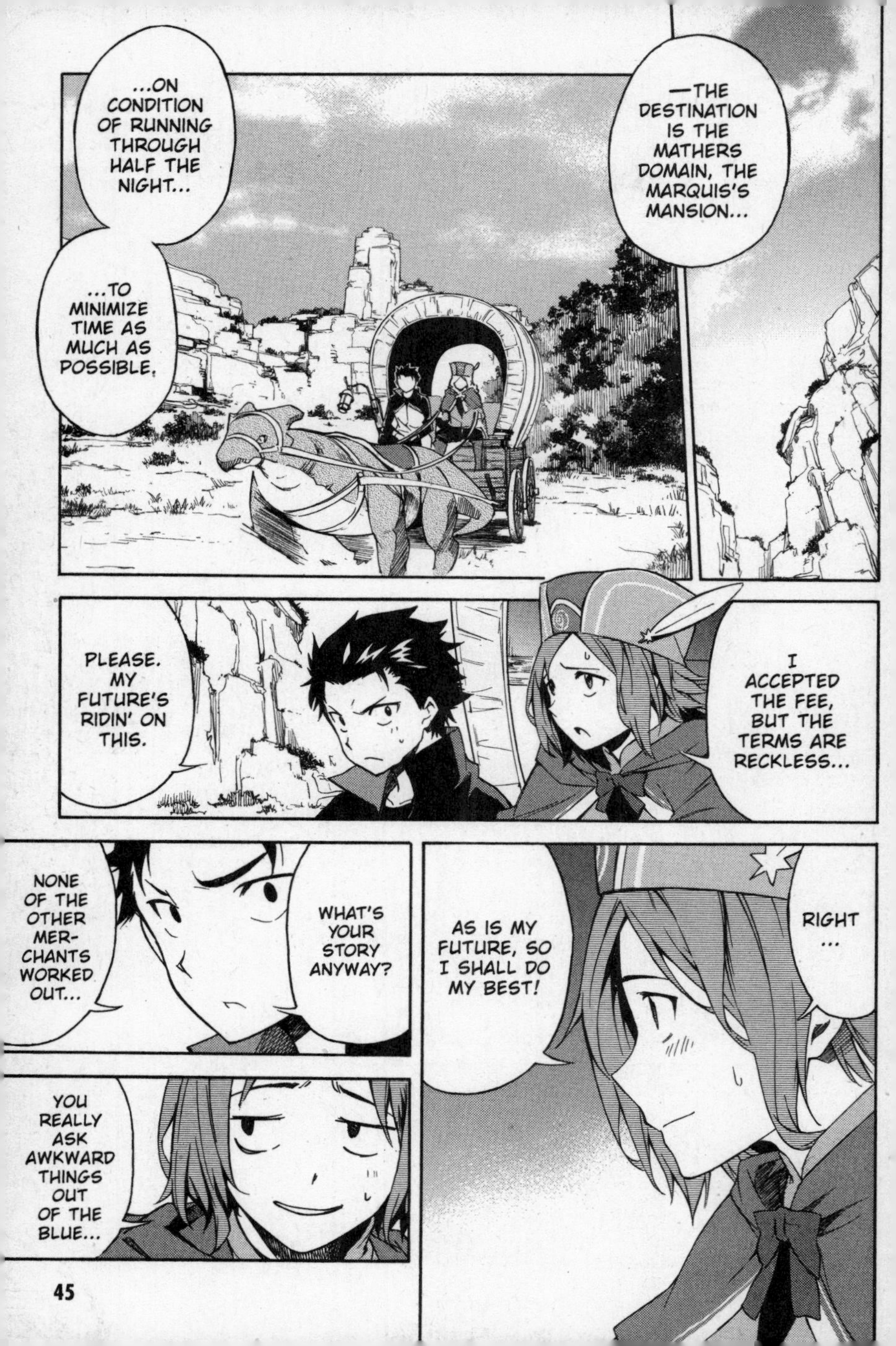
—THE DESTINATION IS THE MATHERS DOMAIN, THE MARQUIS'S MANSION...
...ON CONDITION OF RUNNING THROUGH HALF THE NIGHT...
...TO MINIMIZE TIME AS MUCH AS POSSIBLE.
I ACCEPTED THE FEE, BUT THE TERMS ARE RECKLESS...
PLEASE. MY FUTURE'S RIDIN' ON THIS.
RIGHT ...
AS IS MY FUTURE, SO I SHALL DO MY BEST!
WHAT'S YOUR STORY ANYWAY?
NONE OF THE OTHER MER-CHANTS WORKED OUT...
YOU REALLY ASK AWKWARD THINGS OUT OF THE BLUE...

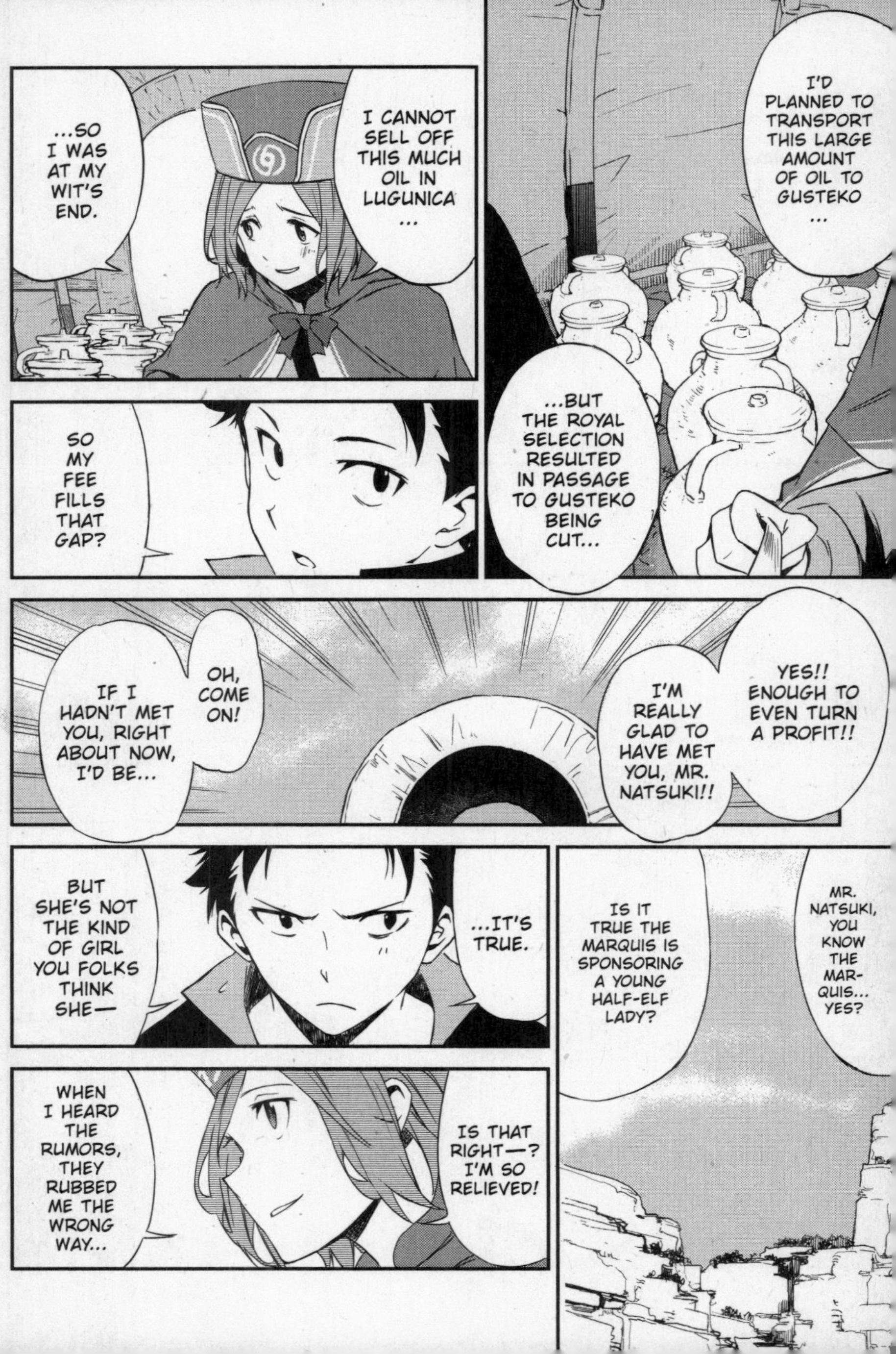
I'D PLANNED TO TRANSPORT THIS LARGE AMOUNT OF OIL TO GUSTEKO ...
...BUT THE ROYAL SELECTION RESULTED IN PASSAGE TO GUSTEKO BEING CUT...
I CANNOT SELL OFF THIS MUCH OIL IN LUGUNICA ...
...SO I WAS AT MY WIT'S END.
SO MY FEE FILLS THAT GAP?
YES!! ENOUGH TO EVEN TURN A PROFIT!!
I'M REALLY GLAD TO HAVE MET YOU, MR. NATSUKI!!
OH, COME ON!
IF I HADN'T MET YOU, RIGHT ABOUT NOW, I'D BE...
MR. NATSUKI, YOU KNOW THE MAR-QUIS... YES?
IS IT TRUE THE MARQUIS IS SPONSORING A YOUNG HALF-ELF LADY?
...IT'S TRUE.
BUT SHE'S NOT THE KIND OF GIRL YOU FOLKS THINK SHE—
IS THAT RIGHT—? I'M SO RELIEVED!
WHEN I HEARD THE RUMORS, THEY RUBBED ME THE WRONG WAY...

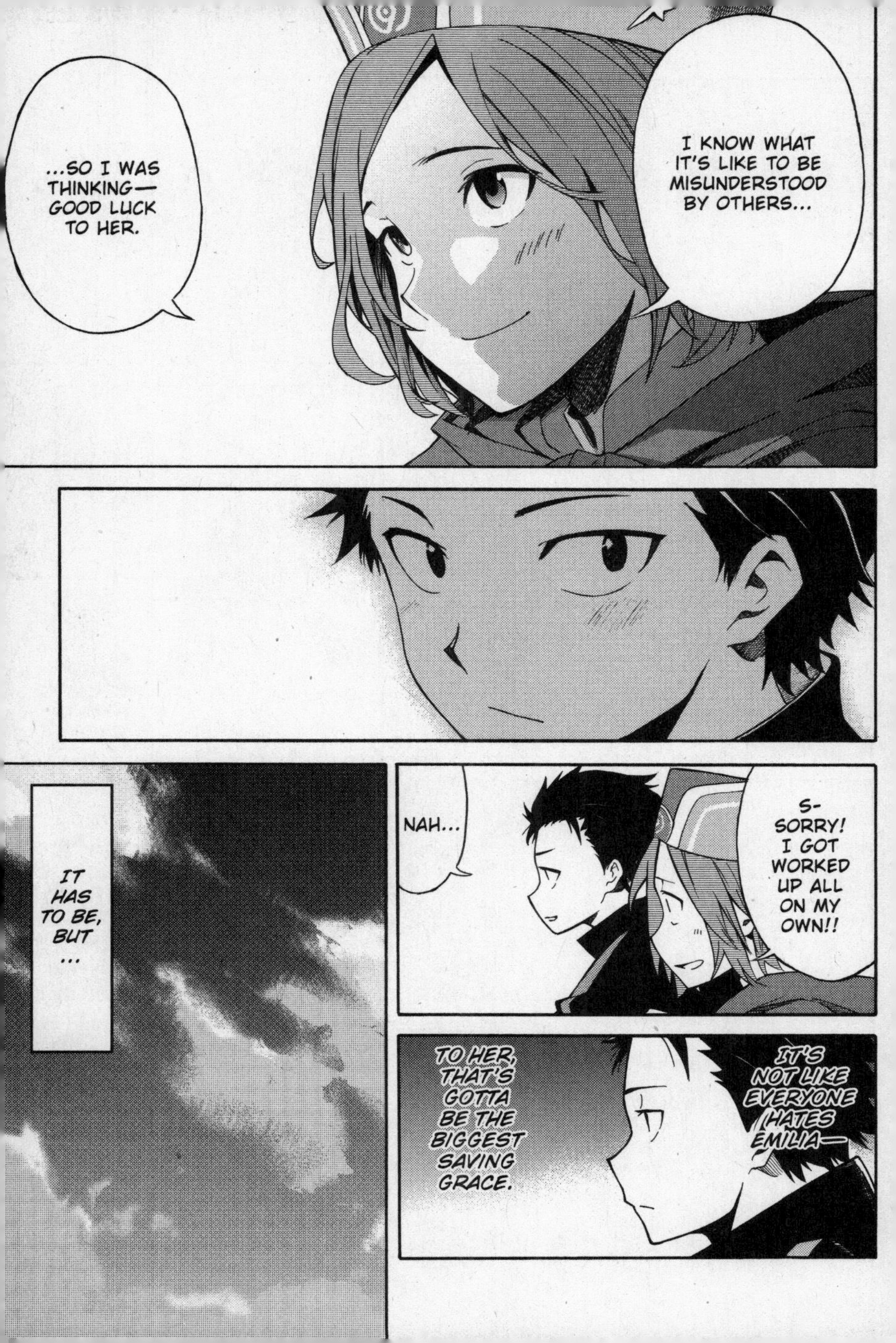
I KNOW WHAT IT'S LIKE TO BE MISUNDERSTOOD BY OTHERS...
...SO I WAS THINKING—GOOD LUCK TO HER.
S-SORRY! I GOT WORKED UP ALL ON MY OWN!!
NAH...
IT'S NOT LIKE EVERYONE HATES EMILIA—
TO HER, THAT'S GOTTA BE THE BIGGEST SAVING GRACE.
IT HAS TO BE, BUT ...

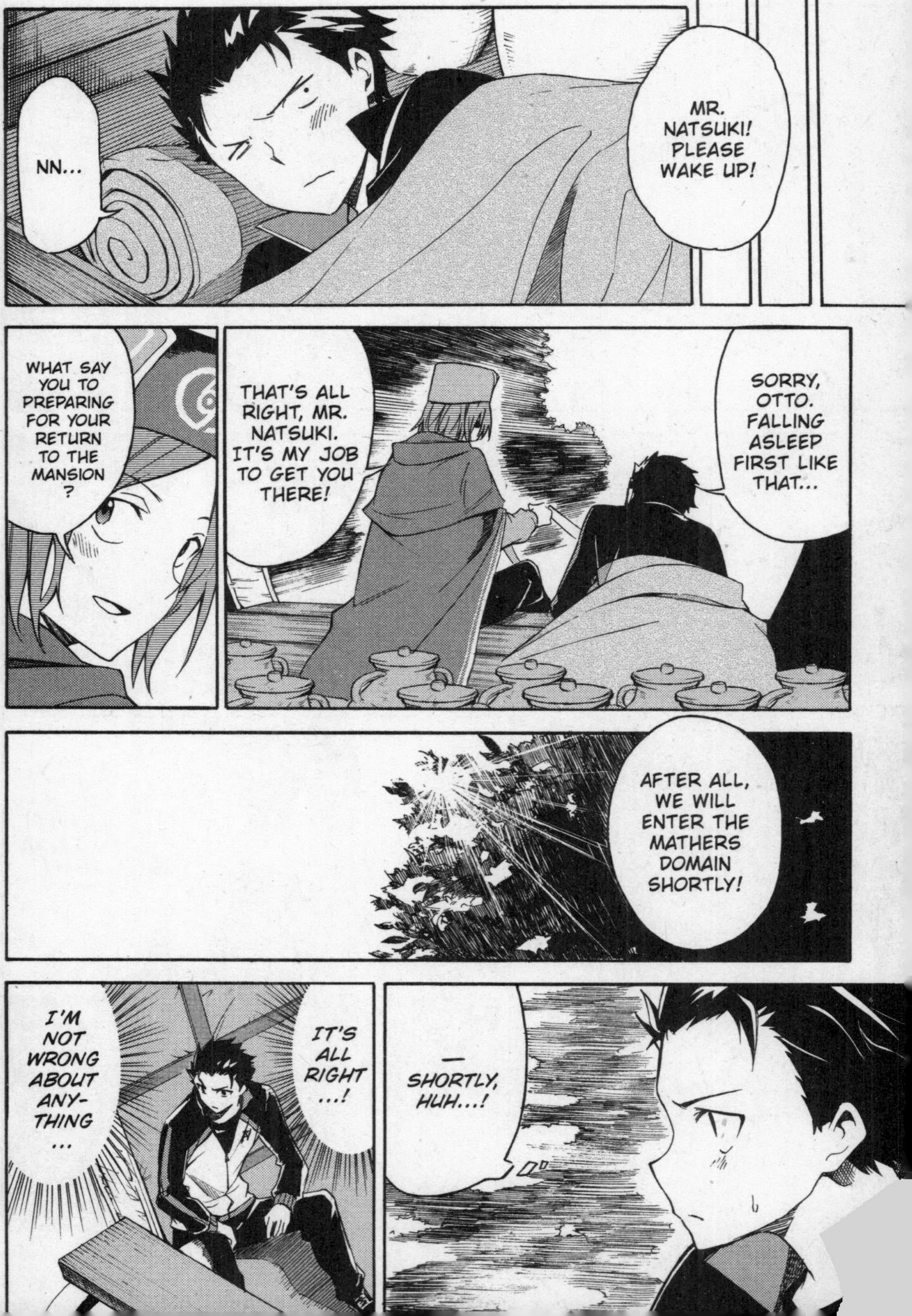
MR. NATSUKI! PLEASE WAKE UP!
NN...
SORRY, OTTO. FALLING ASLEEP FIRST LIKE THAT...
THAT'S ALL RIGHT, MR. NATSUKI. IT'S MY JOB TO GET YOU THERE!
WHAT SAY YOU TO PREPARING FOR YOUR RETURN TO THE MANSION?
AFTER ALL, WE WILL ENTER THE MATHERS DOMAIN SHORTLY!
—SHORTLY, HUH...!
IT'S ALL RIGHT...!
I'M NOT WRONG ABOUT ANY-THING...

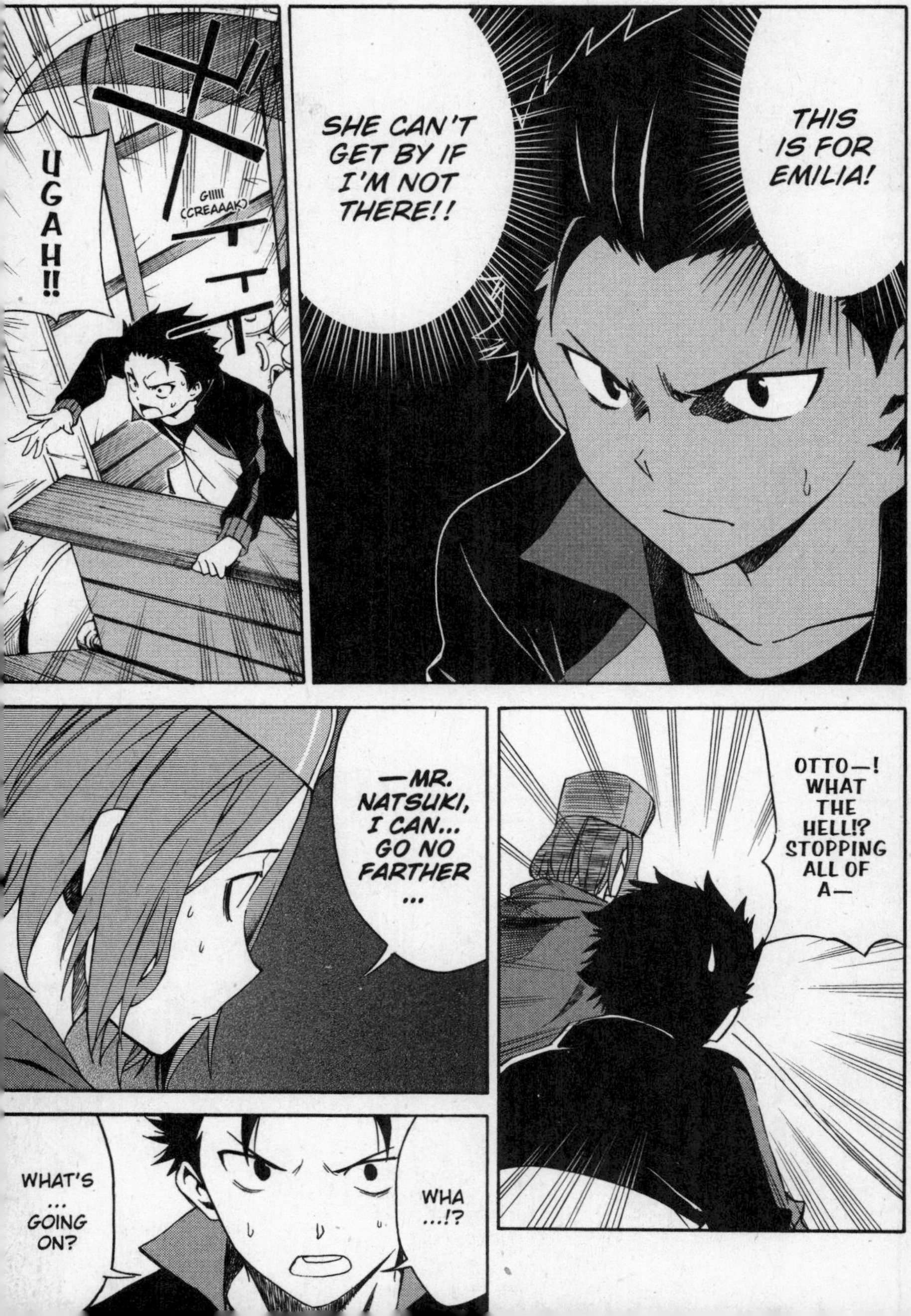
THIS IS FOR EMILIA!
SHE CAN'T GET BY IF I'M NOT THERE!!
GIIII (CREAAAK)
UGAH!!
OTTO—! WHAT THE HELL!? STOPPING ALL OF A—
—MR. NATSUKI, I CAN... GO NO FARTHER ...
WHA ...!?
WHAT'S ... GOING ON?

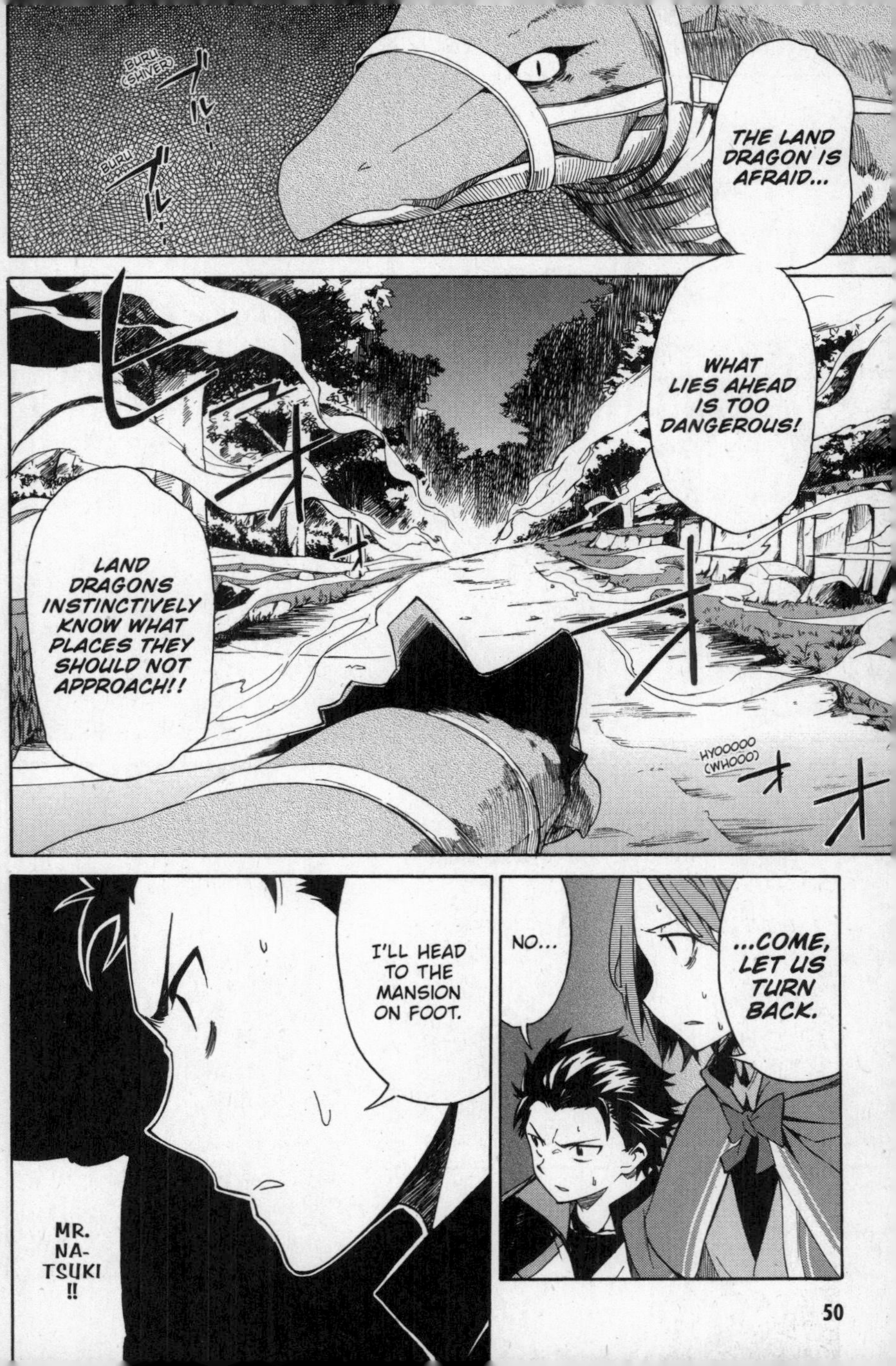
BURU (SHIVER)
BURU
THE LAND DRAGON IS AFRAID...
WHAT LIES AHEAD IS TOO DANGEROUS!
LAND DRAGONS INSTINCTIVELY KNOW WHAT PLACES THEY SHOULD NOT APPROACH!!
HYOOOOO (WHOOO)
...COME, LET US TURN BACK.
NO...
I'LL HEAD TO THE MANSION ON FOOT.
MR. NATSUKI!!

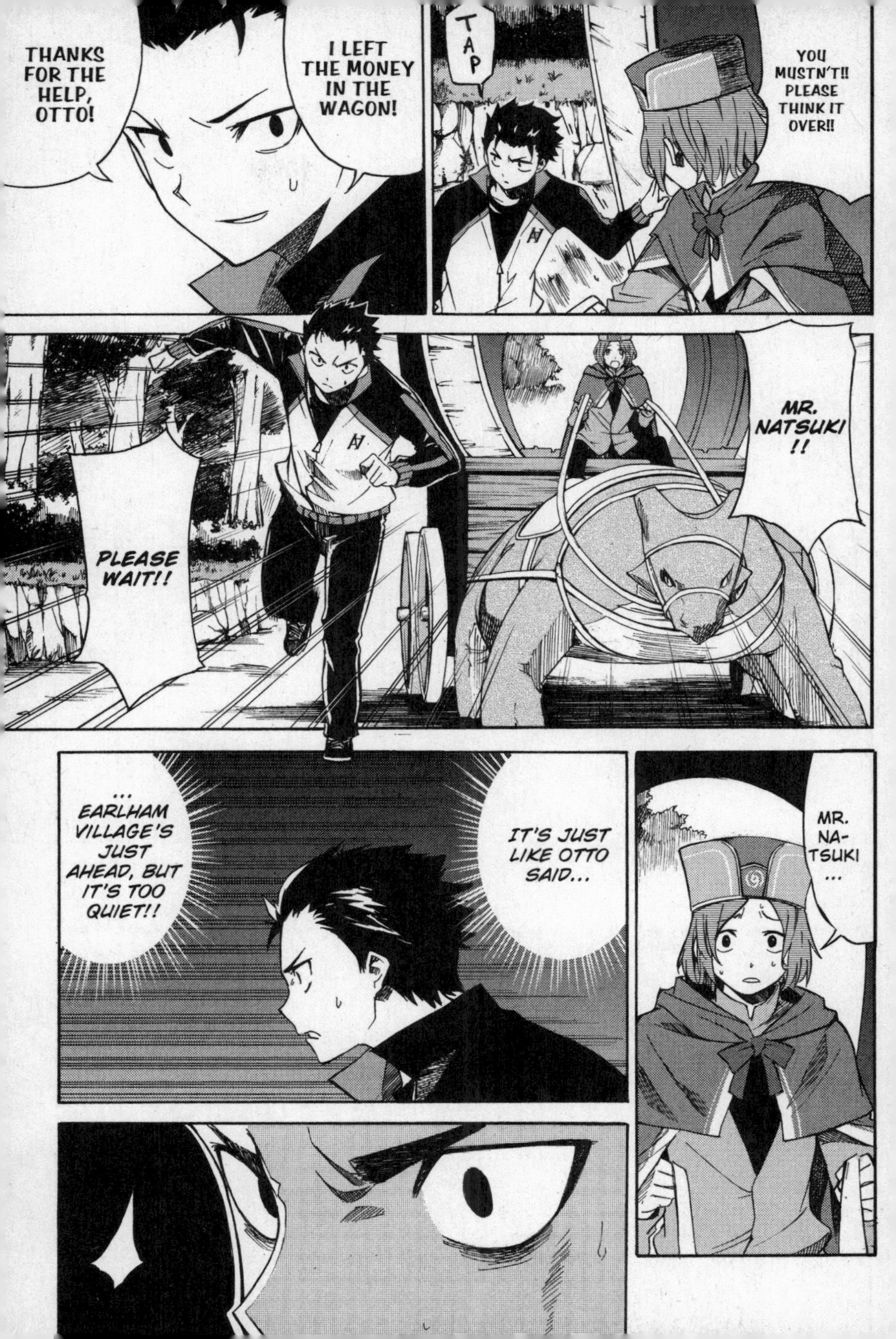
YOU MUSTN'T!! PLEASE THINK IT OVER!!
TAP
I LEFT THE MONEY IN THE WAGON!
THANKS FOR THE HELP, OTTO!
MR. NATSUKI!!
PLEASE WAIT!!
MR. NA-TSUKI...
IT'S JUST LIKE OTTO SAID...
...EARLHAM VILLAGE'S JUST AHEAD, BUT IT'S TOO QUIET!!

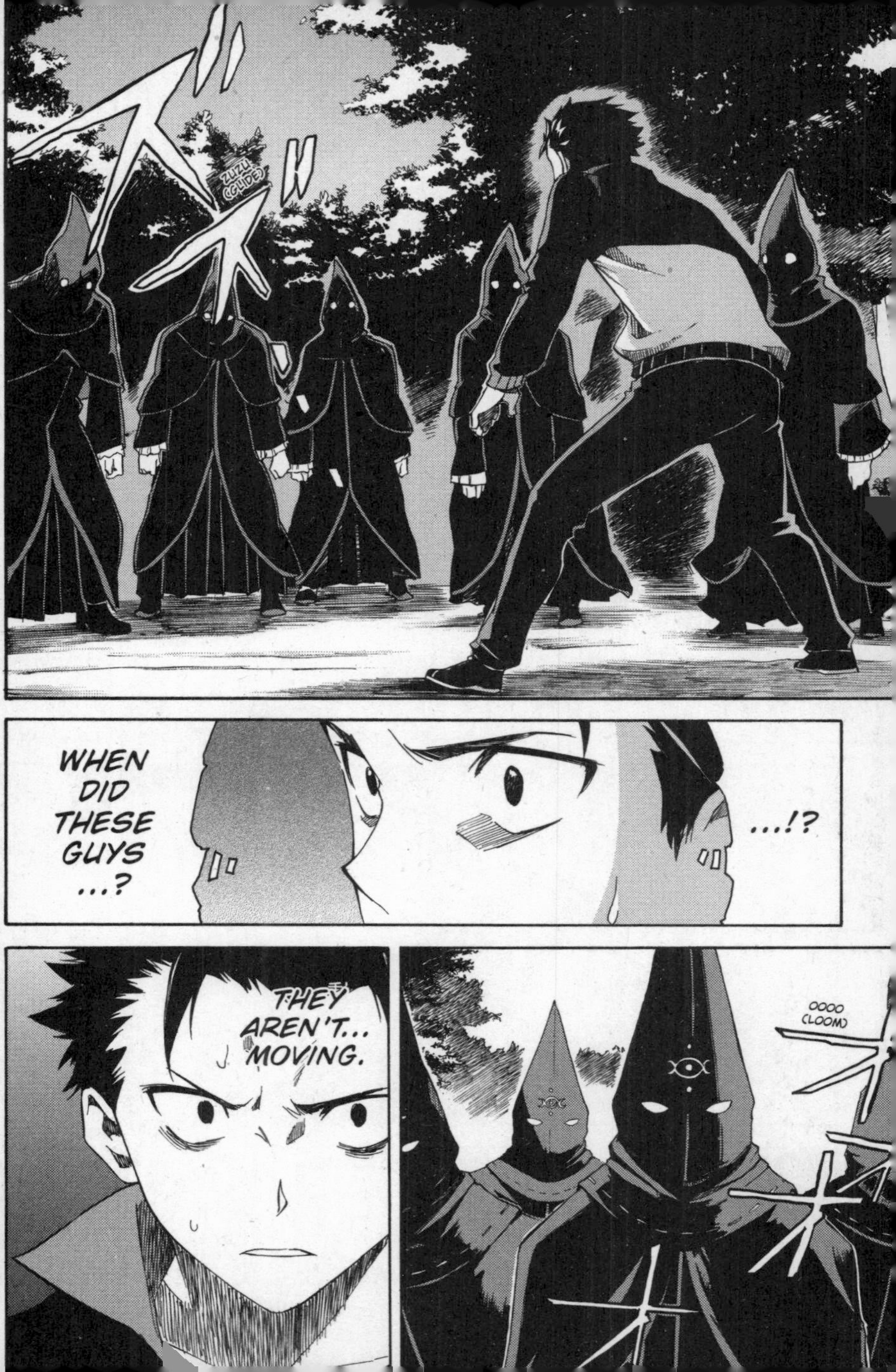
ZUZU (GLIDE)
...!?
WHEN DID THESE GUYS ...?
OOOO (LOOM)
THEY AREN'T... MOVING.

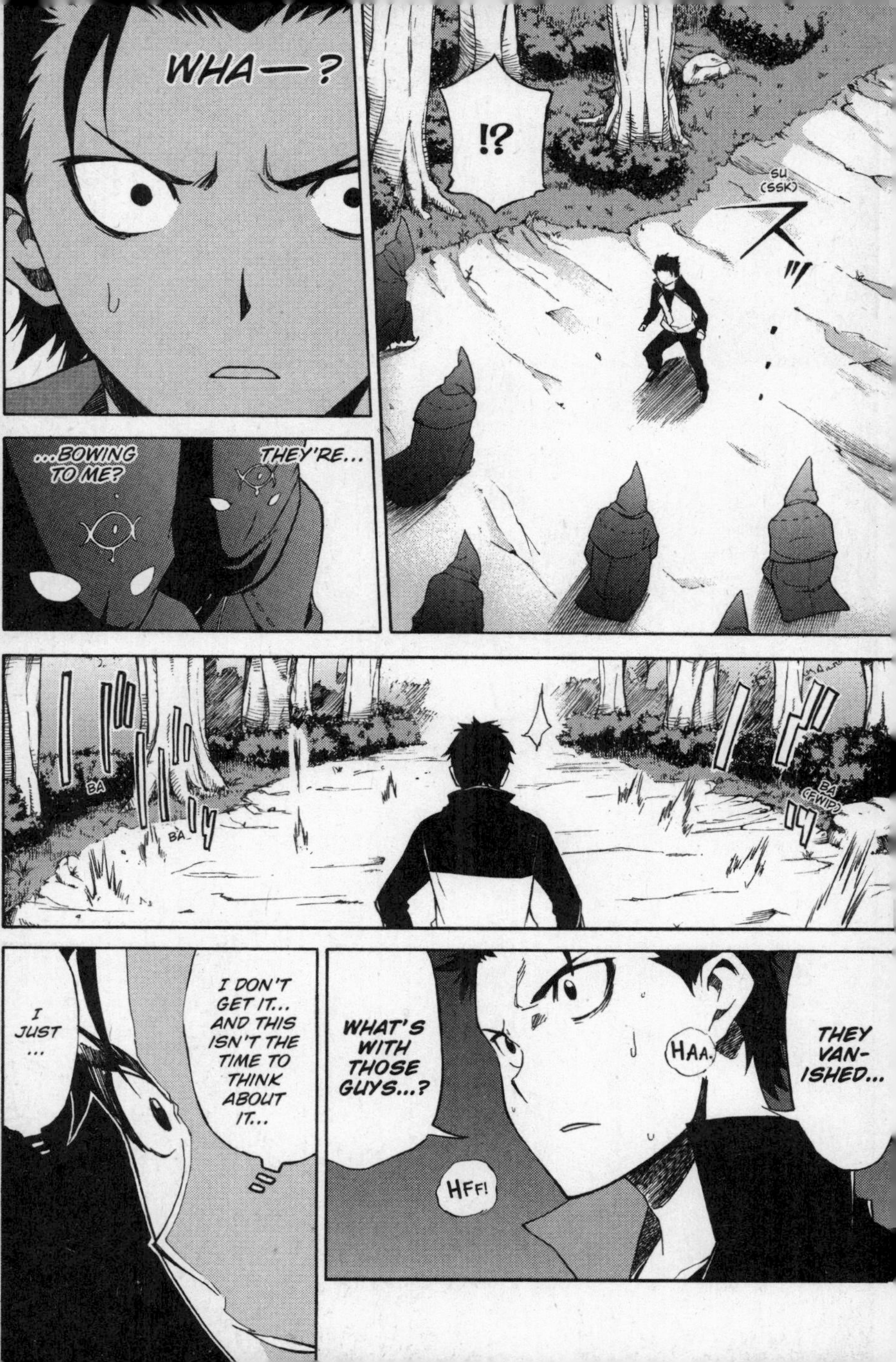
!?
SU (SSK)
WHA—?
THEY'RE...
...BOWING TO ME?
BA (FWIP)
BA
BA
THEY VAN-ISHED...
HAA.
HFF!
WHAT'S WITH THOSE GUYS...?
I DON'T GET IT... AND THIS ISN'T THE TIME TO THINK ABOUT IT...
I JUST ...

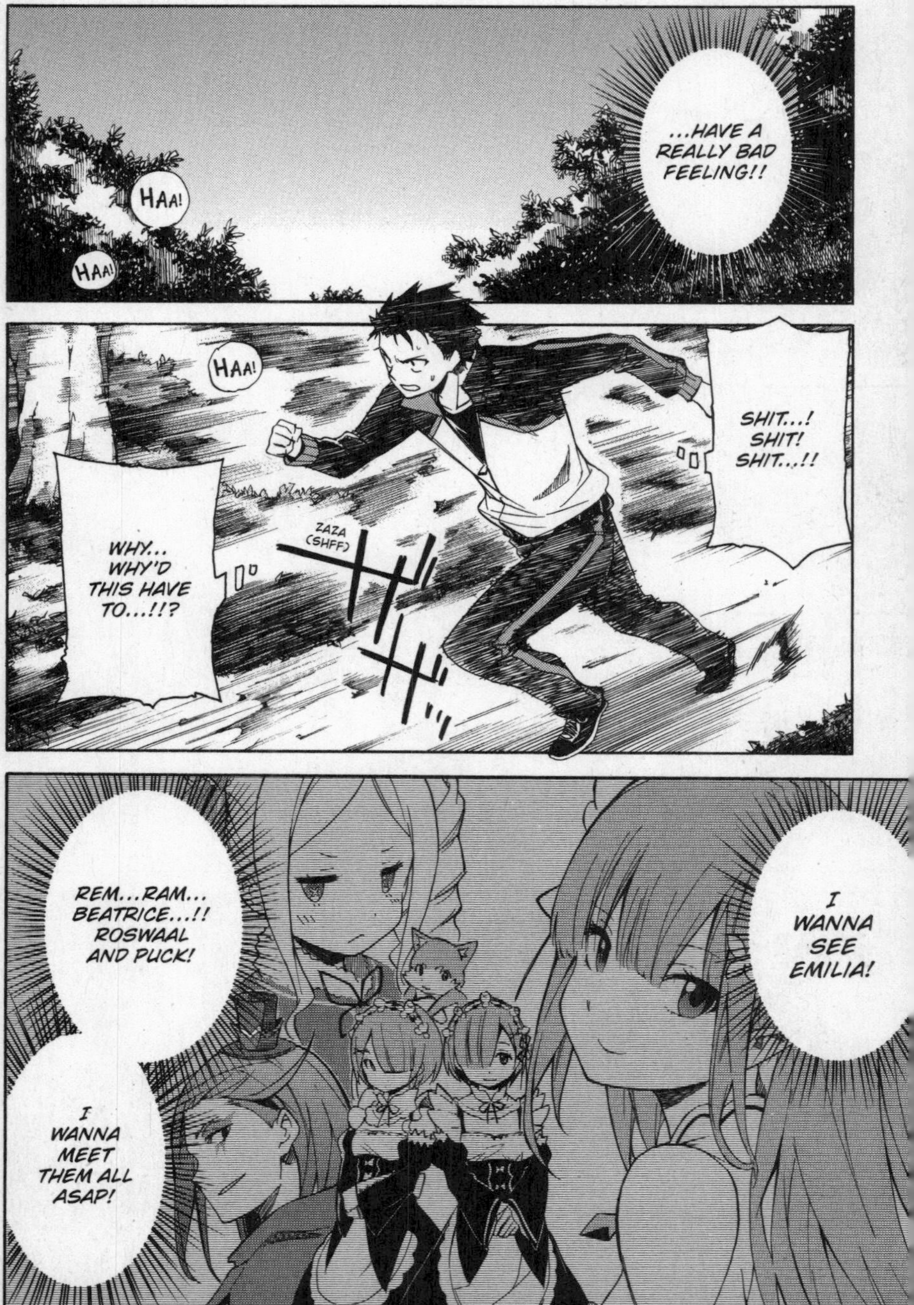
...HAVE A REALLY BAD FEELING!!
HAA!
HAA!
SHIT...! SHIT! SHIT...!!
HAA!
ZAZA (SHFF)
WHY... WHY'D THIS HAVE TO...!!?
I WANNA SEE EMILIA!
REM...RAM... BEATRICE...!! ROSWAAL AND PUCK!
I WANNA MEET THEM ALL ASAP!

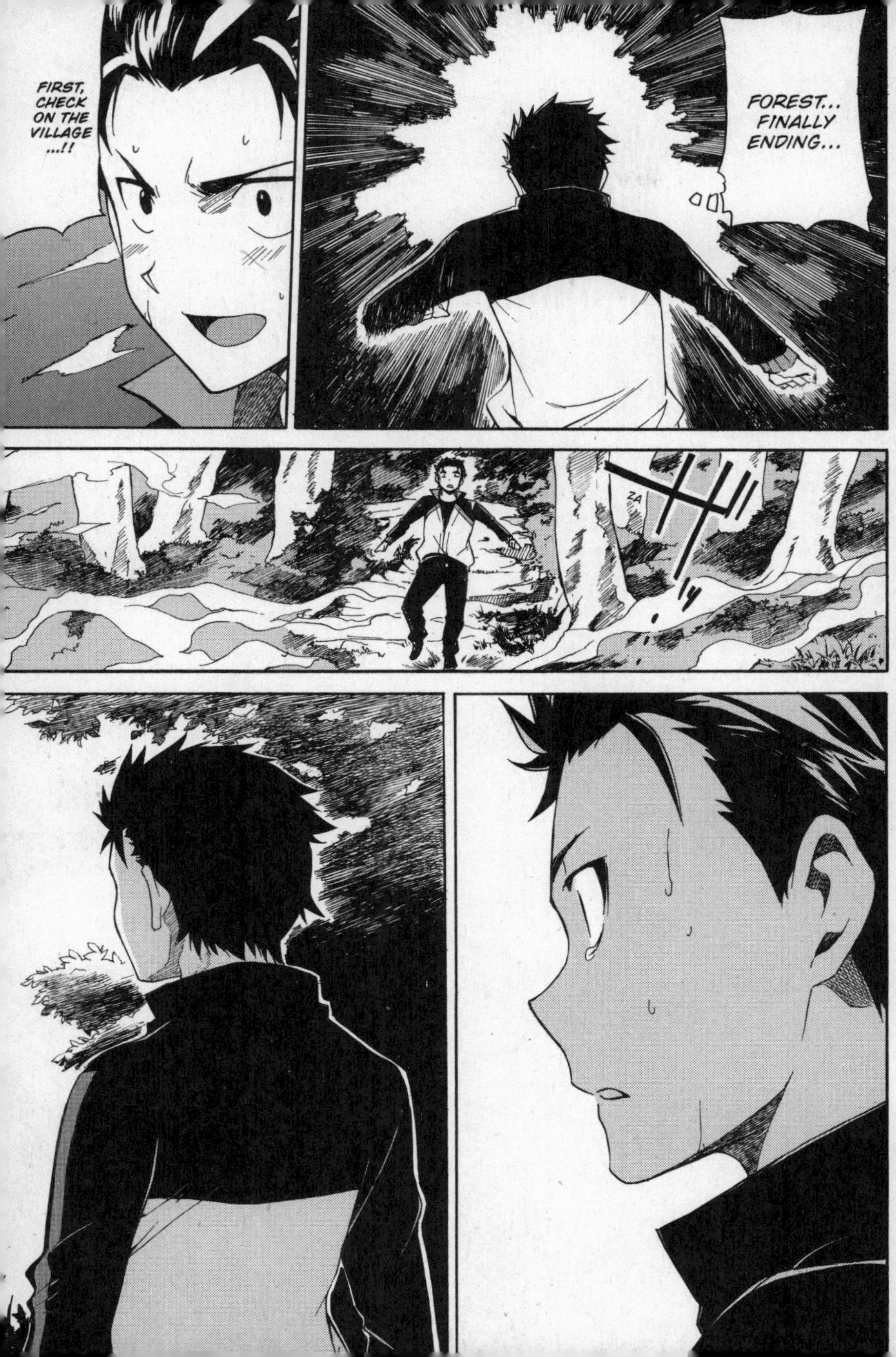
FOREST... FINALLY ENDING...
FIRST, CHECK ON THE VILLAGE ...!!
ZA

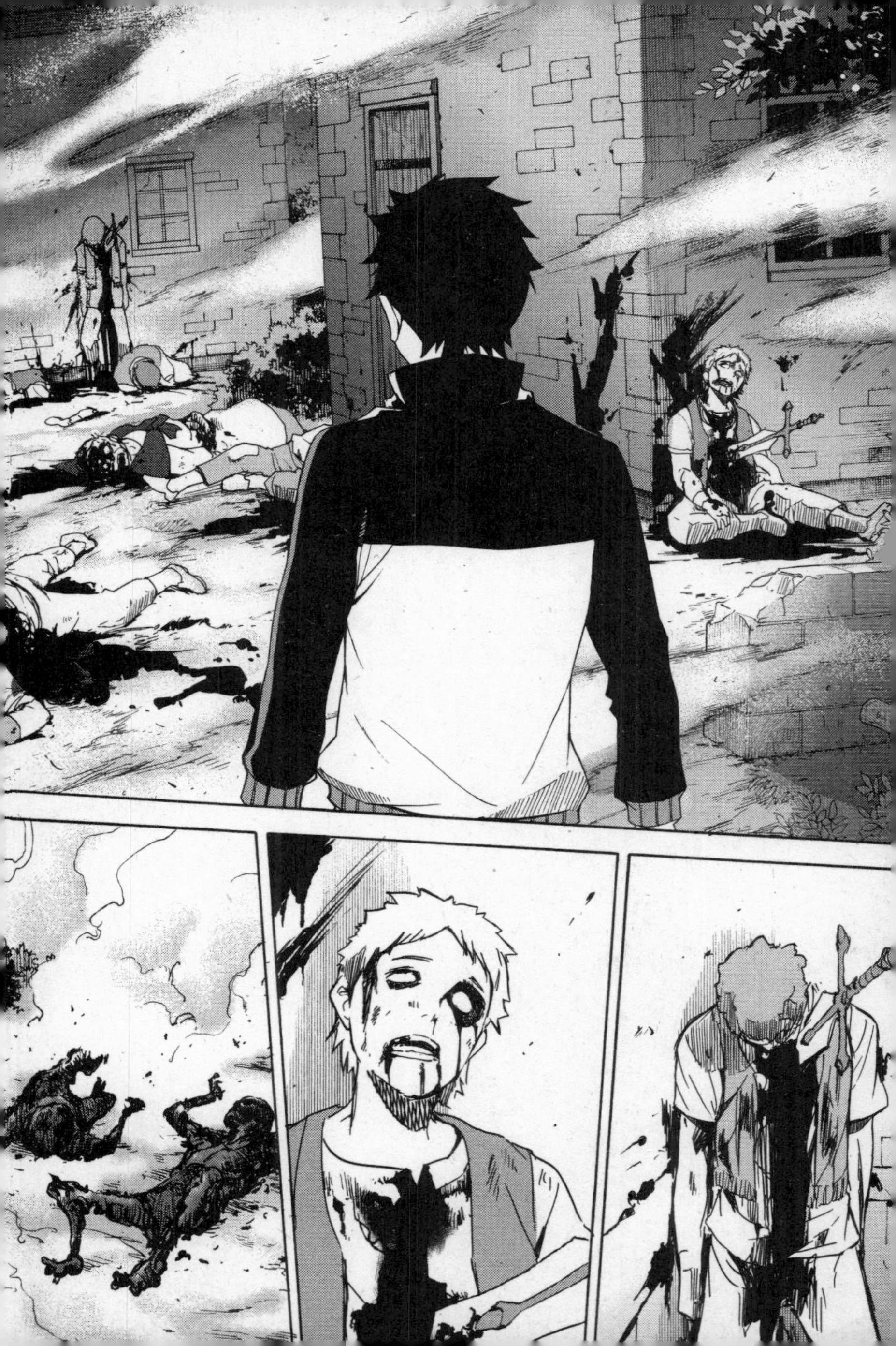

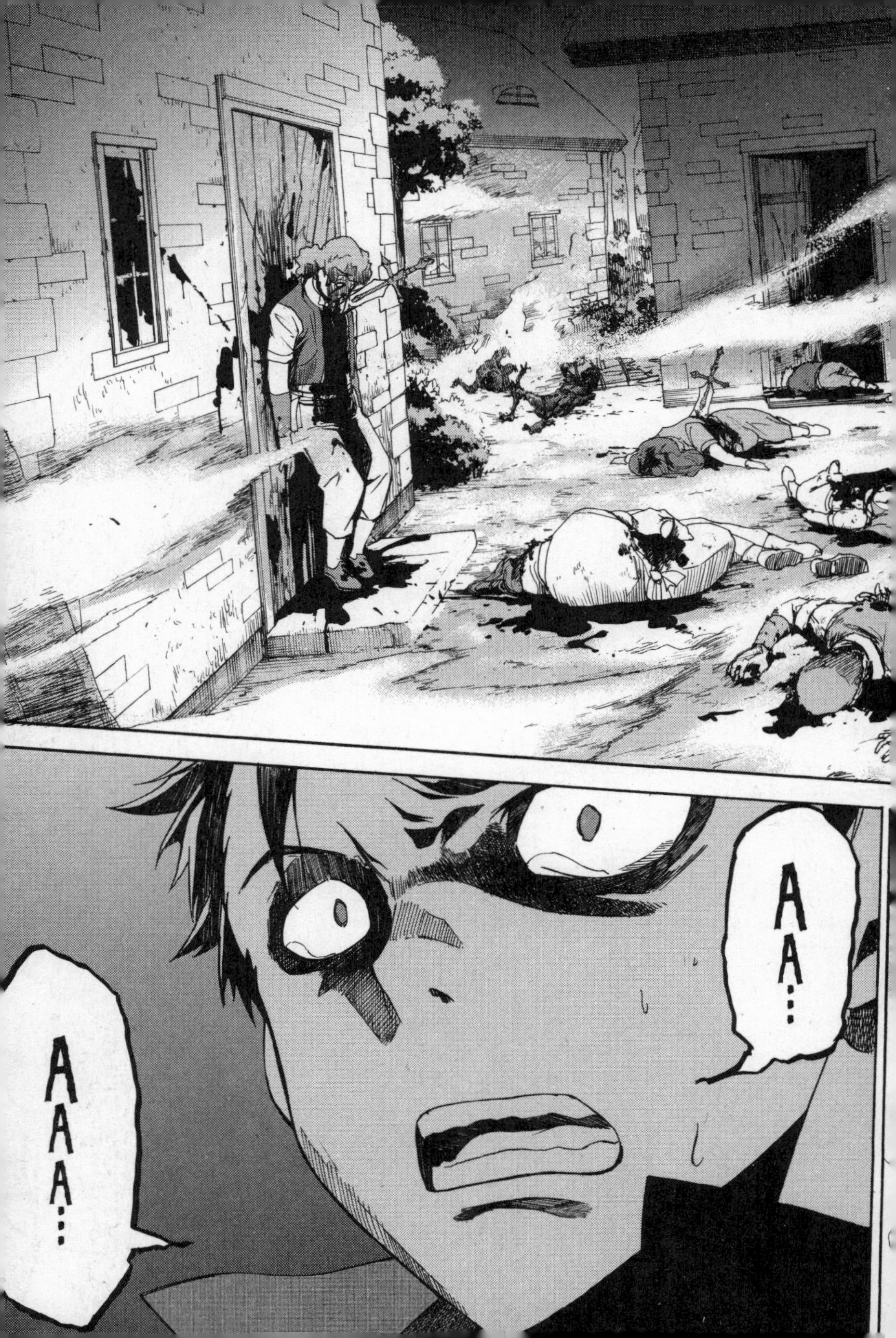
AA...
AAA...

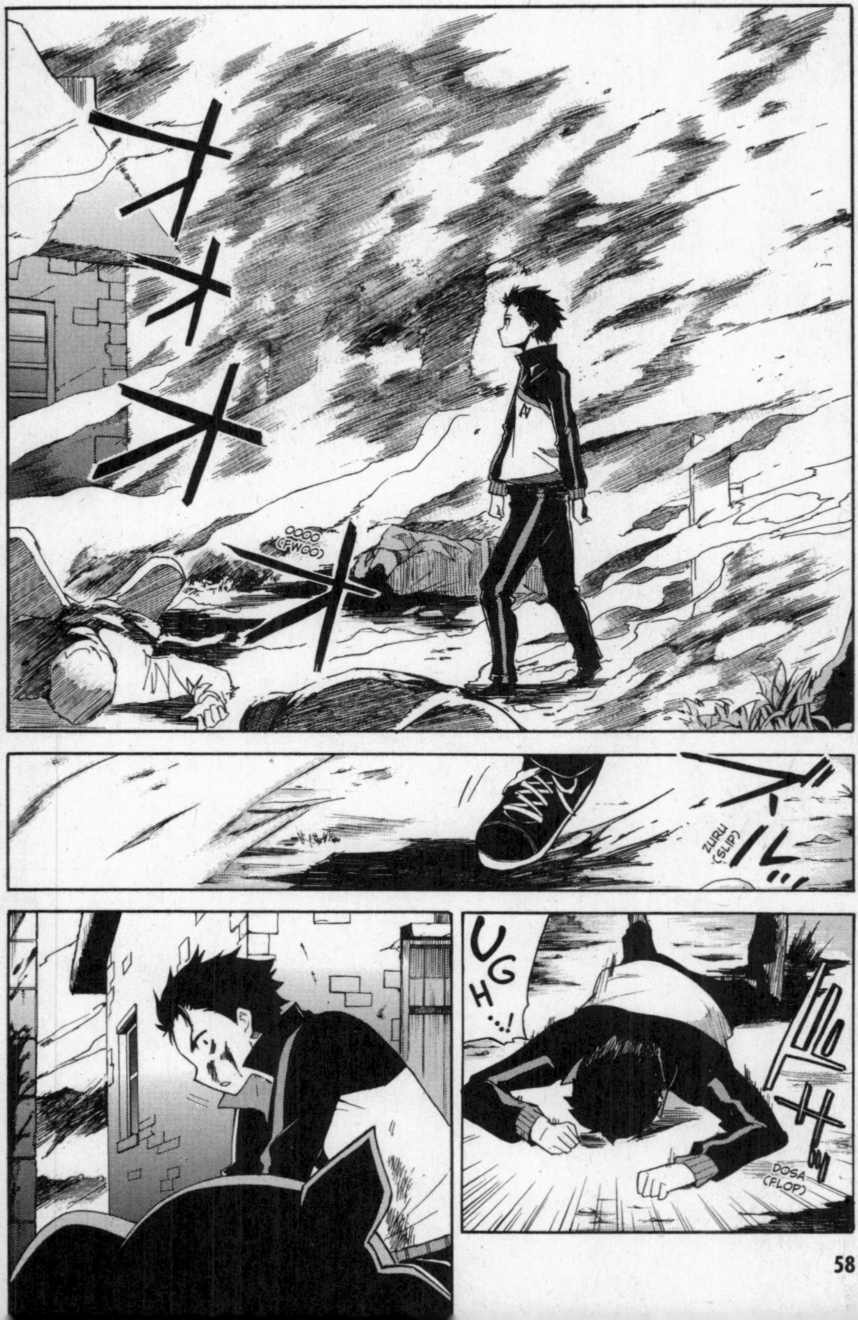
OOOO (FWOO)
ZURU (SLIP)
UGH...!
DOSA (FLOP)

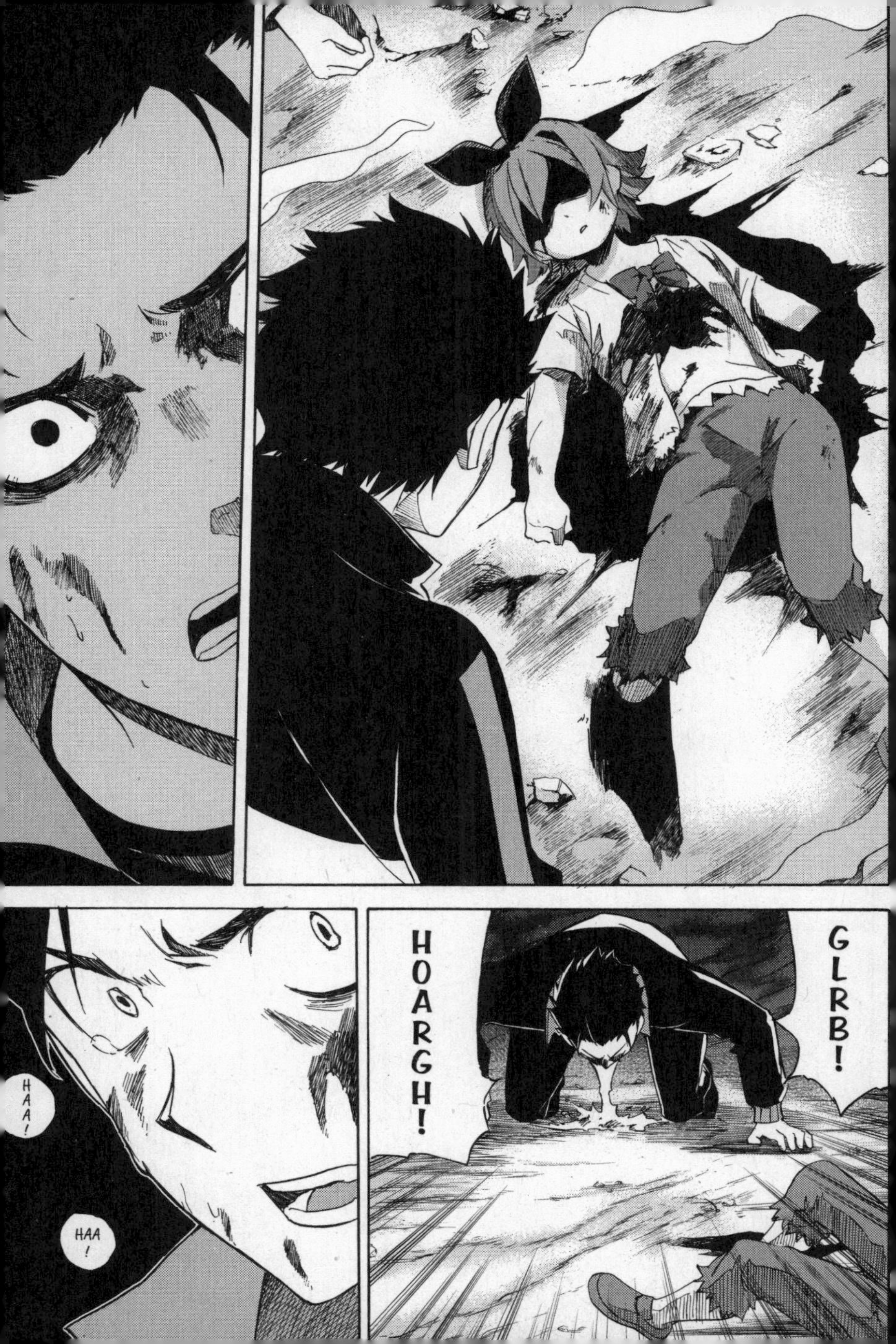
GLRB!
HOARGH!
HAA!
HAA!

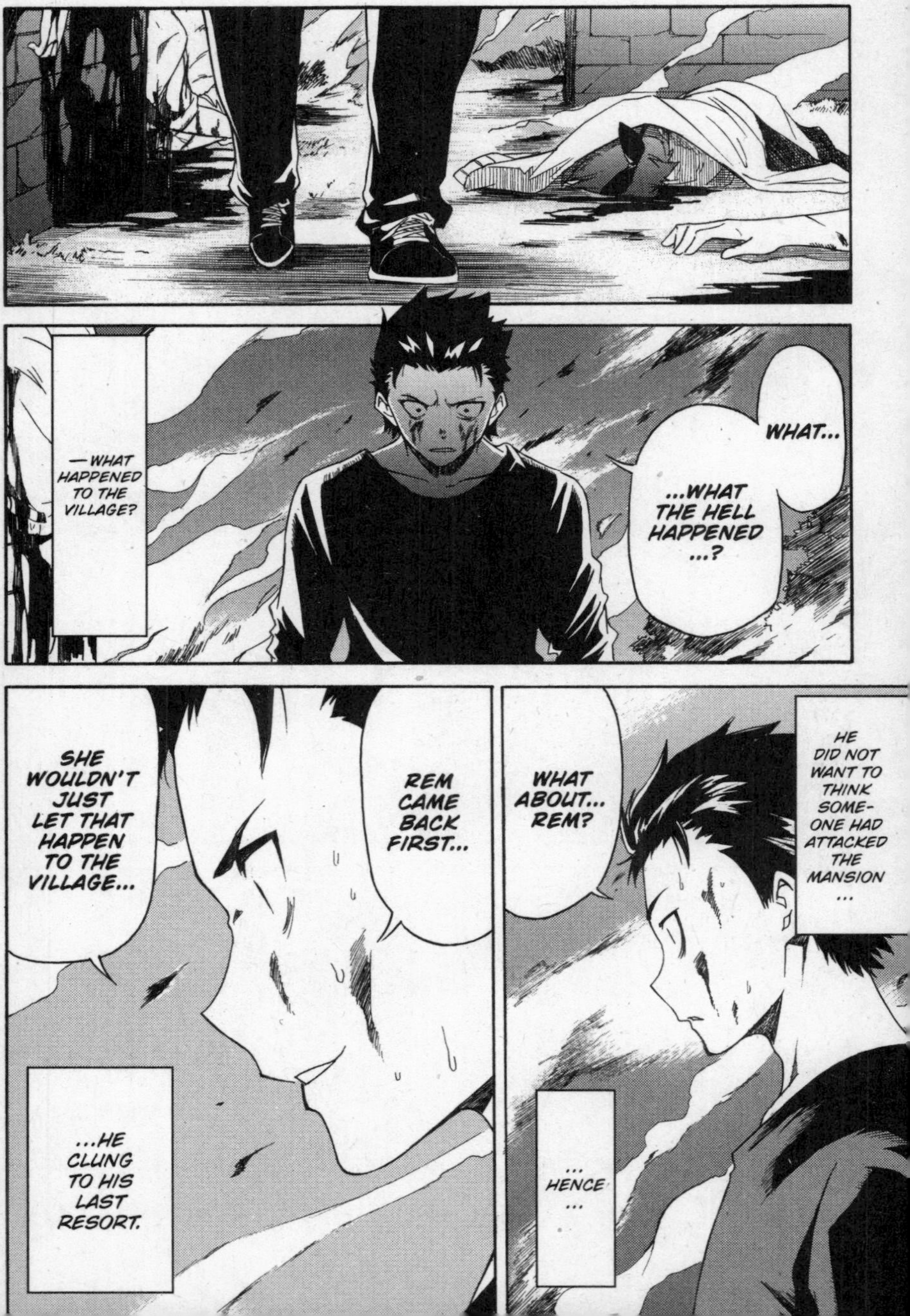
WHAT... ...WHAT THE HELL HAPPENED ...?
—WHAT HAPPENED TO THE VILLAGE?
HE DID NOT WANT TO THINK SOME-ONE HAD ATTACKED THE MANSION ...
WHAT ABOUT... REM?
... HENCE ...
REM CAME BACK FIRST...
SHE WOULDN'T JUST LET THAT HAPPEN TO THE VILLAGE...
...HE CLUNG TO HIS LAST RESORT.

THAT'S RIGHT...!

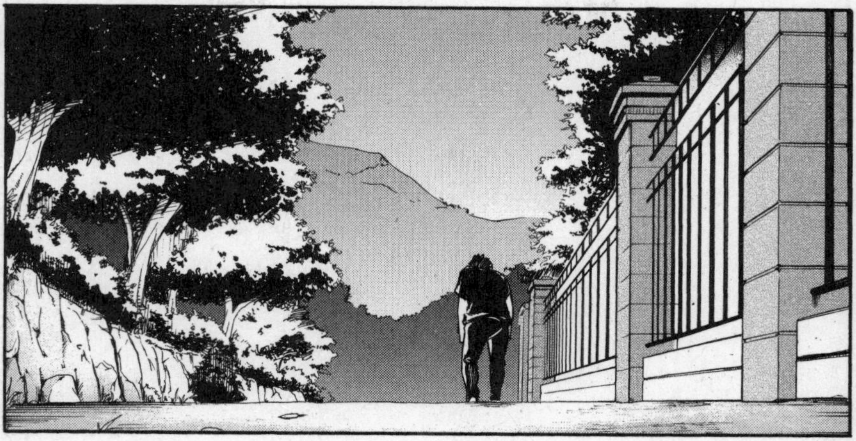

—REM...

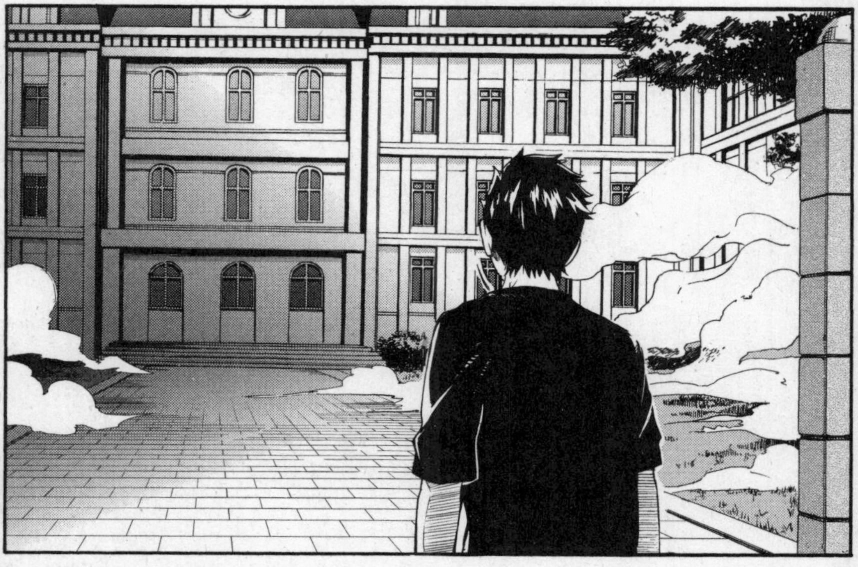

REM...REM...REM, REM, REM...!!!!

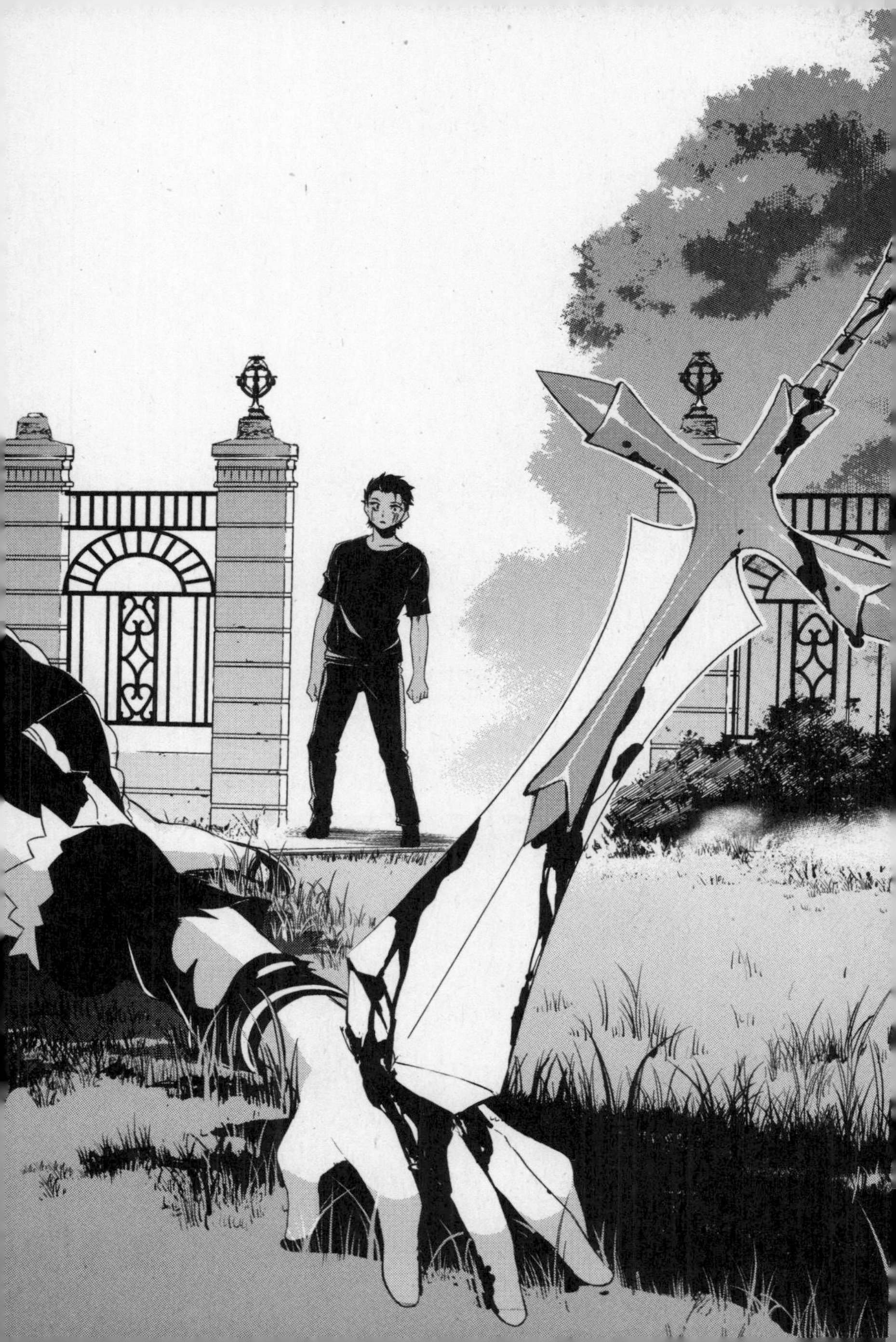

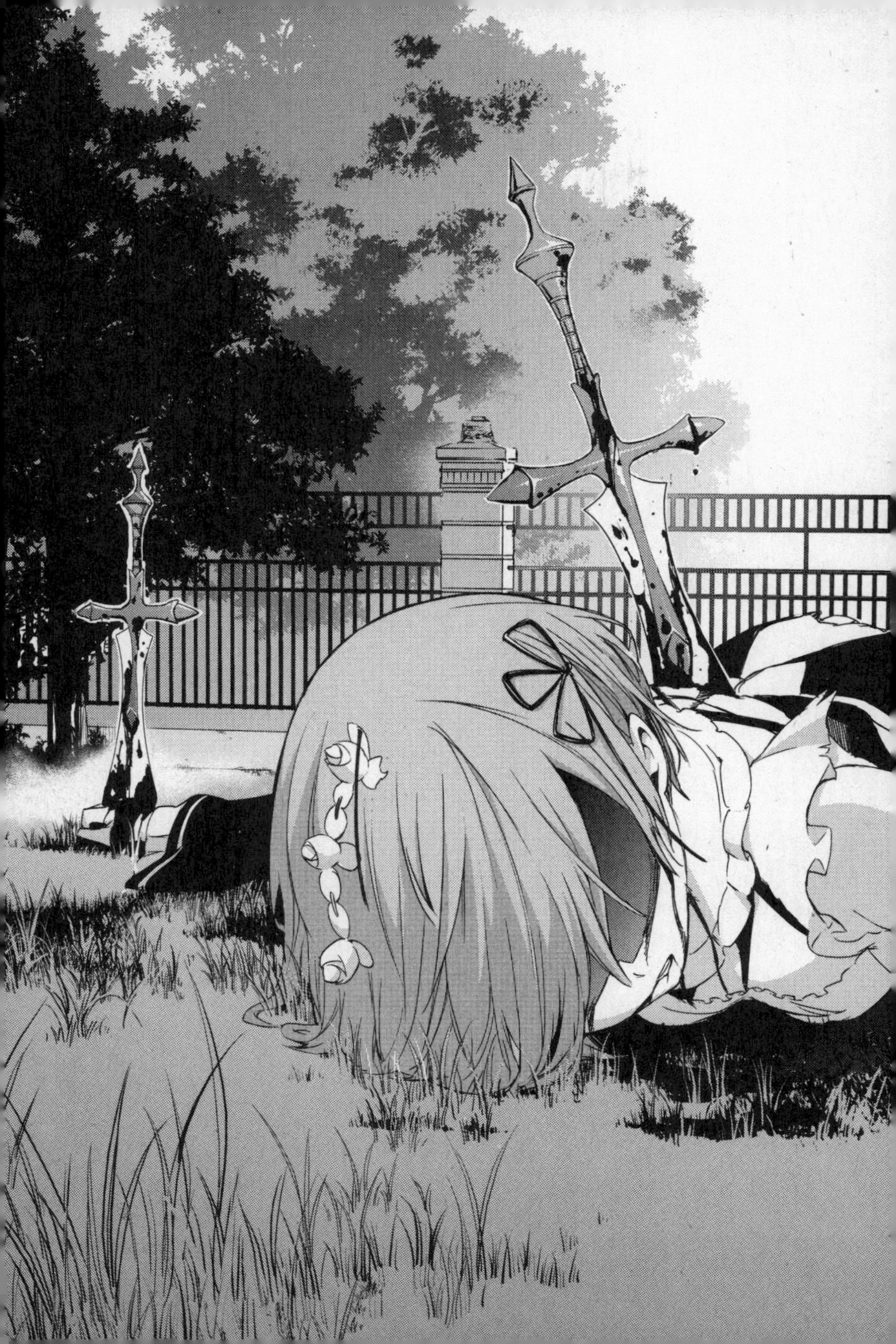

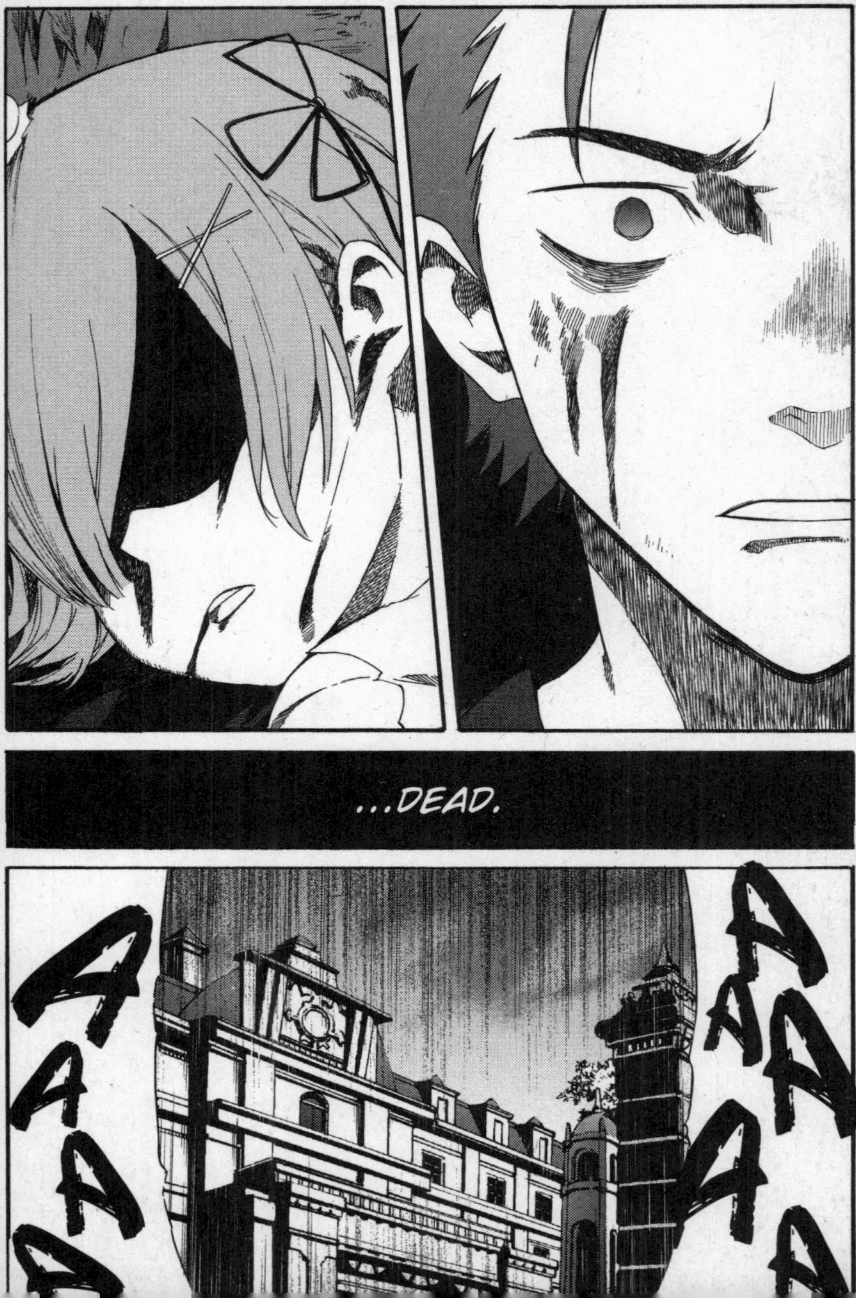
...DEAD.
AAAAAA
AAAAA

Re:ZERO -Starting Life in Another World-

Truth of Zero

The only ability Subaru Natsuki gets when he's summoned to another world is time travel via his own death. But to save her, he'll die as many times as it takes.

Re:ZERO -Starting Life in Another World-

Truth of Zero
The only ability Subaru Natsuki gets when he's summoned to another world is
time travel via his own death. But to save her, he'll die as many times as it takes.

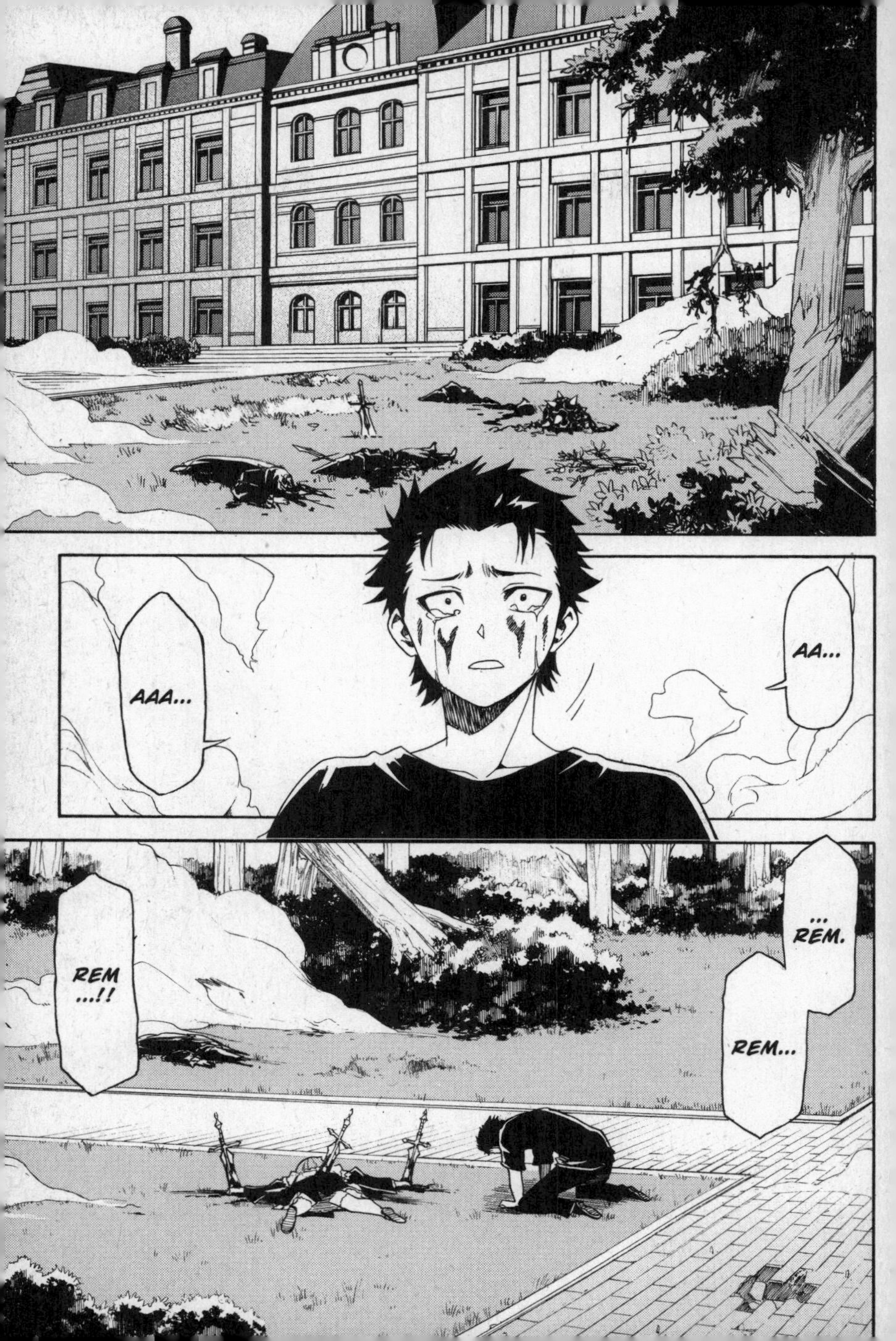
AA...
AAA...
...REM.
REM...
REM ...!!

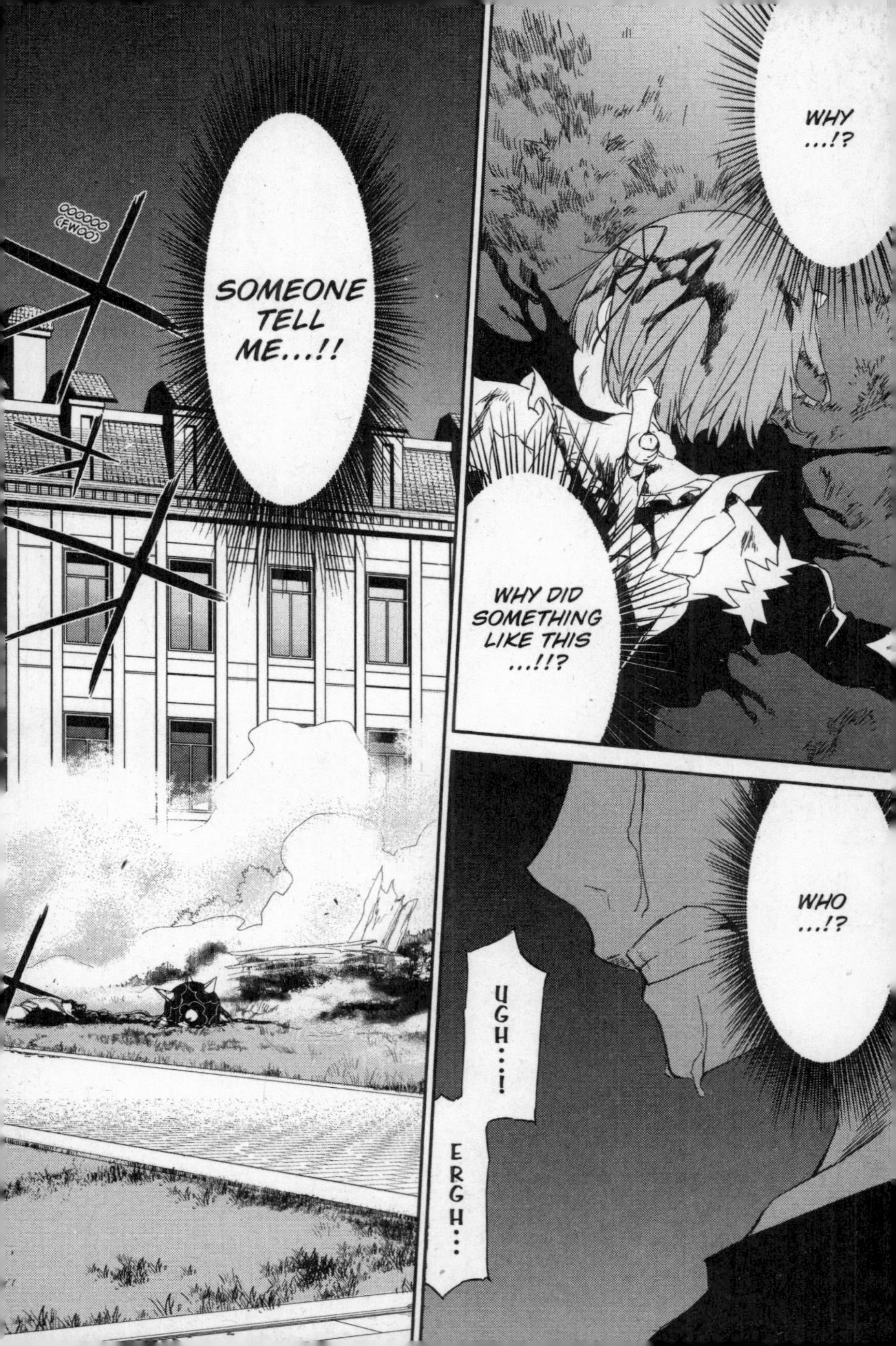
WHY ...!?
WHY DID SOMETHING LIKE THIS ...!!?
WHO ...!?
UGH...!
ERGH...
SOMEONE TELL ME...!!
OOOOOO (FWOO)

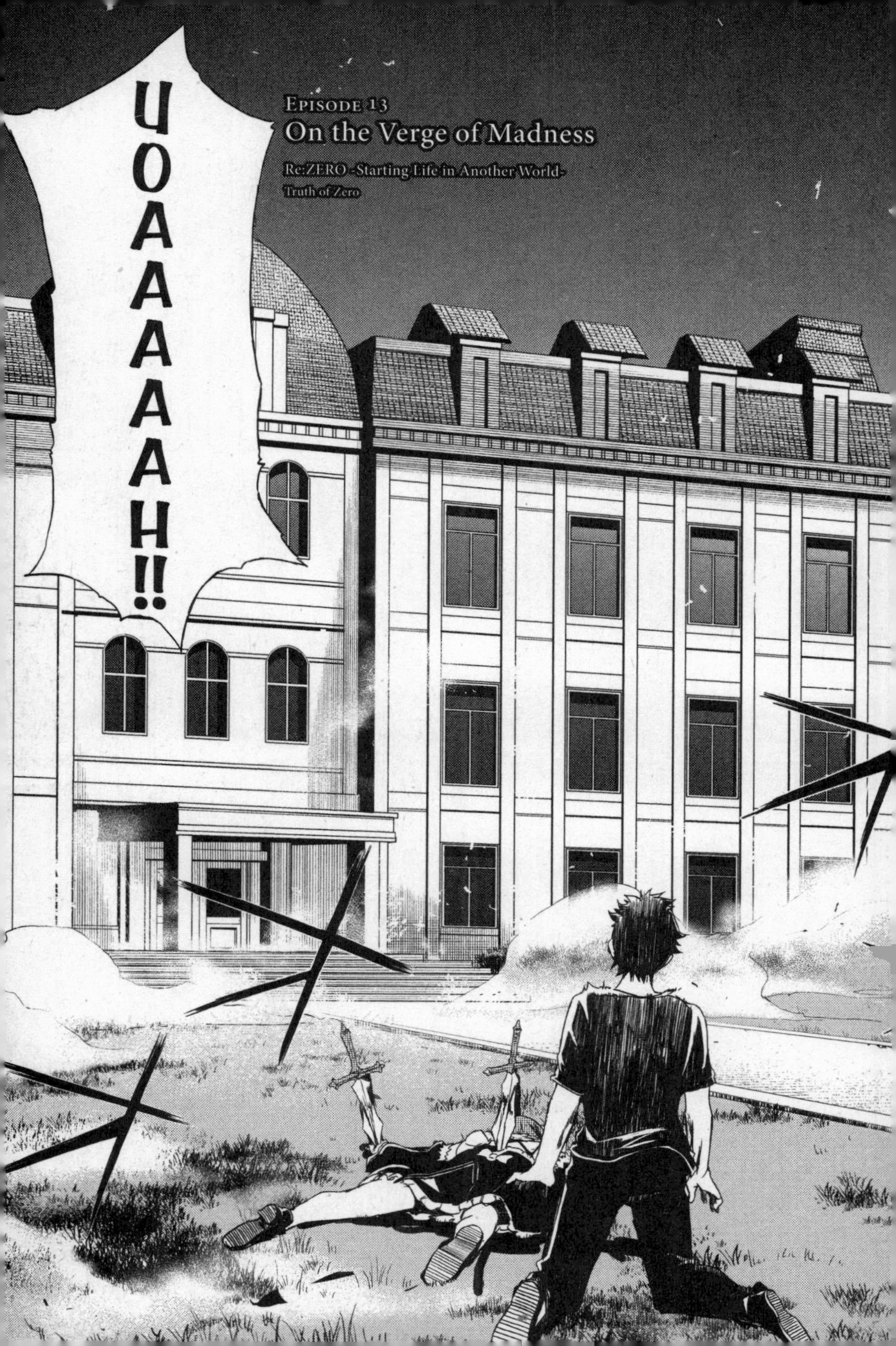

Episode 13
On the Verge of Madness
Re:ZERO -Starting Life in Another World-
Truth of Zero
UOAAAAAH!!

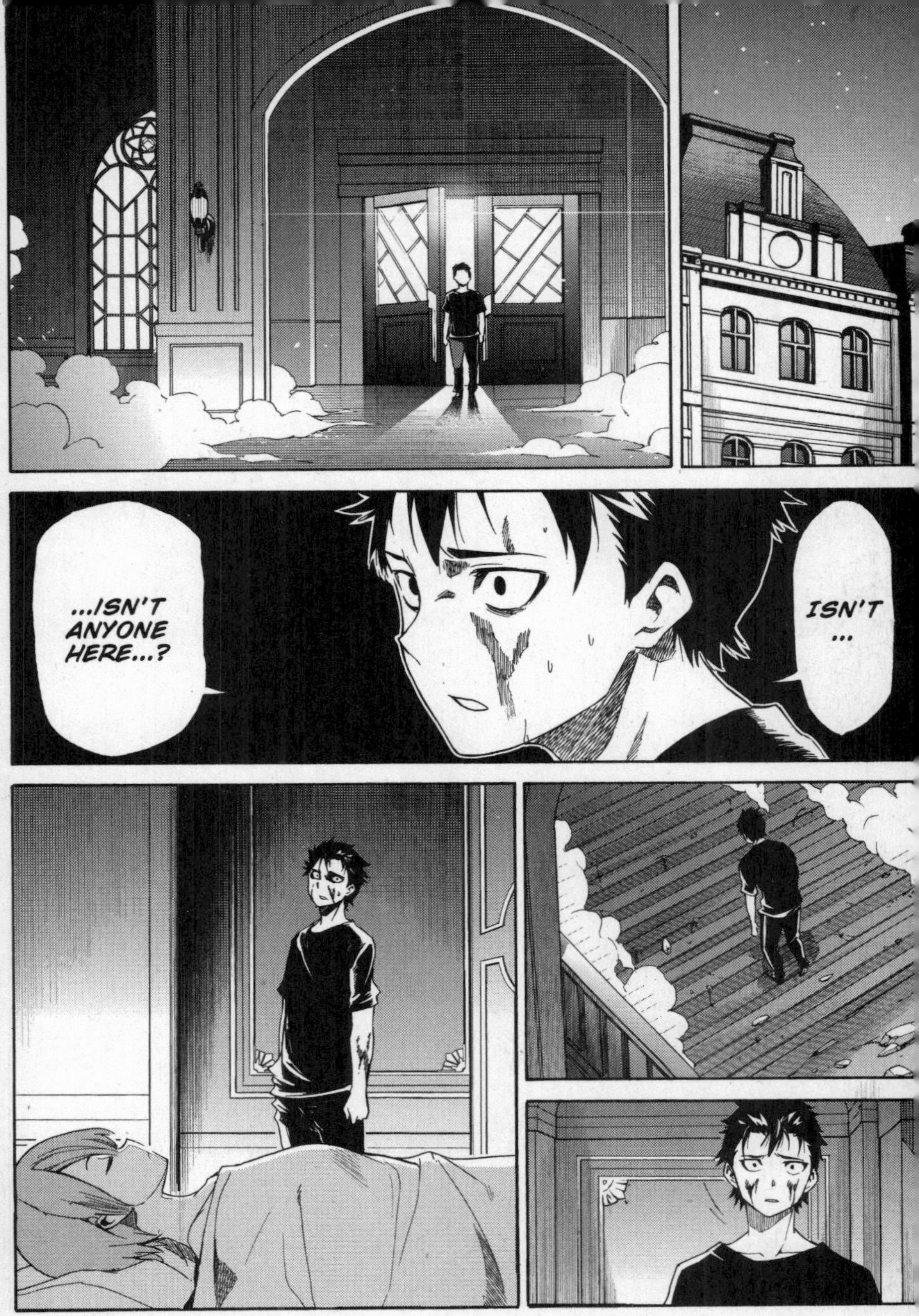
ISN'T ...
...ISN'T ANYONE HERE...?

—IN THE BACK ROOM ON THE SECOND FLOOR...

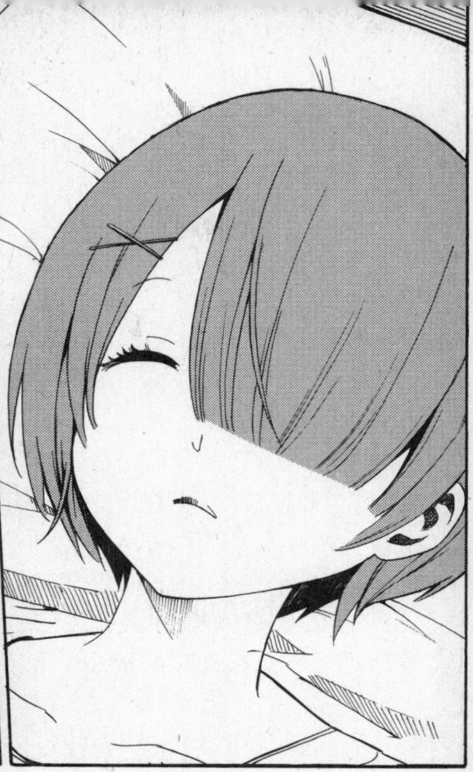

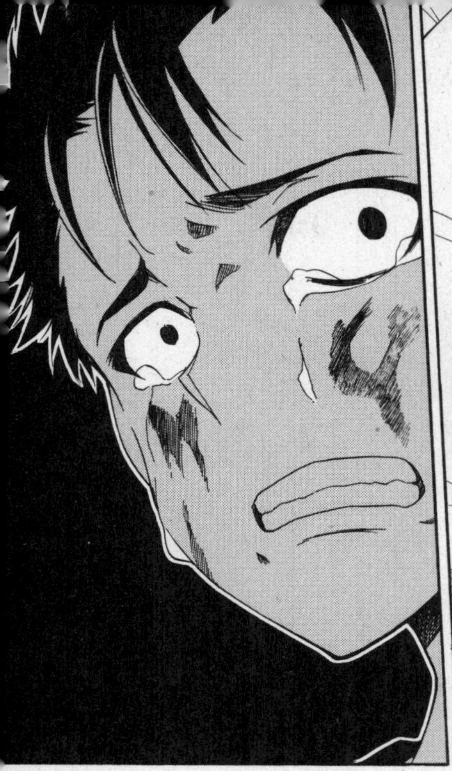

...HE FOUND RAM'S CORPSE.

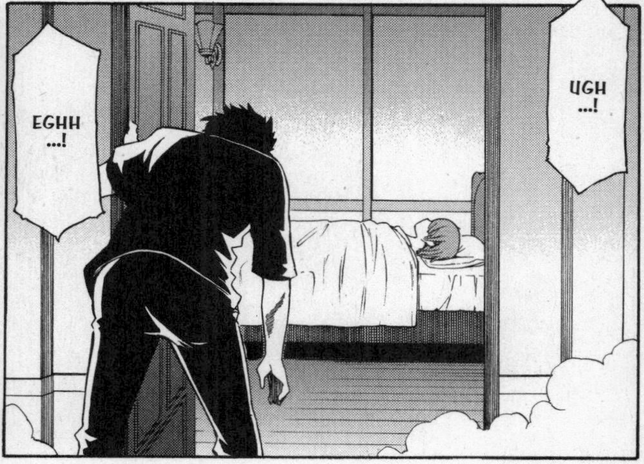
UGH ...!
EGHH ...!

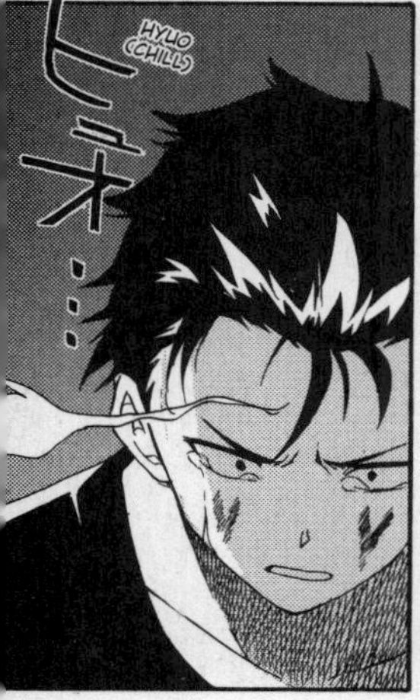
HYUO (CHILL)
ヒュオ…

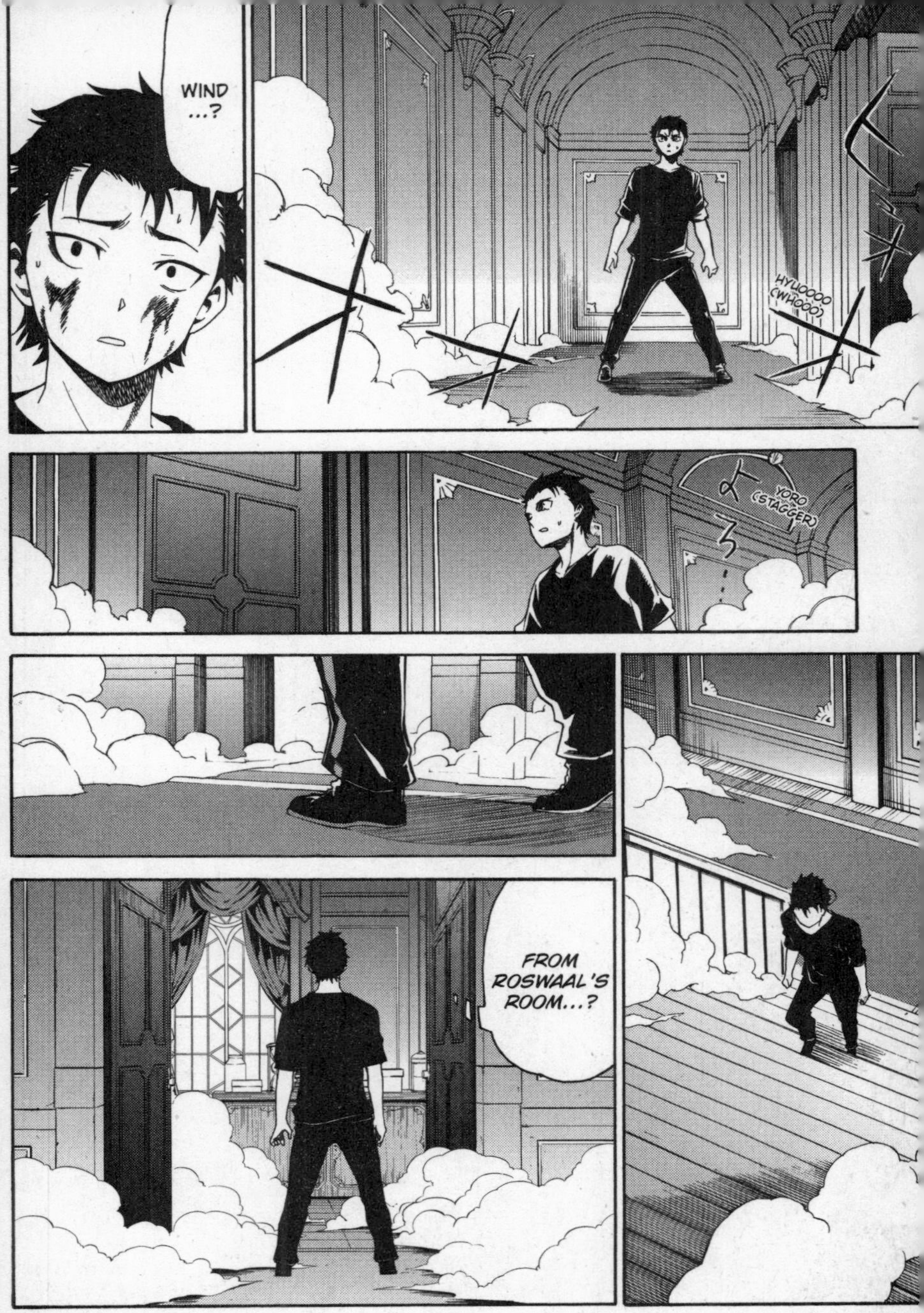
HYUOOOO (WHOOO)
WIND ...?
YORO (STAGGER)
FROM ROSWAAL'S ROOM...?

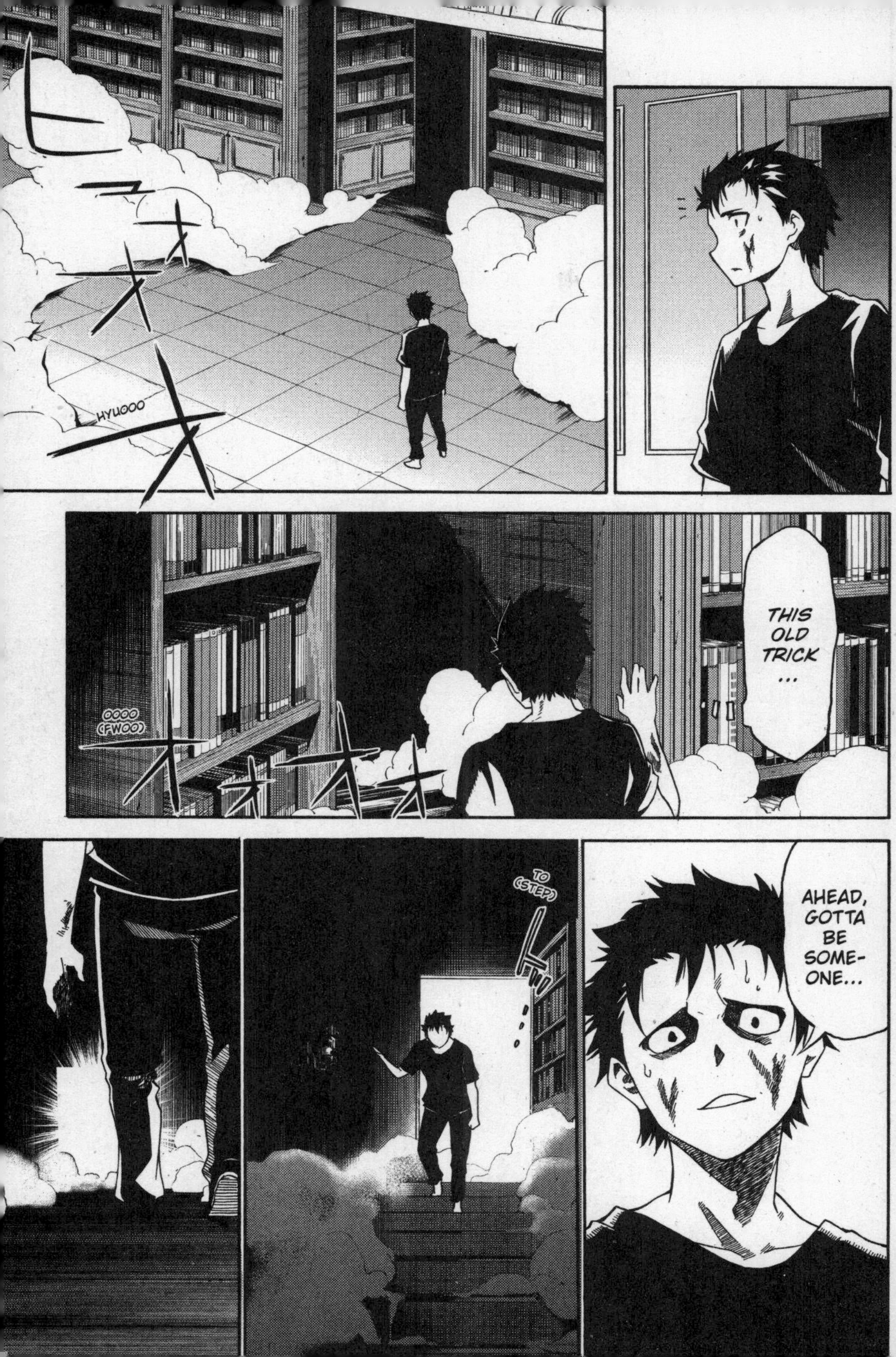
HYUOOO
THIS OLD TRICK...
OOOO (FWOO)
AHEAD, GOTTA BE SOME-ONE...
TO (STEP)

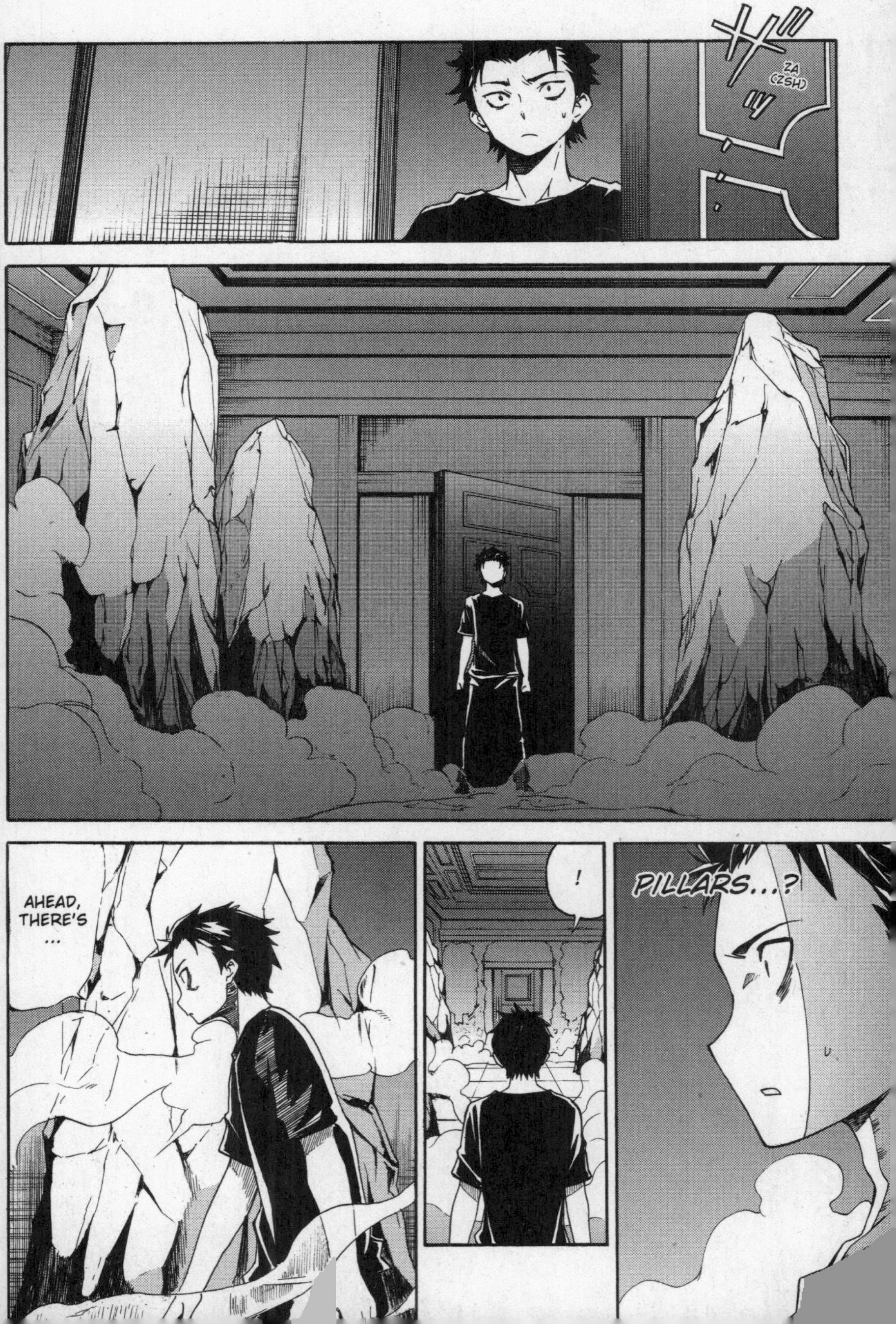
ZA
(ZSH)
PILLARS...?
!
AHEAD, THERE'S ...

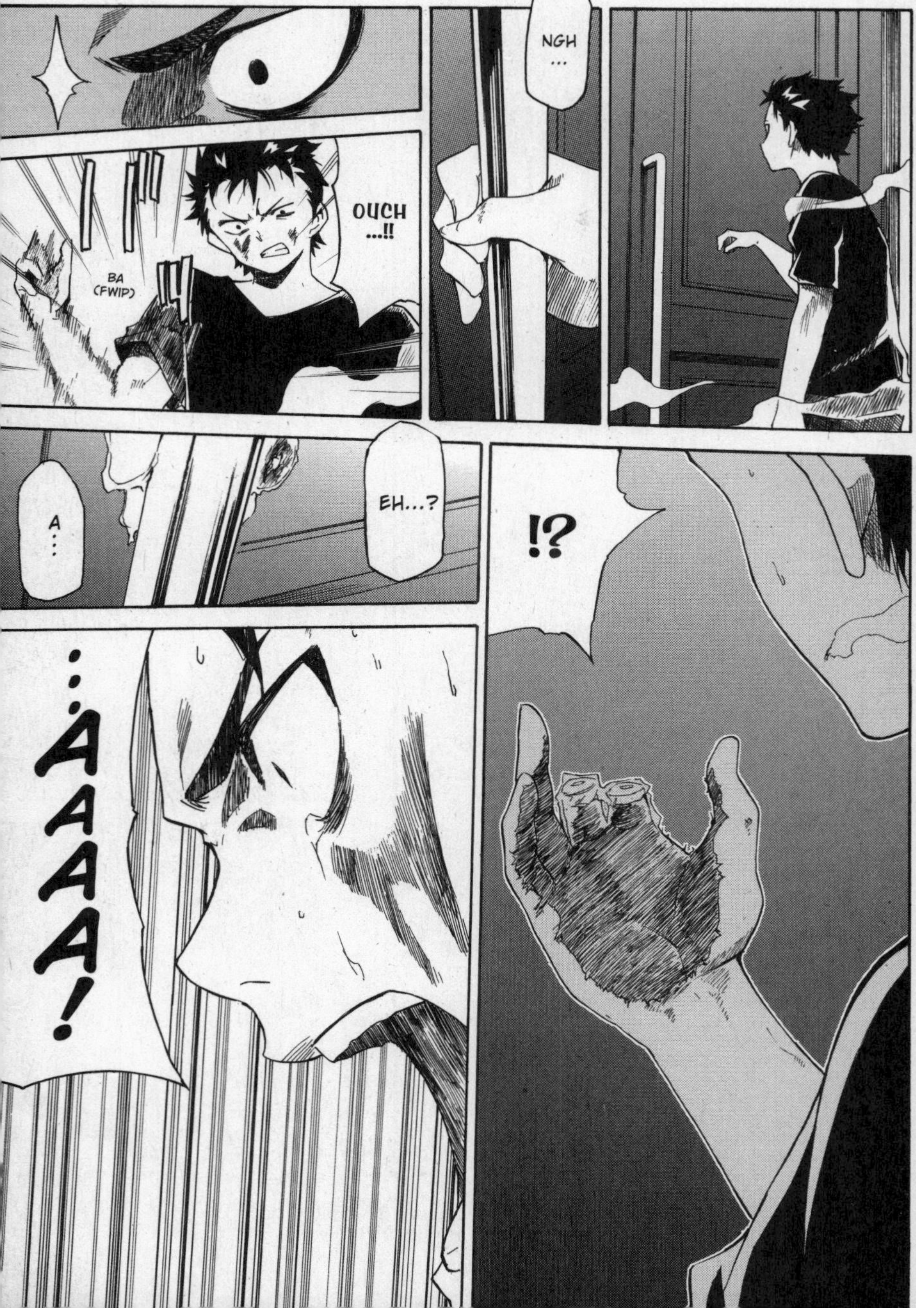
NGH ...
OUCH ...!!
BA (FWIP)
!?
EH...?
A...
...AAAA!

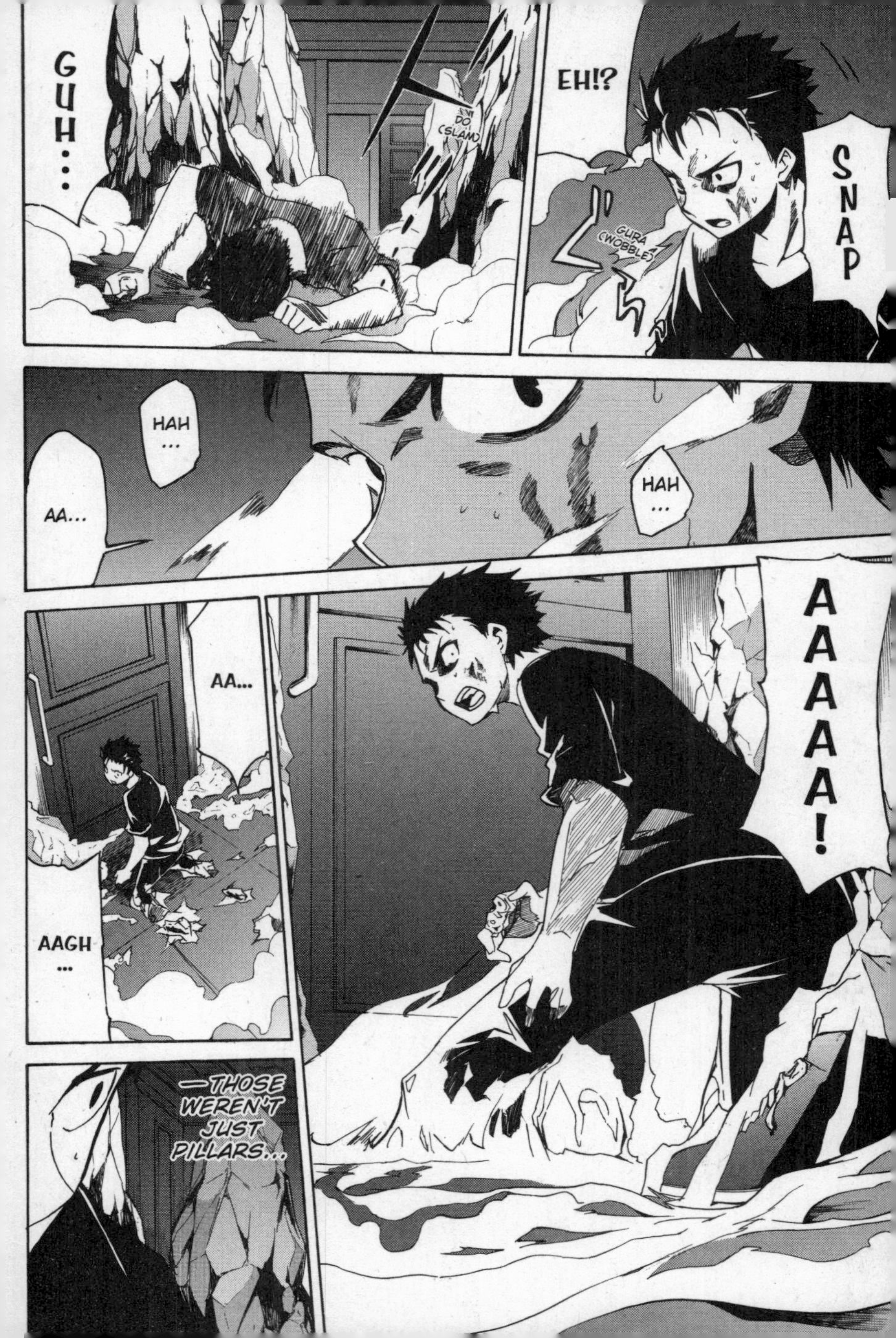
SNAP
EH!?
GURA (WOBBLE)
DO (SLAM)
GUH...
HAH...
HAH...
AA...
AAAAA!
AA...
AAGH...
—THOSE WEREN'T JUST PILLARS...

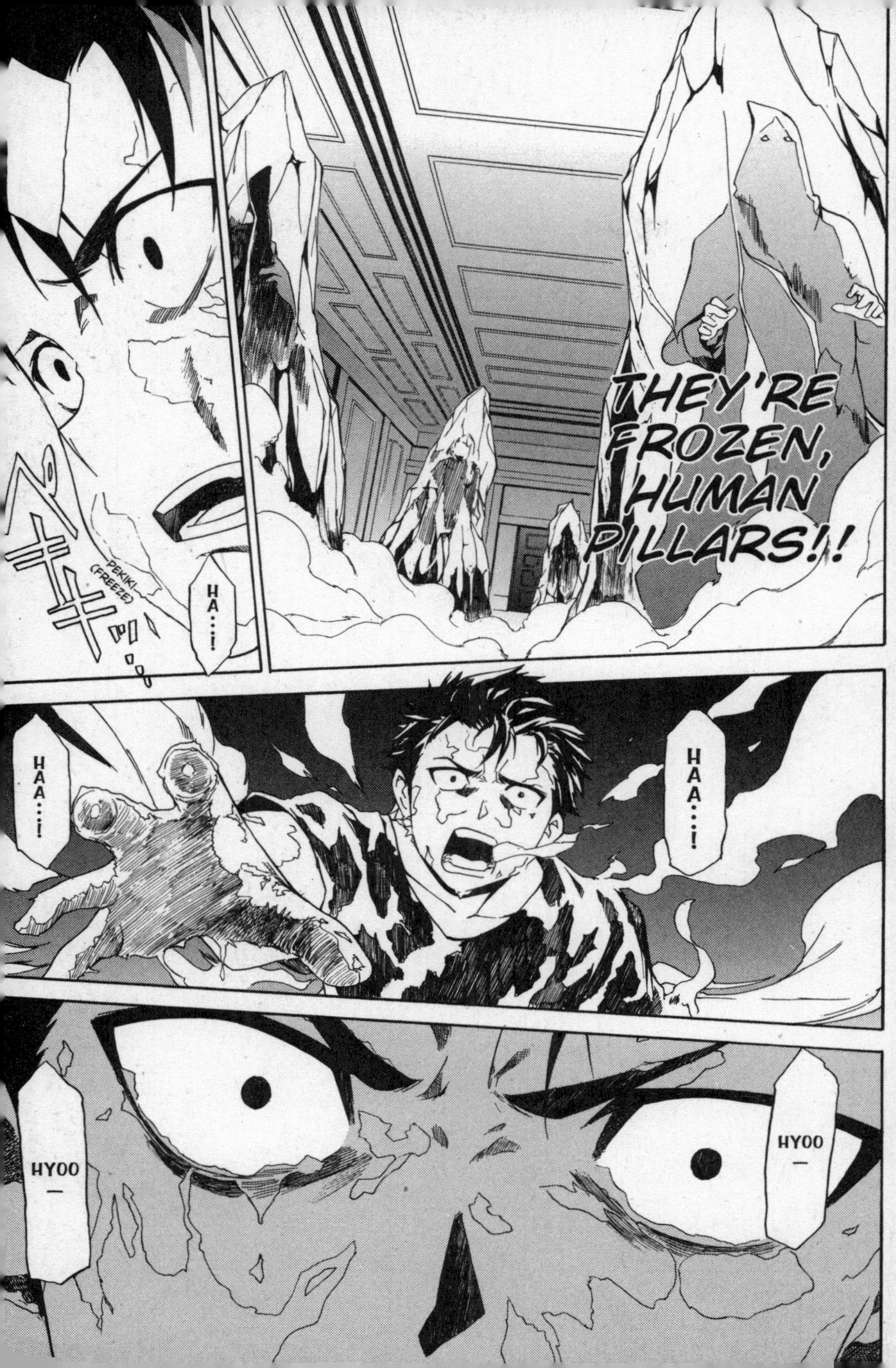
THEY'RE FROZEN, HUMAN PILLARS!!
HA...!
PEKIKI (FREEZE)
HAA...!
HAA...!
HYOO—
HYOO—

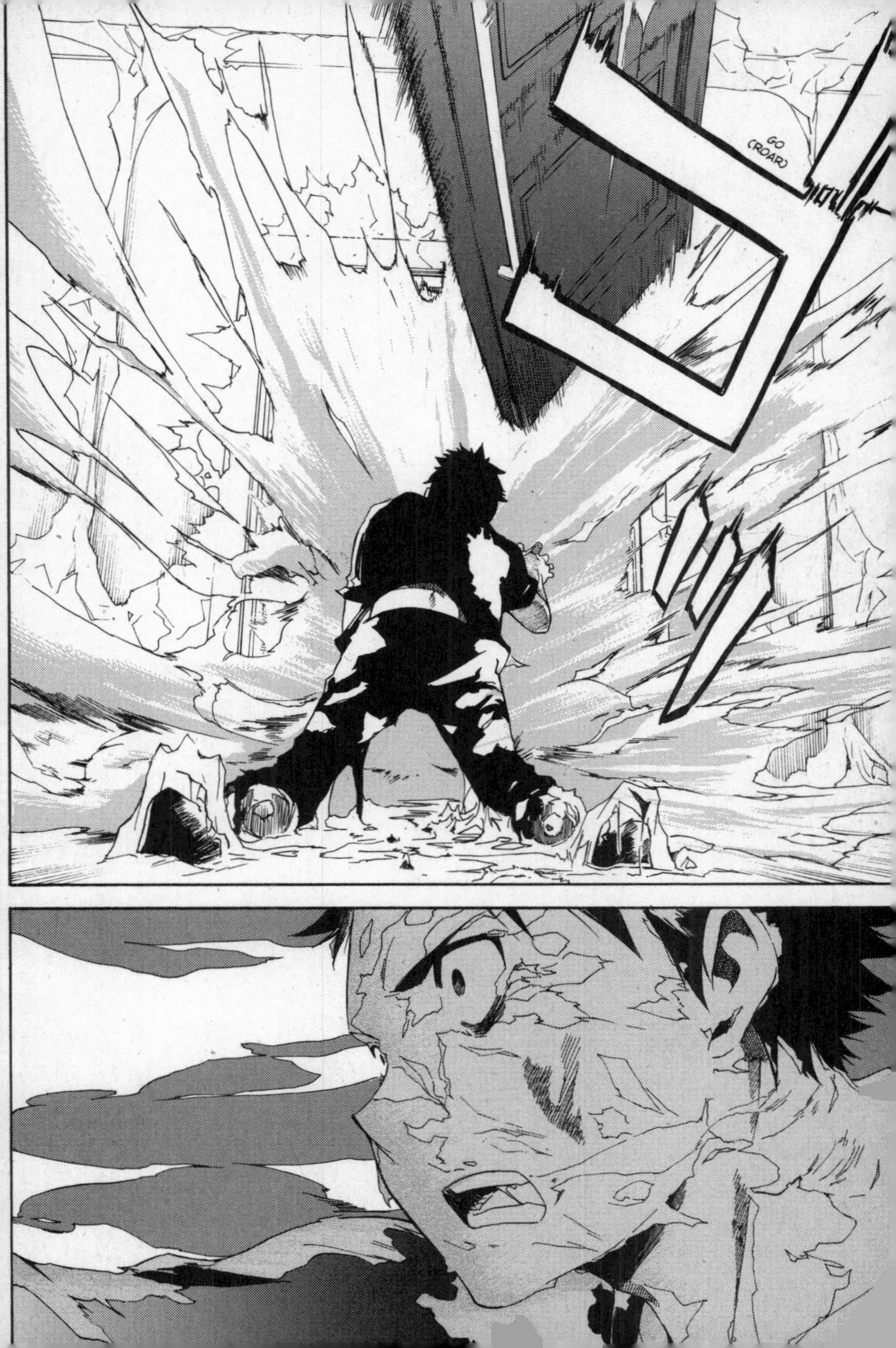
GO
(ROAR)

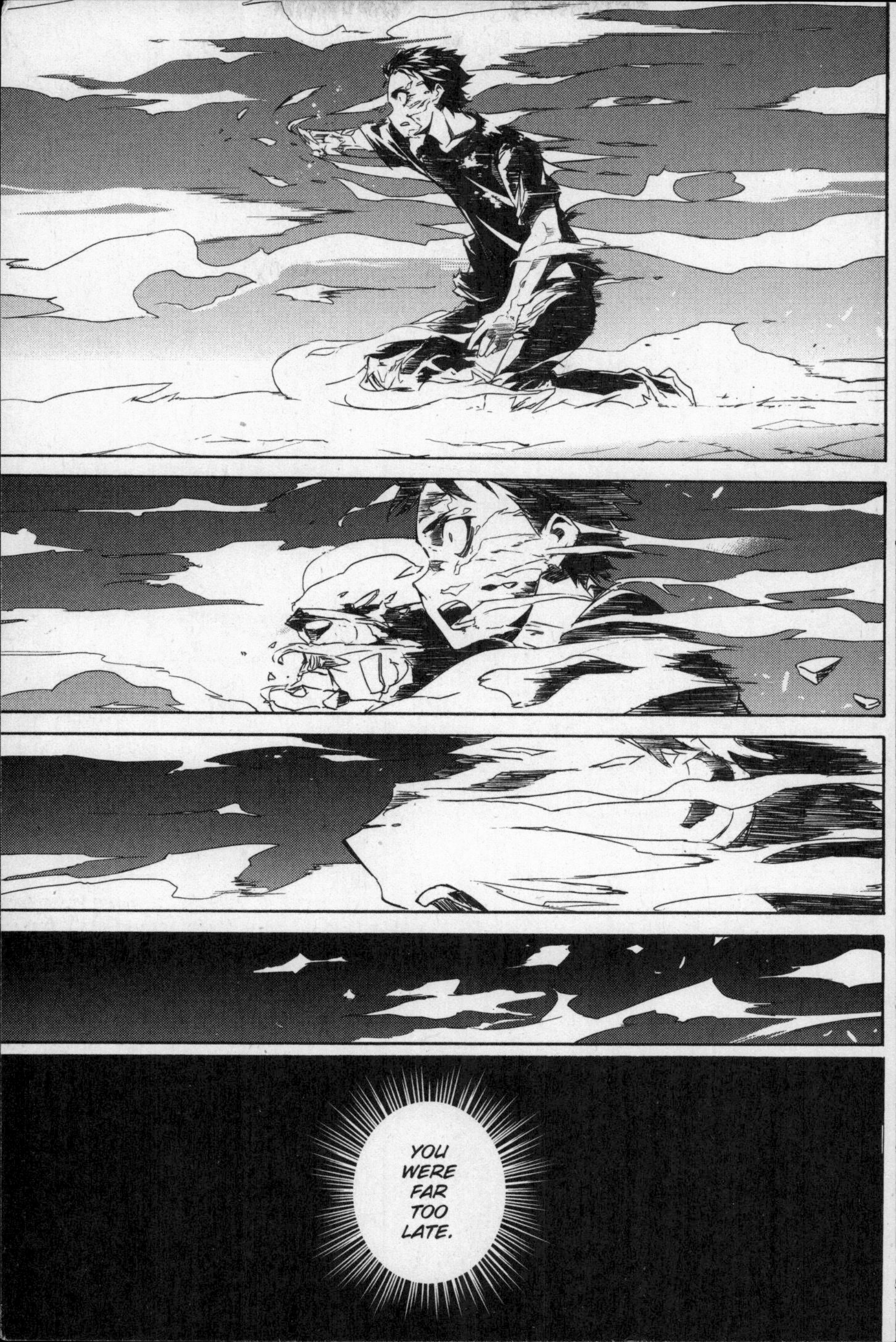
YOU WERE FAR TOO LATE.

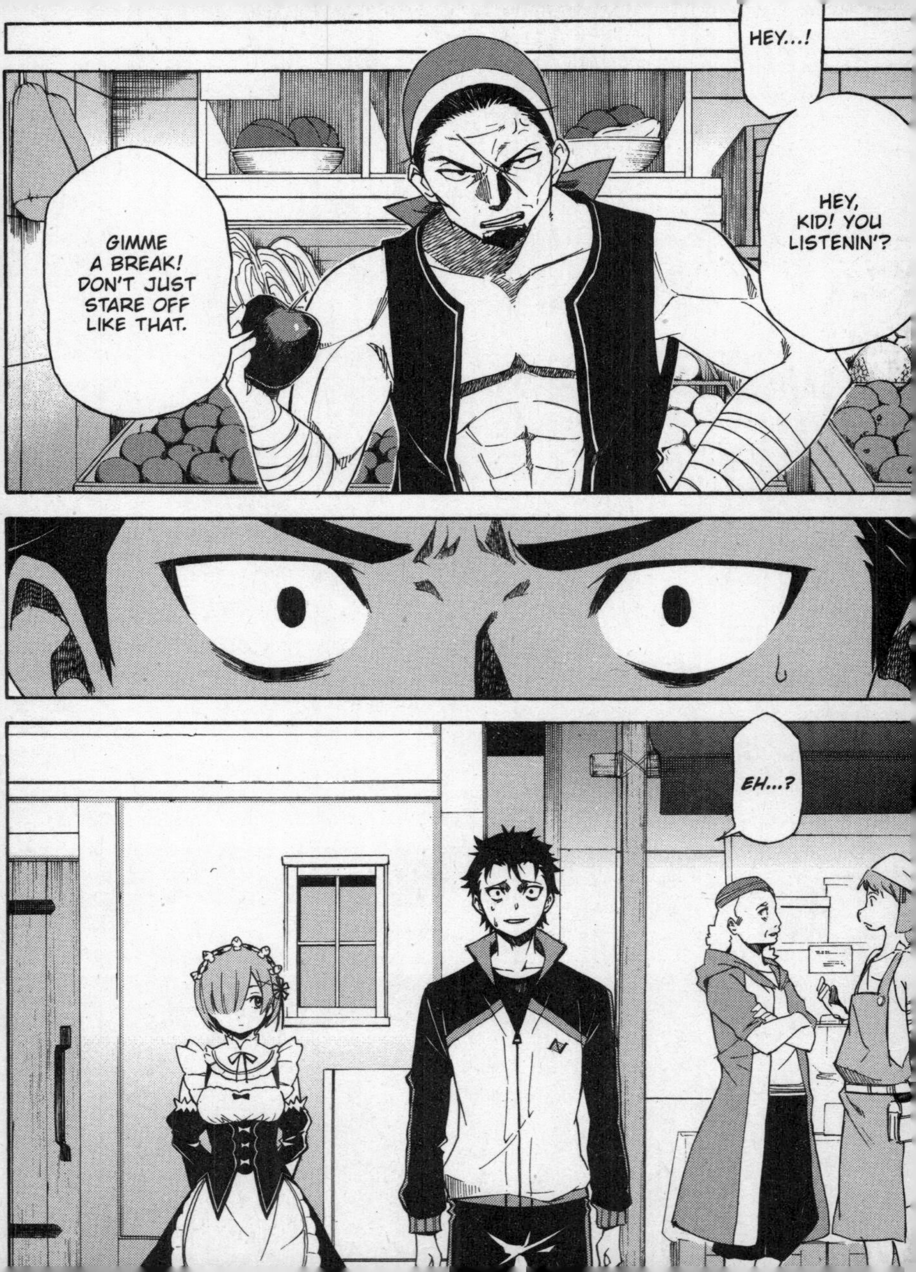
HEY...!
HEY, KID! YOU LISTENIN'?
GIMME A BREAK! DON'T JUST STARE OFF LIKE THAT.
EH...?

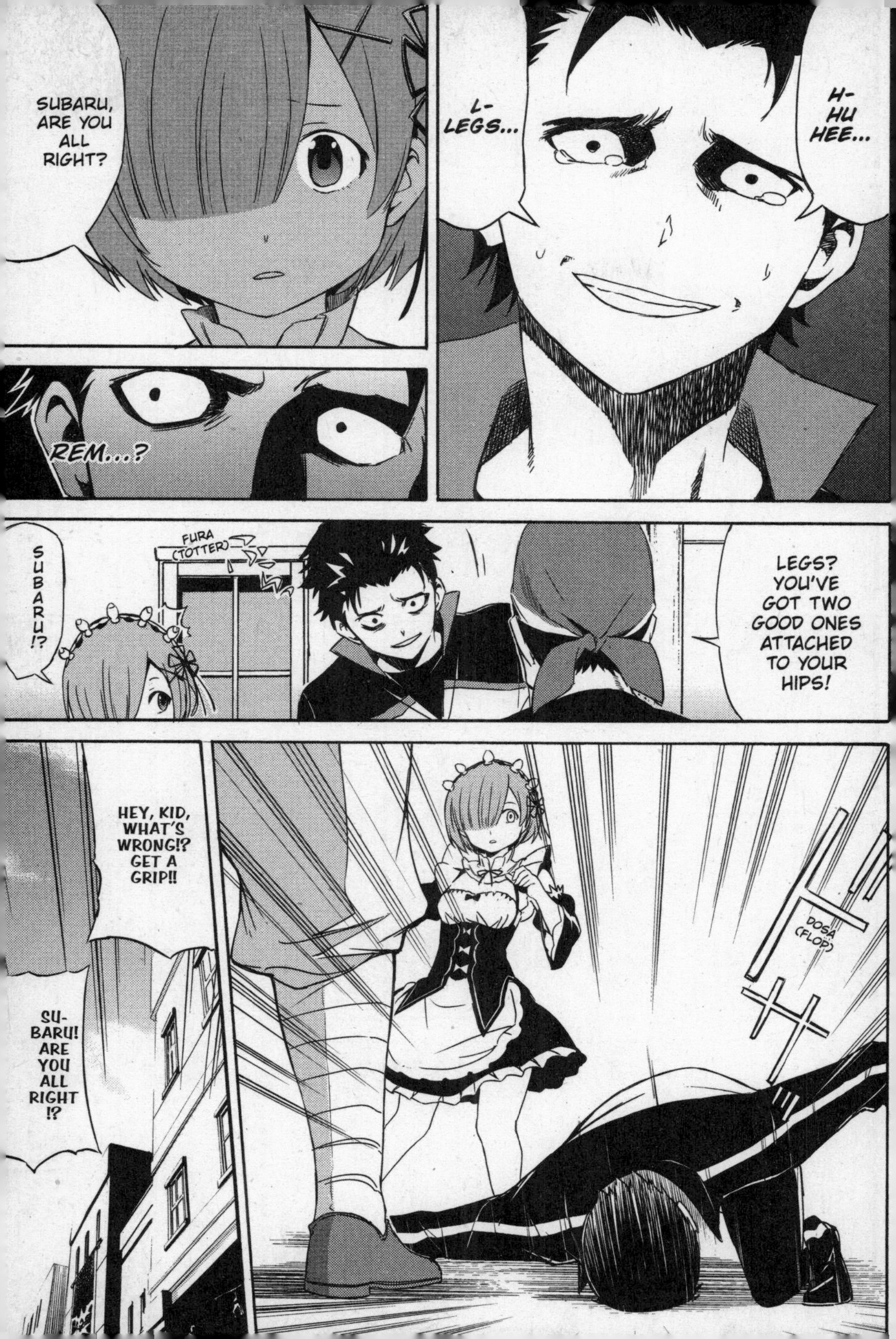
H-HU HEE...
L-LEGS...
SUBARU, ARE YOU ALL RIGHT?
REM...?
LEGS? YOU'VE GOT TWO GOOD ONES ATTACHED TO YOUR HIPS!
FURA (TOTTER)
SUBARU!?
DOSA (FLOP)
HEY, KID, WHAT'S WRONG!? GET A GRIP!!
SU-BARU! ARE YOU ALL RIGHT!?

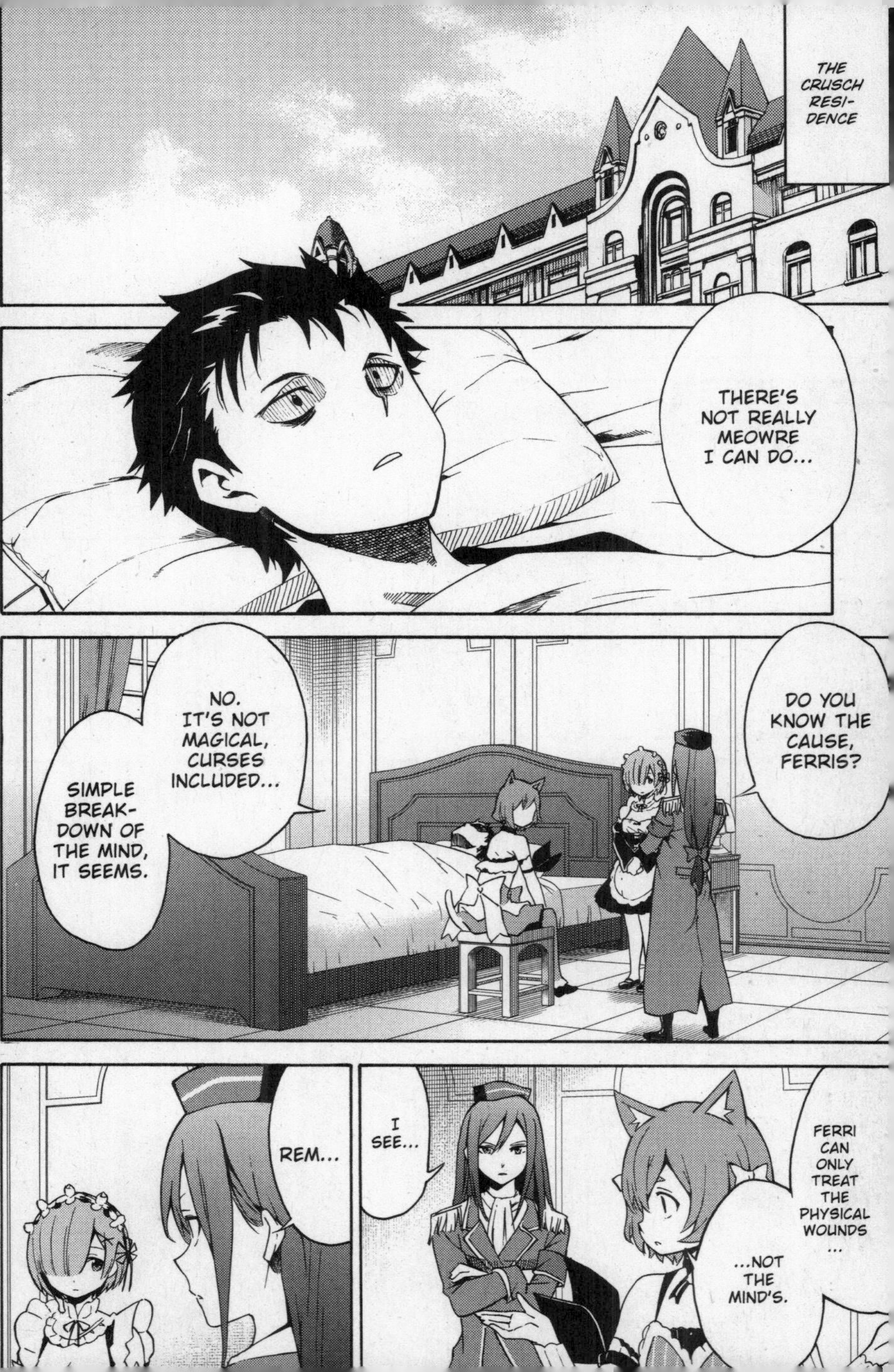
THE CRUSCH RESIDENCE
THERE'S NOT REALLY MEOWRE I CAN DO...
DO YOU KNOW THE CAUSE, FERRIS?
NO. IT'S NOT MAGICAL, CURSES INCLUDED...
SIMPLE BREAKDOWN OF THE MIND, IT SEEMS.
FERRI CAN ONLY TREAT THE PHYSICAL WOUNDS ...
...NOT THE MIND'S.
I SEE...
REM...

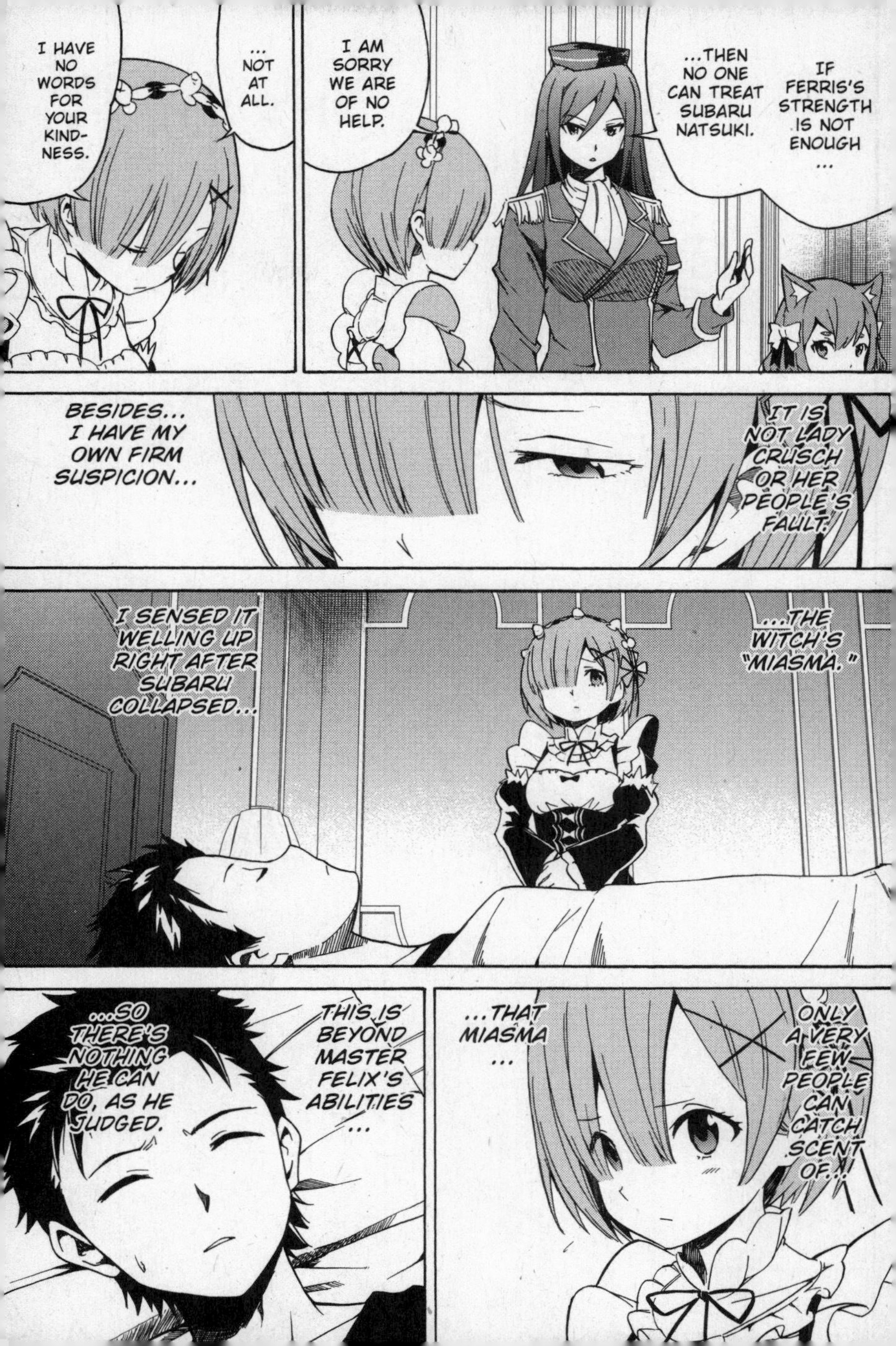
IF FERRIS'S STRENGTH IS NOT ENOUGH...
...THEN NO ONE CAN TREAT SUBARU NATSUKI.
I AM SORRY WE ARE OF NO HELP.
...NOT AT ALL.
I HAVE NO WORDS FOR YOUR KINDNESS.
IT IS NOT LADY CRUSCH OR HER PEOPLE'S FAULT.
BESIDES... I HAVE MY OWN FIRM SUSPICION...
...THE WITCH'S "MIASMA."
I SENSED IT WELLING UP RIGHT AFTER SUBARU COLLAPSED...
ONLY A VERY FEW PEOPLE CAN CATCH SCENT OF...
...THAT MIASMA...
THIS IS BEYOND MASTER FELIX'S ABILITIES...
...SO THERE'S NOTHING HE CAN DO, AS HE JUDGED.

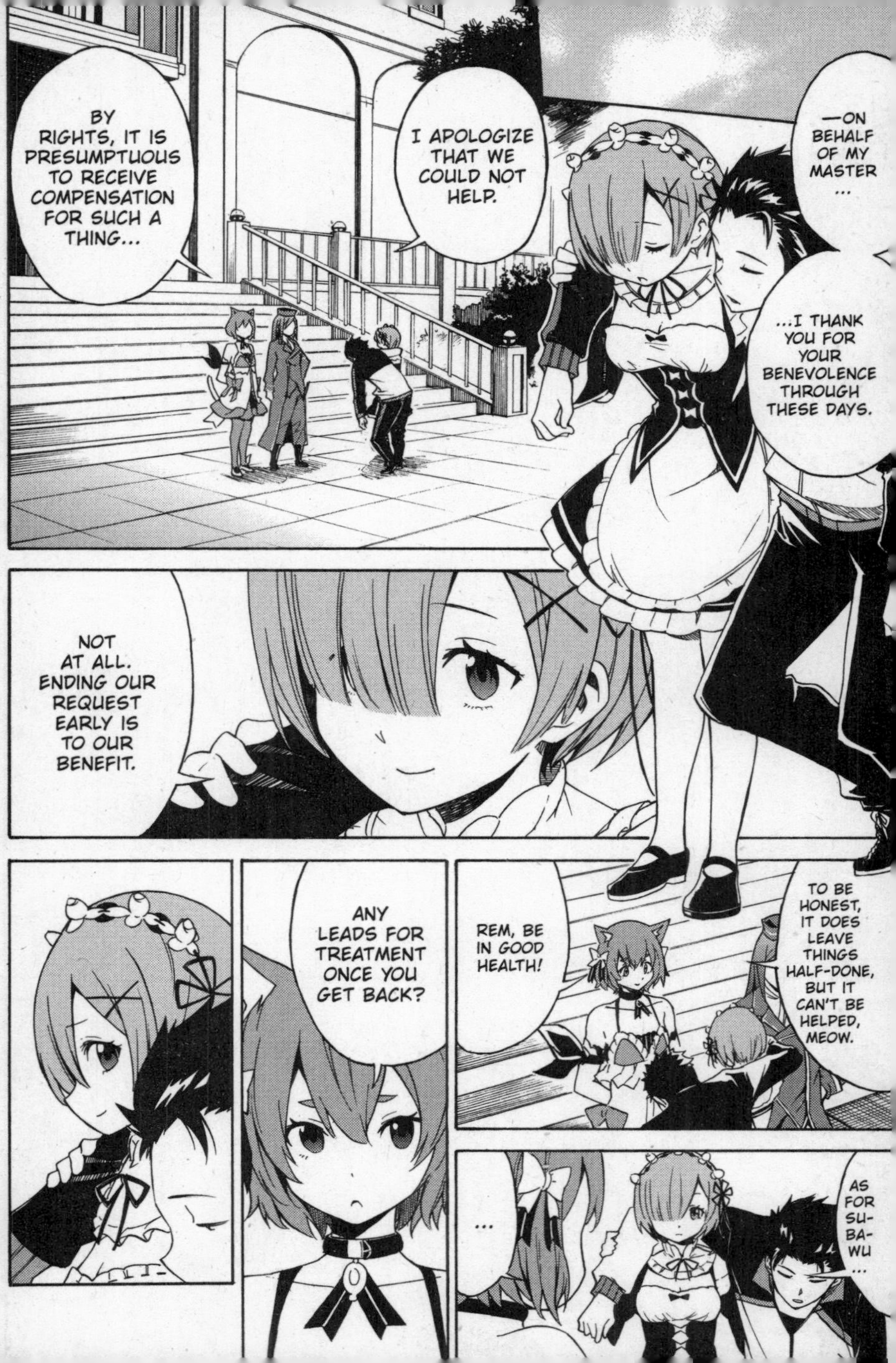
—ON BEHALF OF MY MASTER...
...I THANK YOU FOR YOUR BENEVOLENCE THROUGH THESE DAYS.
I APOLOGIZE THAT WE COULD NOT HELP.
BY RIGHTS, IT IS PRESUMPTUOUS TO RECEIVE COMPENSATION FOR SUCH A THING...
NOT AT ALL. ENDING OUR REQUEST EARLY IS TO OUR BENEFIT.
TO BE HONEST, IT DOES LEAVE THINGS HALF-DONE, BUT IT CAN'T BE HELPED, MEOW.
REM, BE IN GOOD HEALTH!
AS FOR SU-BA-WU...
...
ANY LEADS FOR TREATMENT ONCE YOU GET BACK?

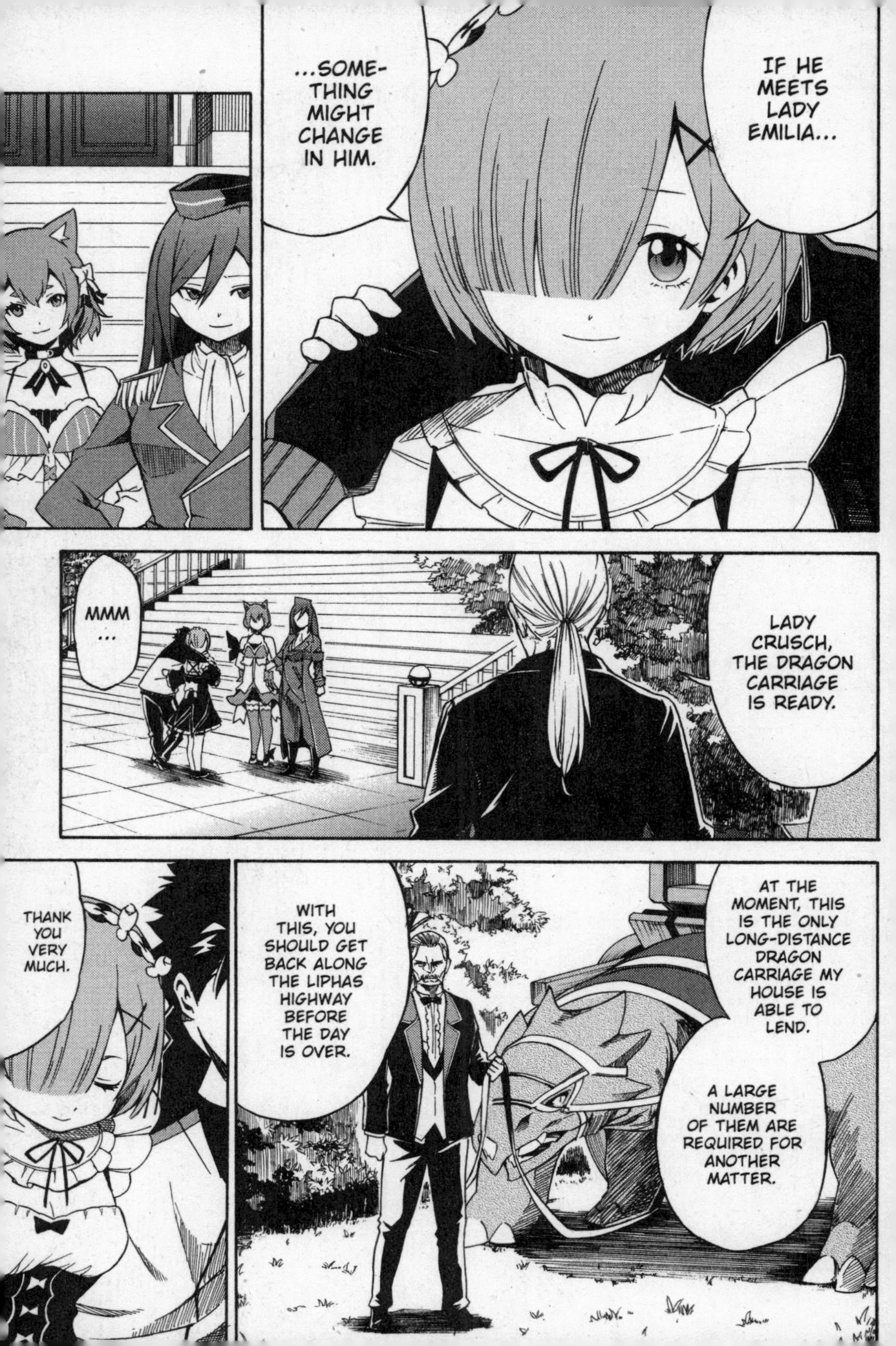
IF HE MEETS LADY EMILIA...
...SOME-THING MIGHT CHANGE IN HIM.
LADY CRUSCH, THE DRAGON CARRIAGE IS READY.
MMM ...
AT THE MOMENT, THIS IS THE ONLY LONG-DISTANCE DRAGON CARRIAGE MY HOUSE IS ABLE TO LEND.
A LARGE NUMBER OF THEM ARE REQUIRED FOR ANOTHER MATTER.
WITH THIS, YOU SHOULD GET BACK ALONG THE LIPHAS HIGHWAY BEFORE THE DAY IS OVER.
THANK YOU VERY MUCH.

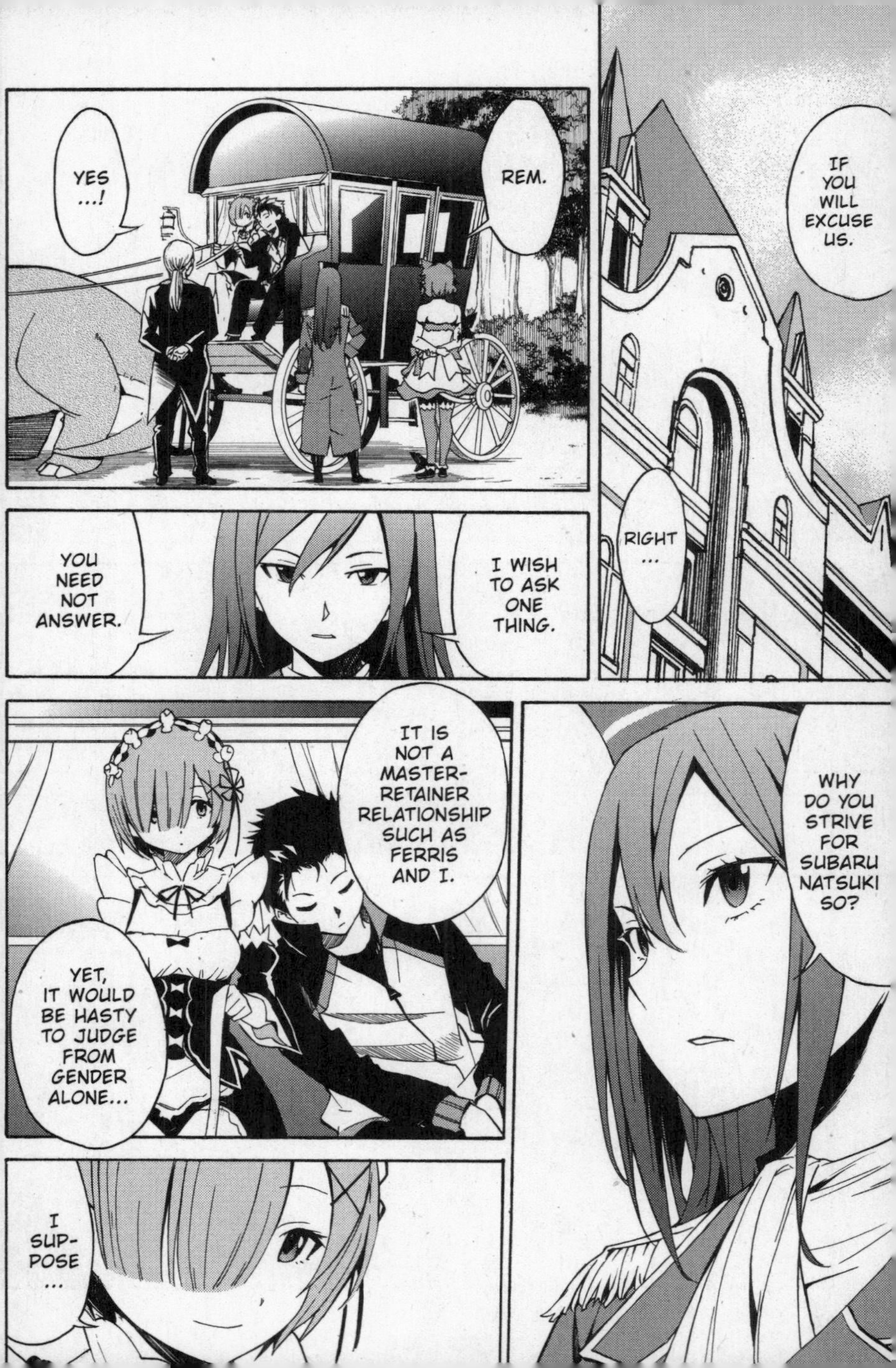
IF YOU WILL EXCUSE US.
RIGHT...
REM.
YES...!
I WISH TO ASK ONE THING.
YOU NEED NOT ANSWER.
WHY DO YOU STRIVE FOR SUBARU NATSUKI SO?
IT IS NOT A MASTER-RETAINER RELATIONSHIP SUCH AS FERRIS AND I.
YET, IT WOULD BE HASTY TO JUDGE FROM GENDER ALONE...
I SUP-POSE...

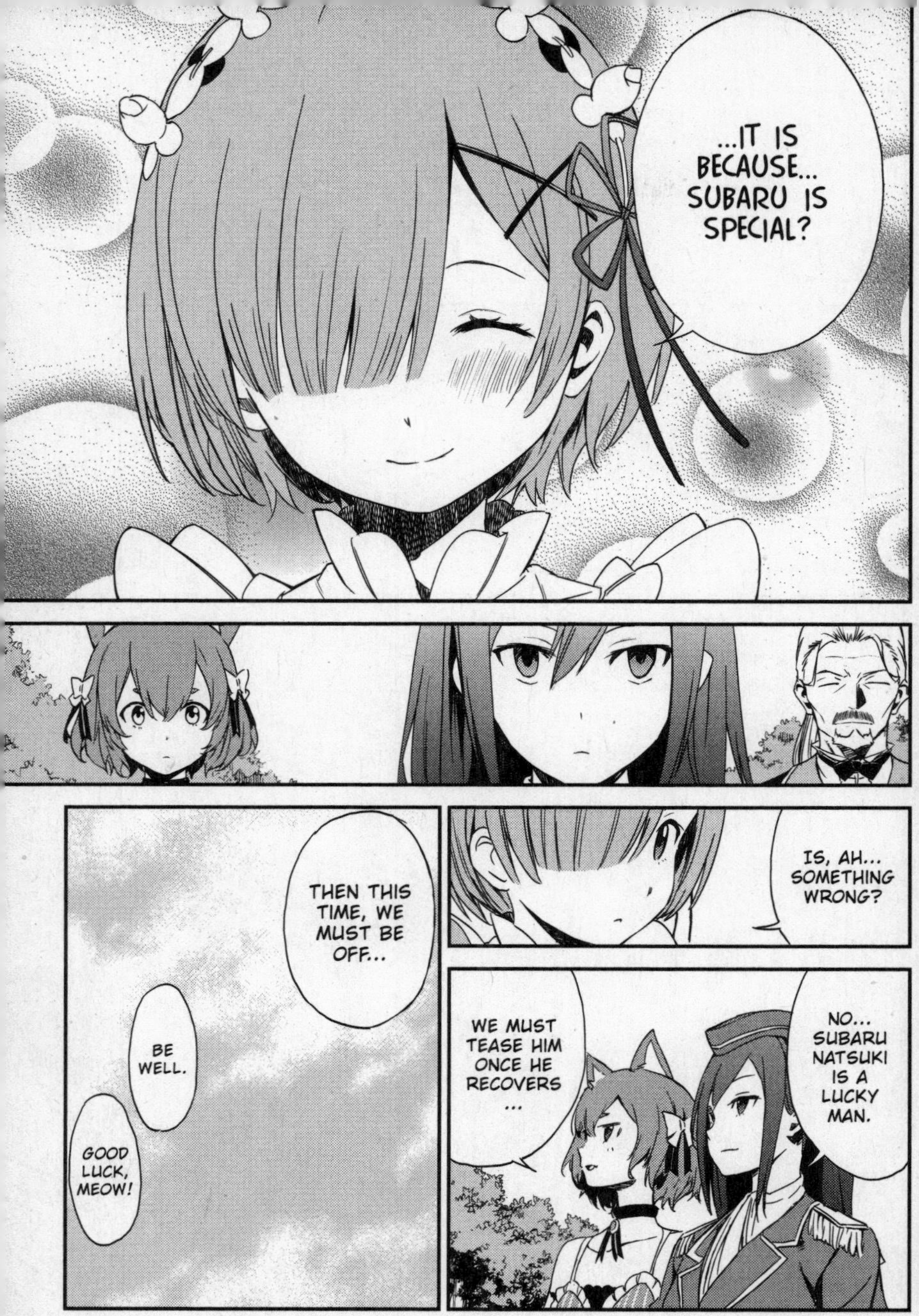
...IT IS BECAUSE... SUBARU IS SPECIAL?
IS, AH... SOMETHING WRONG?
NO... SUBARU NATSUKI IS A LUCKY MAN.
WE MUST TEASE HIM ONCE HE RECOVERS ...
THEN THIS TIME, WE MUST BE OFF...
BE WELL.
GOOD LUCK, MEOW!

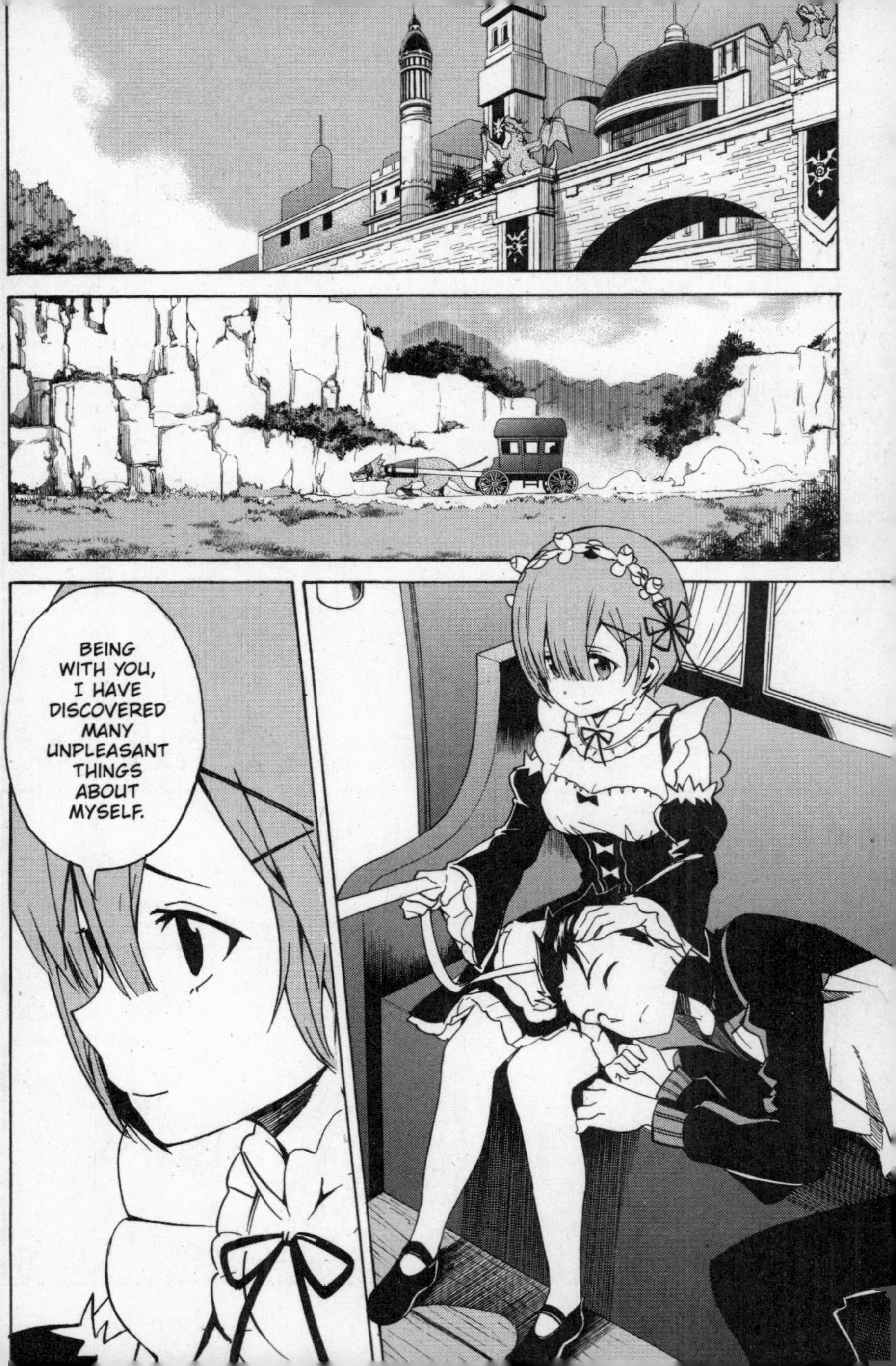
BEING WITH YOU, I HAVE DISCOVERED MANY UNPLEASANT THINGS ABOUT MYSELF.

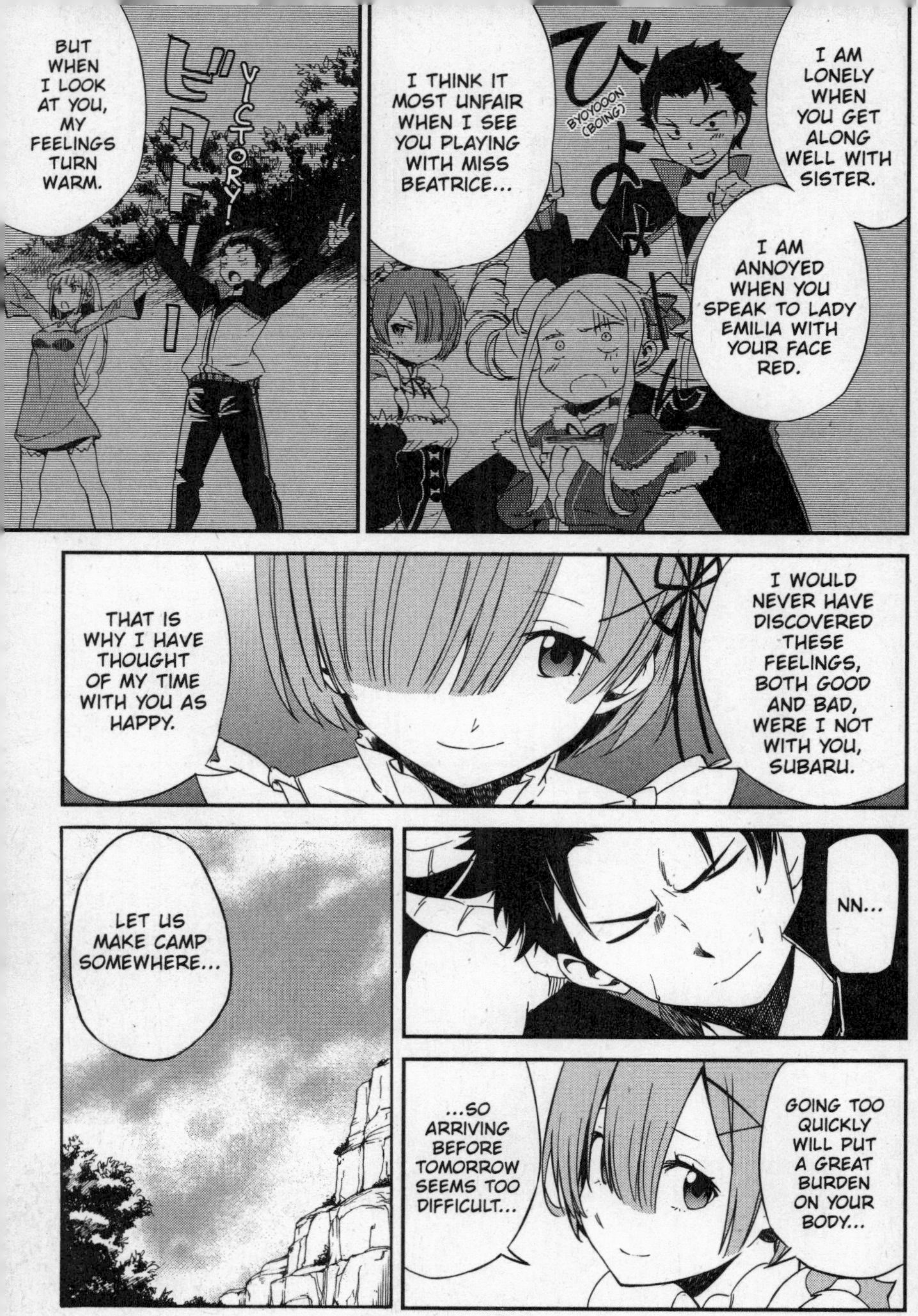
I AM LONELY WHEN YOU GET ALONG WELL WITH SISTER.
I AM ANNOYED WHEN YOU SPEAK TO LADY EMILIA WITH YOUR FACE RED.
BYOYOOON (BOING)
I THINK IT MOST UNFAIR WHEN I SEE YOU PLAYING WITH MISS BEATRICE...
VICTORY!
BUT WHEN I LOOK AT YOU, MY FEELINGS TURN WARM.
I WOULD NEVER HAVE DISCOVERED THESE FEELINGS, BOTH GOOD AND BAD, WERE I NOT WITH YOU, SUBARU.
THAT IS WHY I HAVE THOUGHT OF MY TIME WITH YOU AS HAPPY.
NN...
GOING TOO QUICKLY WILL PUT A GREAT BURDEN ON YOUR BODY...
...SO ARRIVING BEFORE TOMORROW SEEMS TOO DIFFICULT...
LET US MAKE CAMP SOMEWHERE...

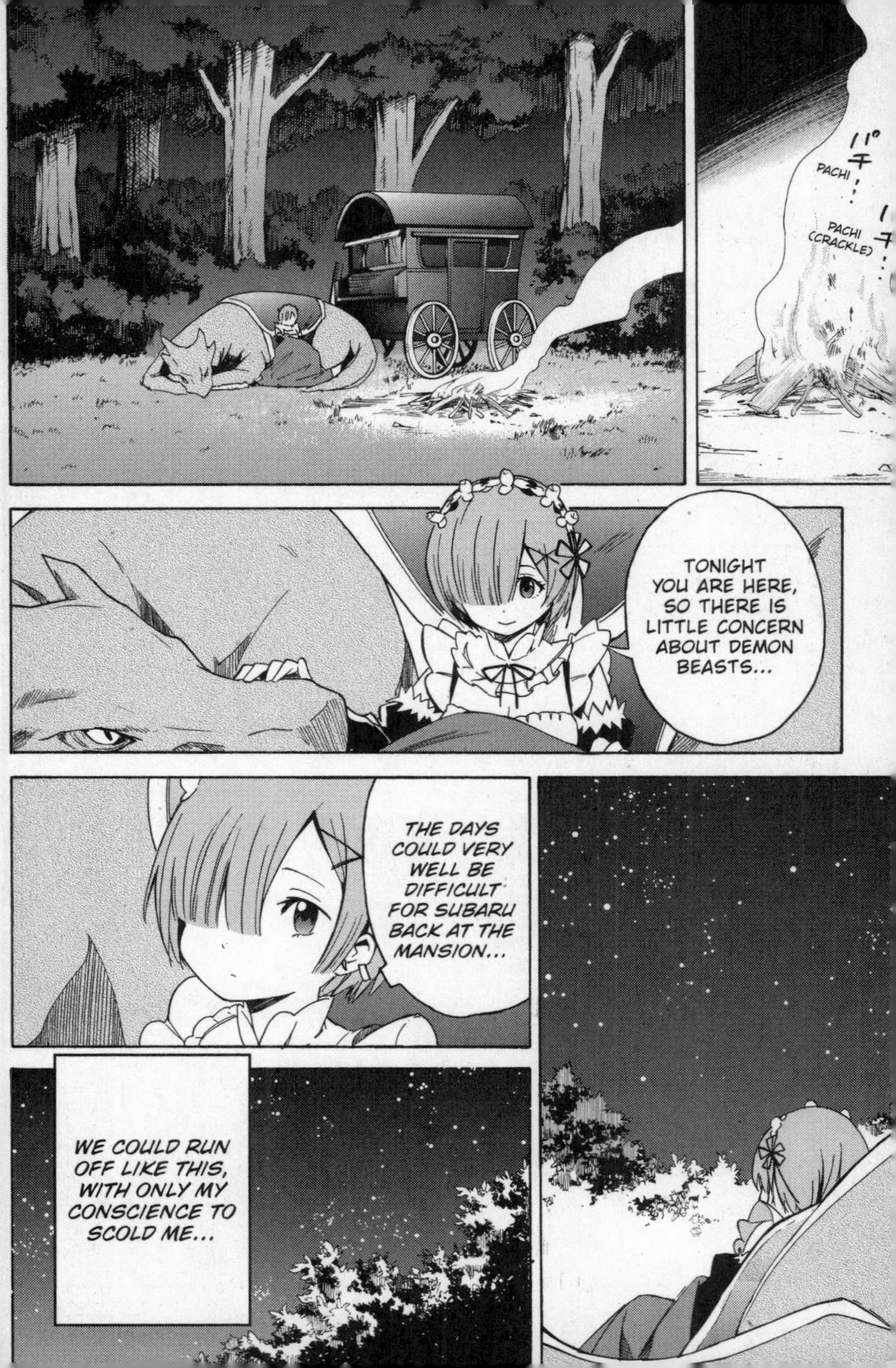
パチ…
PACHI
パチ…
PACHI (CRACKLE)
TONIGHT YOU ARE HERE, SO THERE IS LITTLE CONCERN ABOUT DEMON BEASTS...
THE DAYS COULD VERY WELL BE DIFFICULT FOR SUBARU BACK AT THE MANSION...
WE COULD RUN OFF LIKE THIS, WITH ONLY MY CONSCIENCE TO SCOLD ME...

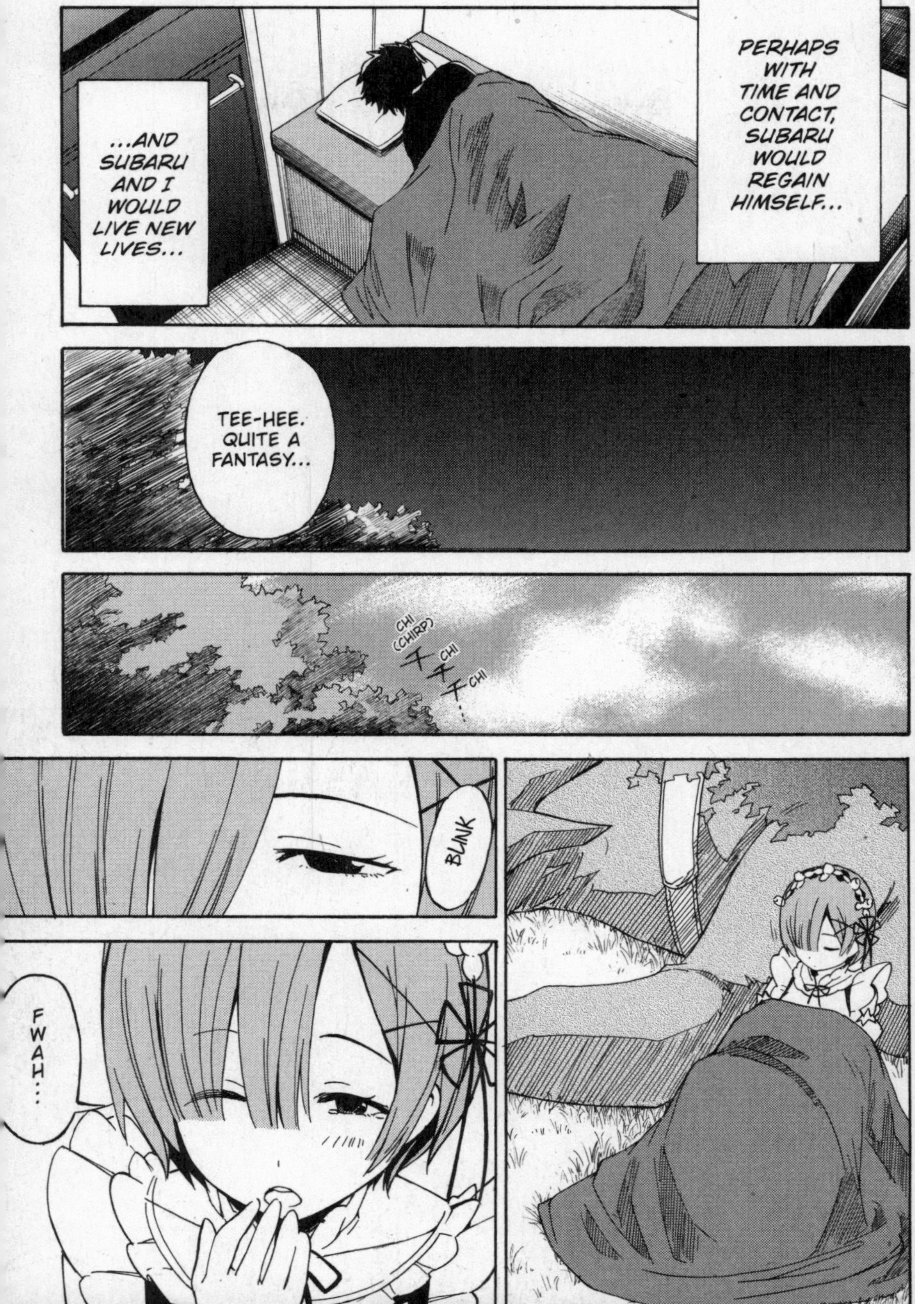
PERHAPS WITH TIME AND CONTACT, SUBARU WOULD REGAIN HIMSELF...
...AND SUBARU AND I WOULD LIVE NEW LIVES...
TEE-HEE. QUITE A FANTASY...
CHI (CHIRP) CHI CHI
BLINK
FWAH...

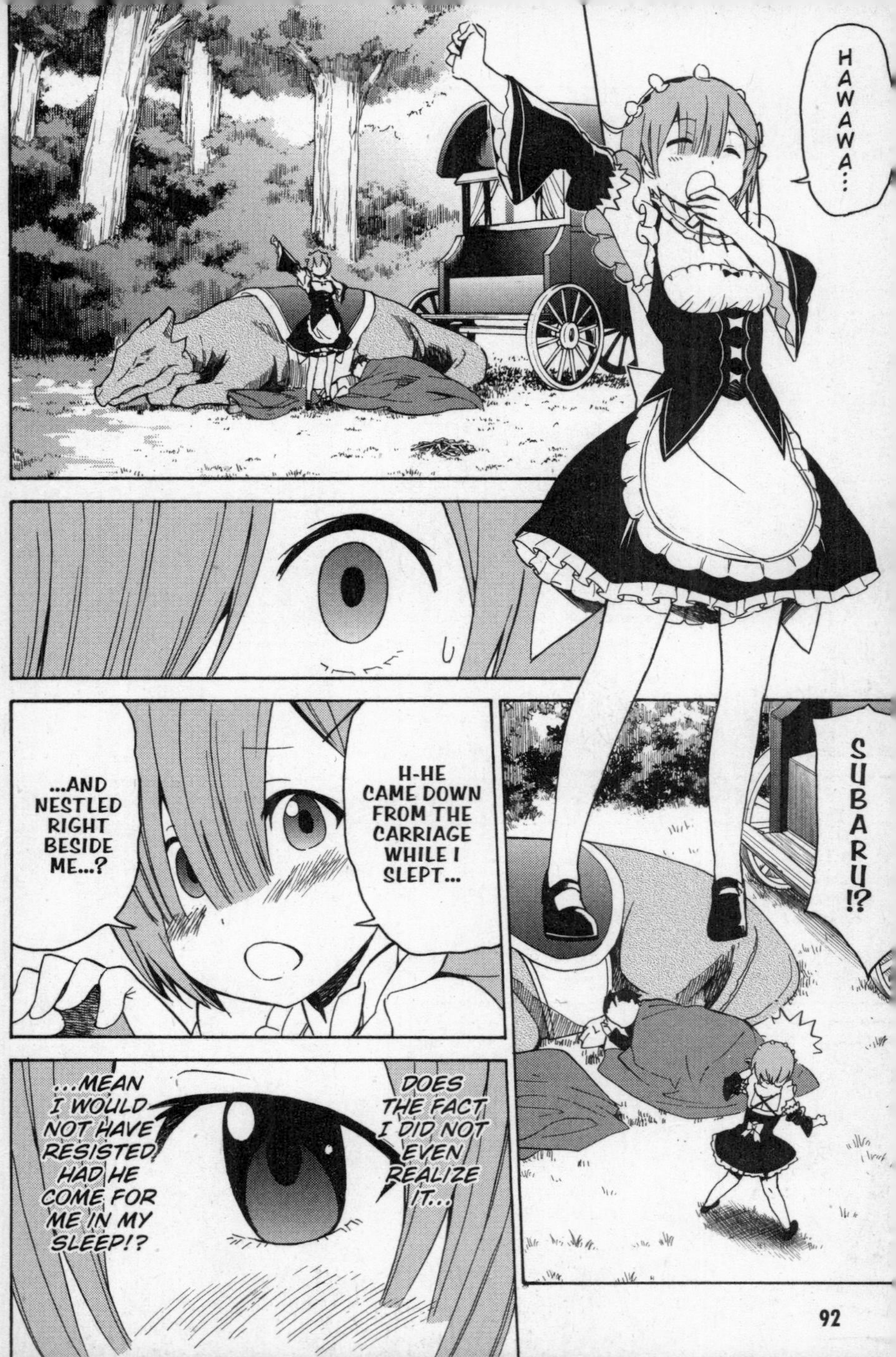
HAWAWA...
SUBARU!?
H-HE CAME DOWN FROM THE CARRIAGE WHILE I SLEPT...
...AND NESTLED RIGHT BESIDE ME...?
DOES THE FACT I DID NOT EVEN REALIZE IT...
...MEAN I WOULD NOT HAVE RESISTED HAD HE COME FOR ME IN MY SLEEP!?

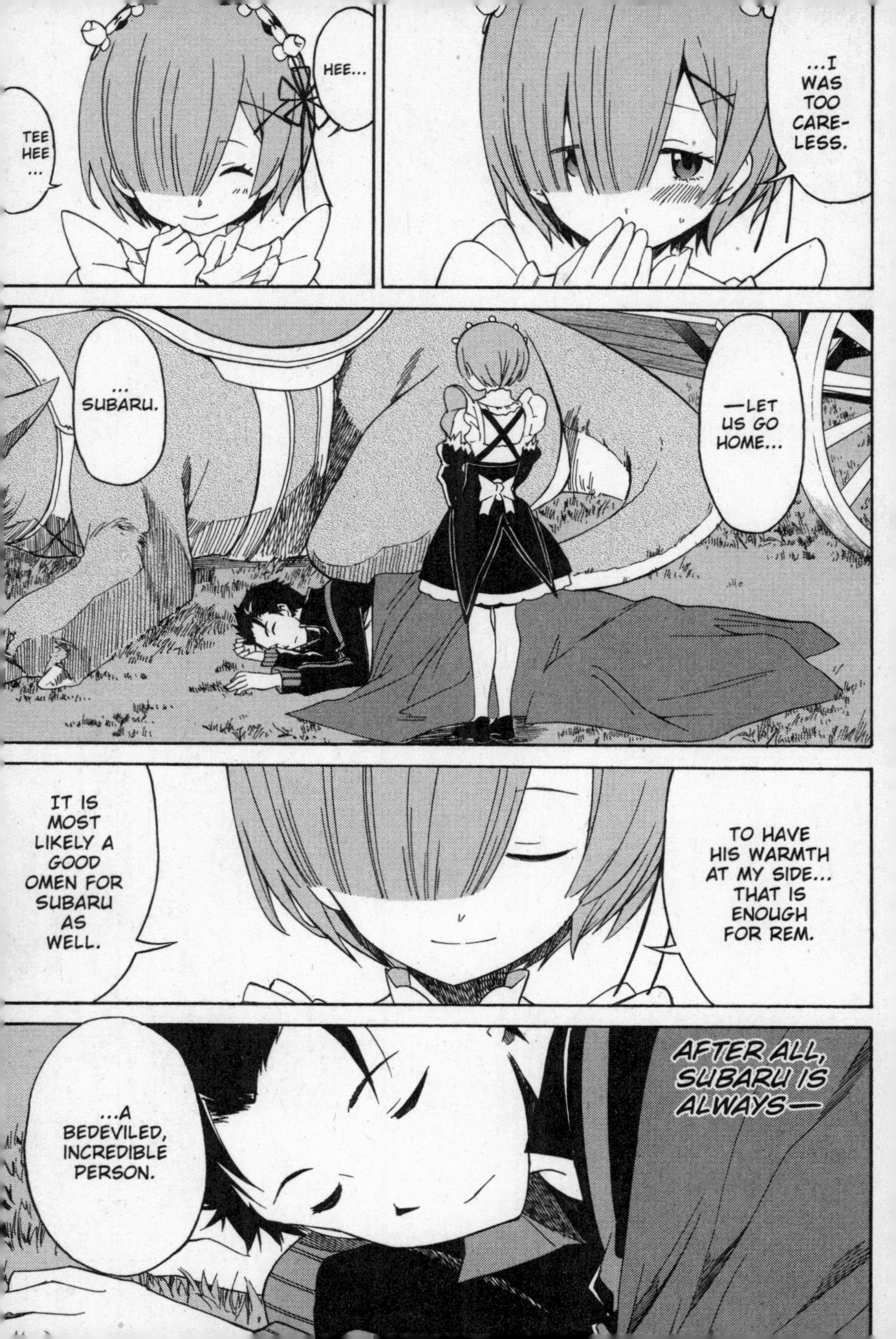
...I WAS TOO CARE-LESS.
HEE...
TEE HEE ...
—LET US GO HOME...
... SUBARU.
TO HAVE HIS WARMTH AT MY SIDE... THAT IS ENOUGH FOR REM.
IT IS MOST LIKELY A GOOD OMEN FOR SUBARU AS WELL.
AFTER ALL, SUBARU IS ALWAYS—
...A BEDEVILED, INCREDIBLE PERSON.

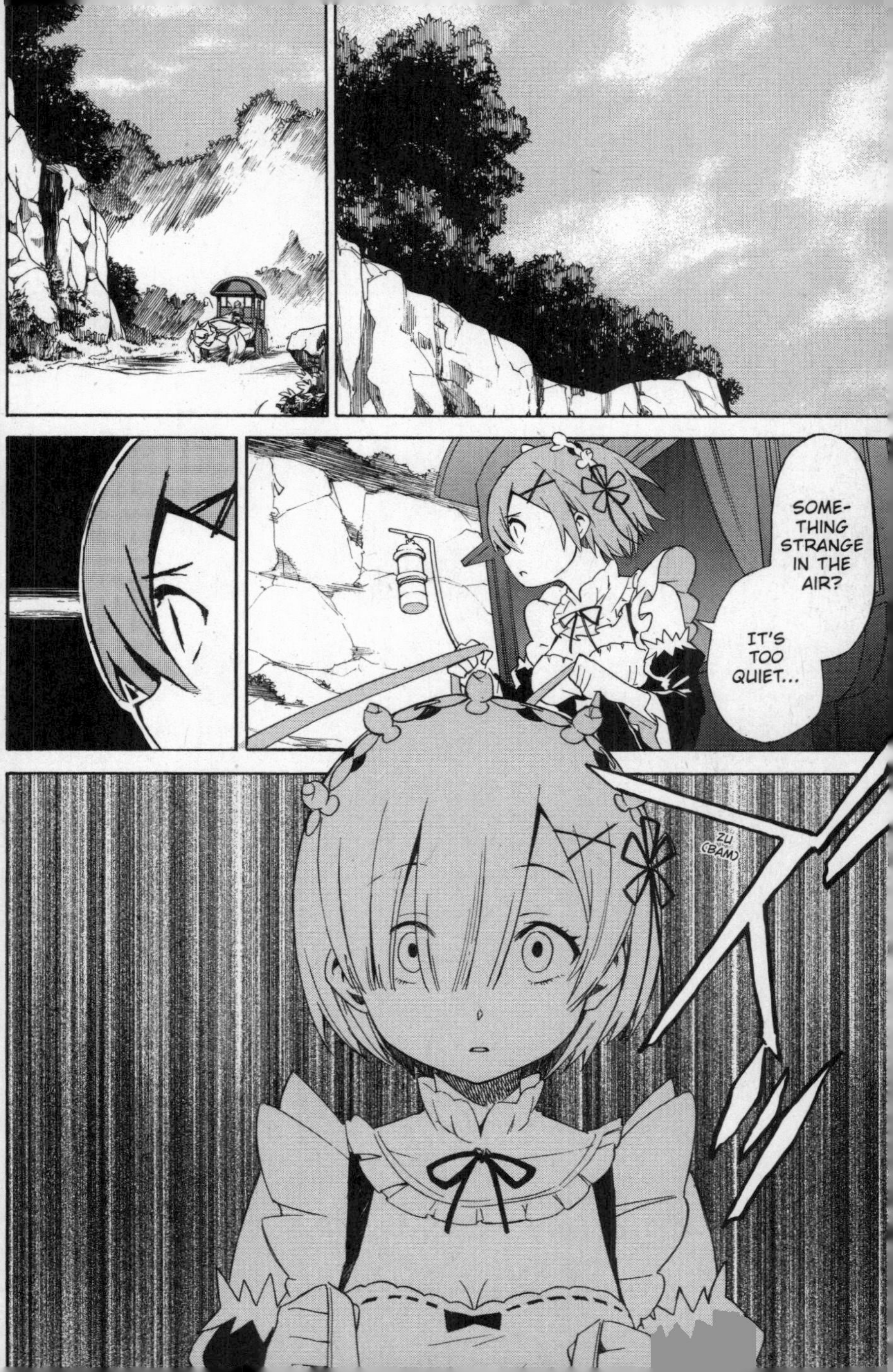
SOME-THING STRANGE IN THE AIR?
IT'S TOO QUIET...
ZU (BAM)

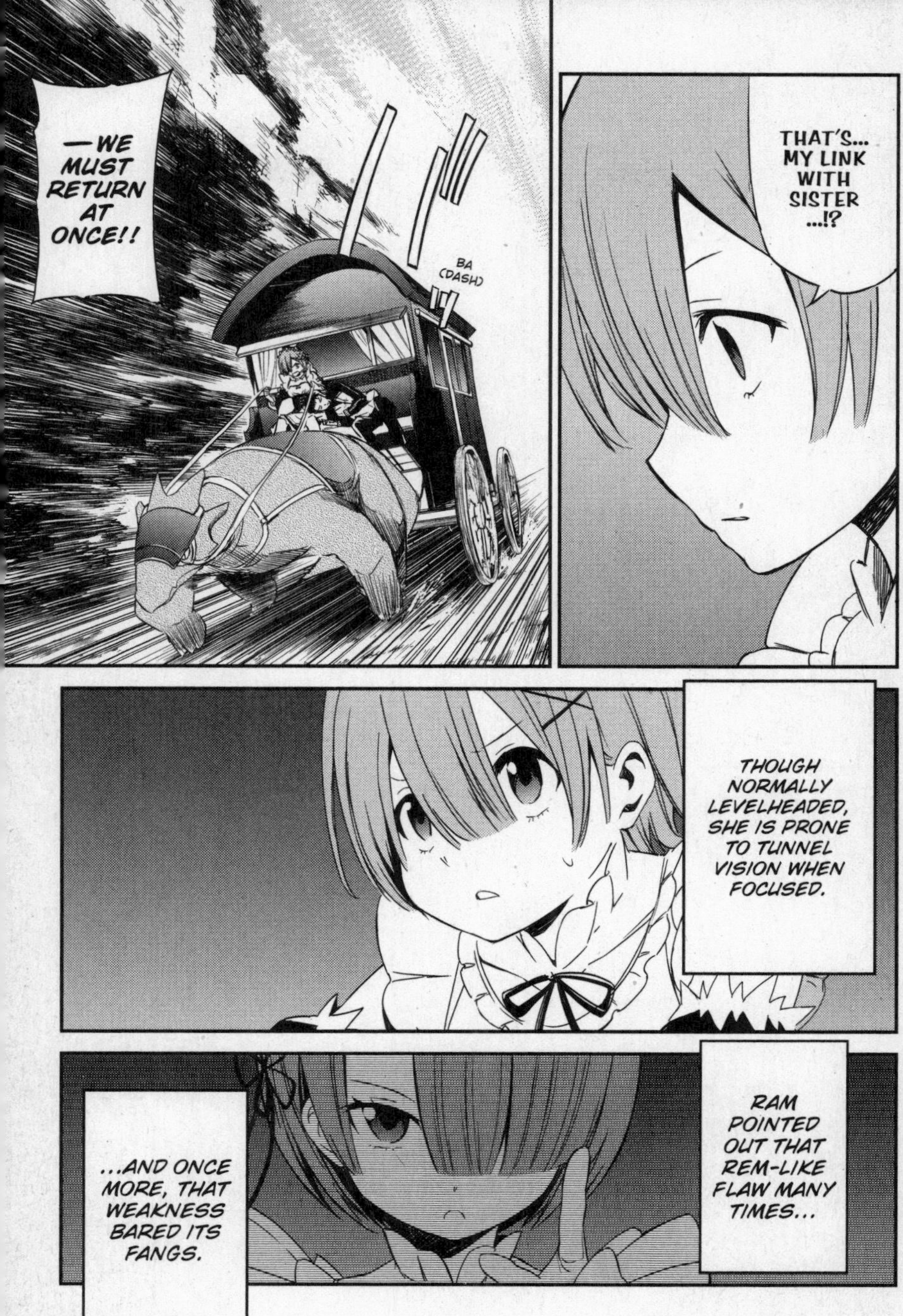
THAT'S... MY LINK WITH SISTER ...!?
—WE MUST RETURN AT ONCE!!
BA (DASH)
THOUGH NORMALLY LEVELHEADED, SHE IS PRONE TO TUNNEL VISION WHEN FOCUSED.
RAM POINTED OUT THAT REM-LIKE FLAW MANY TIMES...
...AND ONCE MORE, THAT WEAKNESS BARED ITS FANGS.

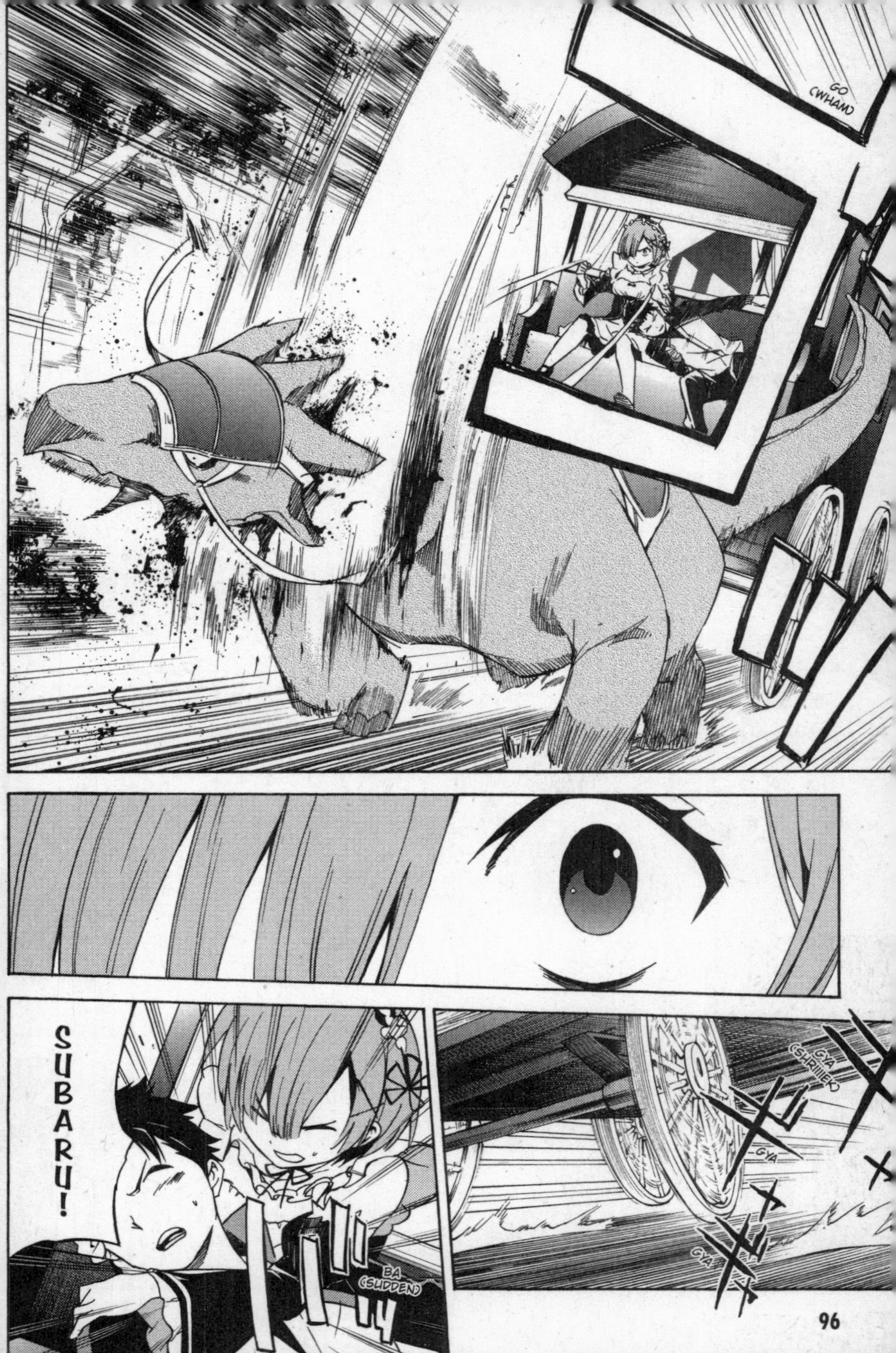
GO (WHAM)
GYA (SHRIIIEK)
GYA
GYA
SUBARU!
BA (SUDDEN)

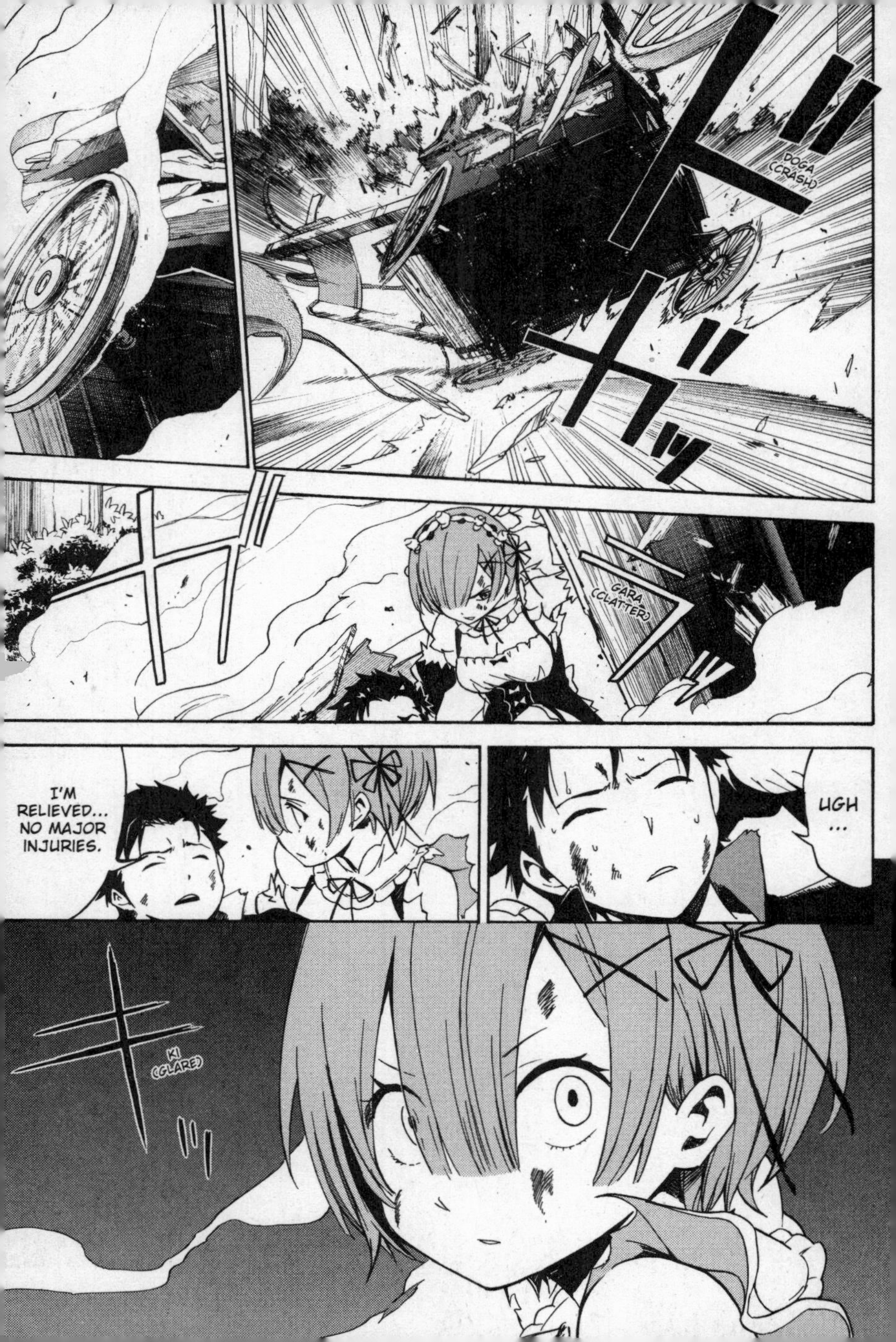
DOGA (CRASH)
GARA (CLATTER)
UGH ...
I'M RELIEVED... NO MAJOR INJURIES.
KI (GLARE)

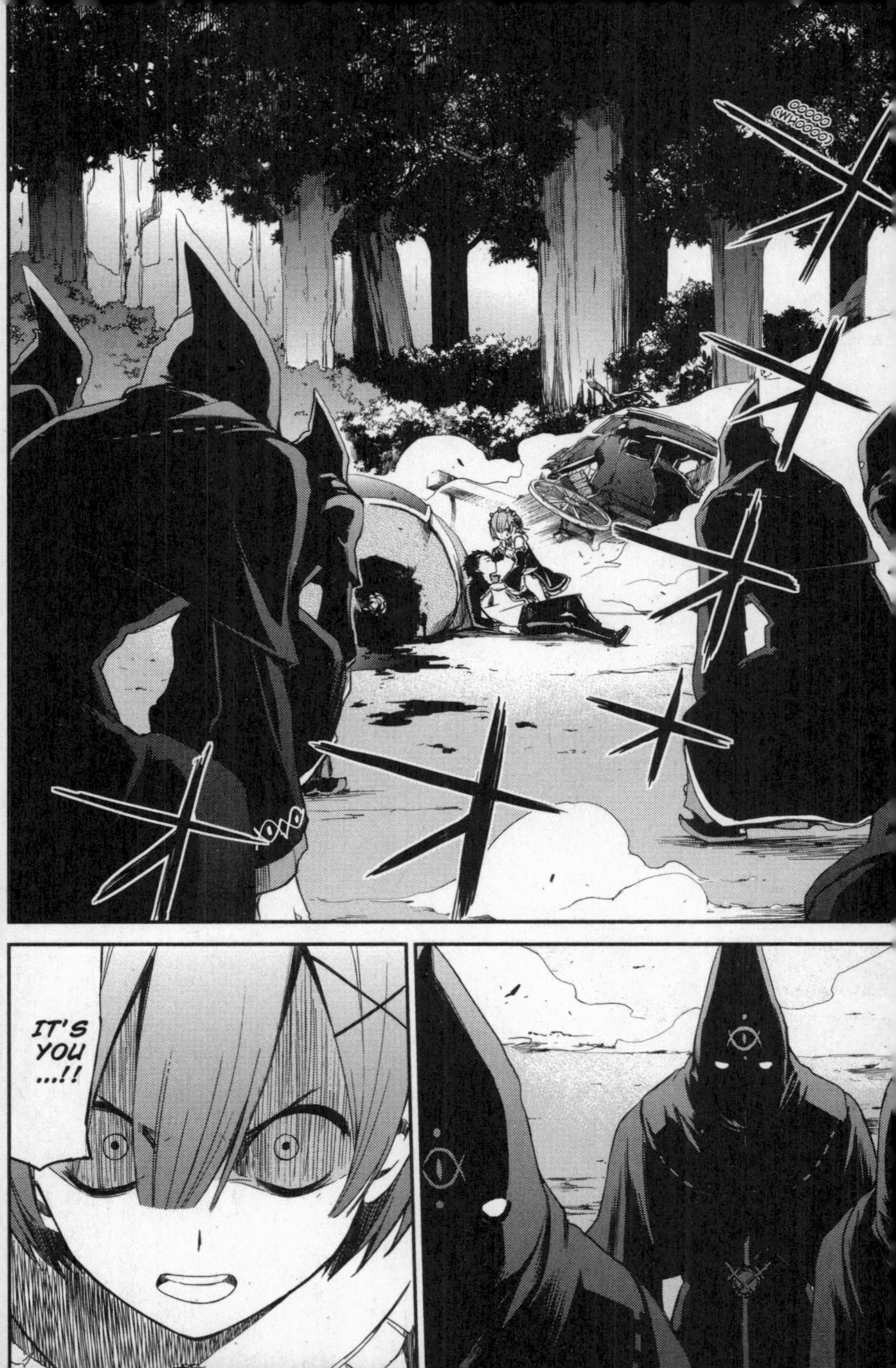
OOOOO
(WHOOOOO)
IT'S YOU ...!!

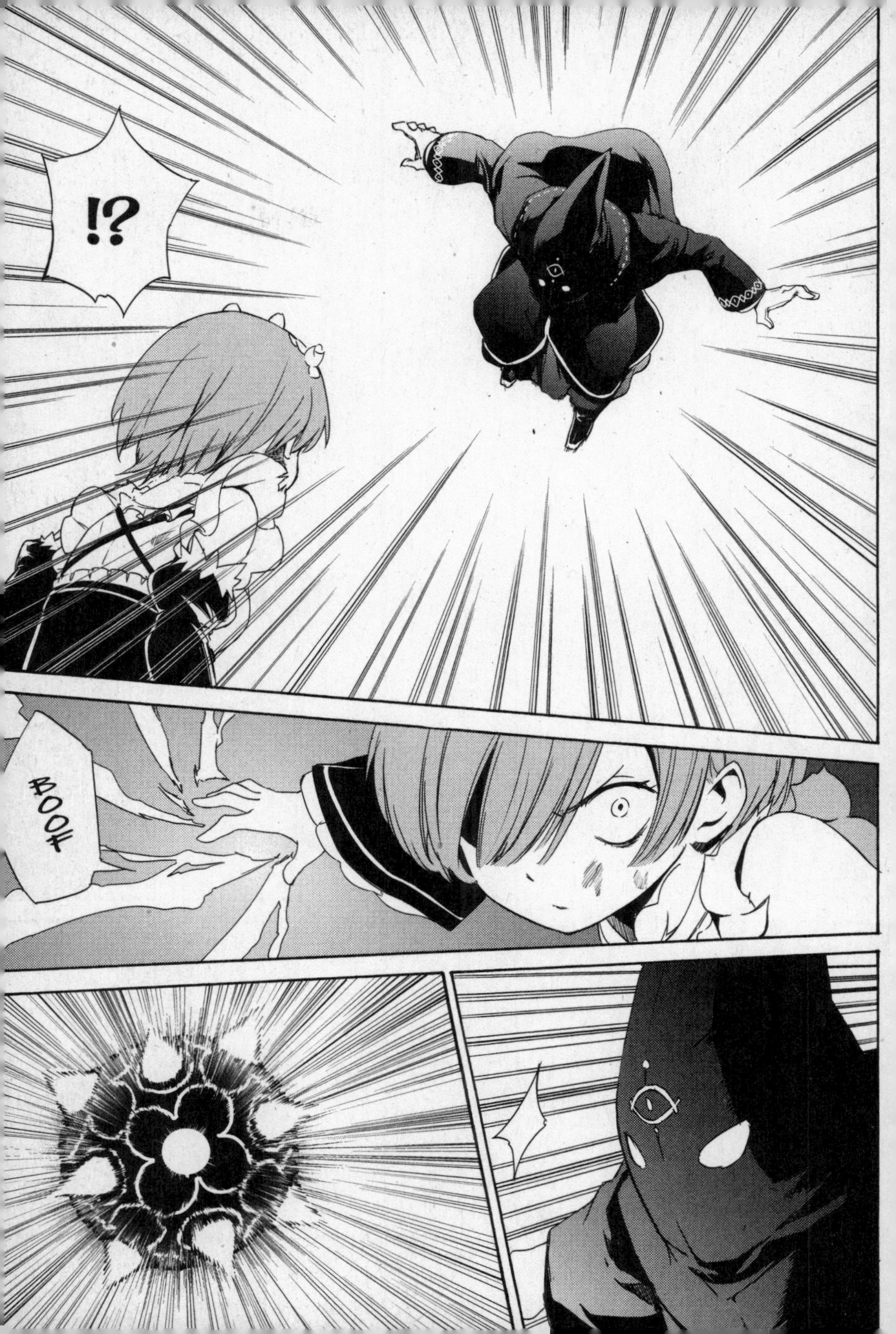
!?
BOOF

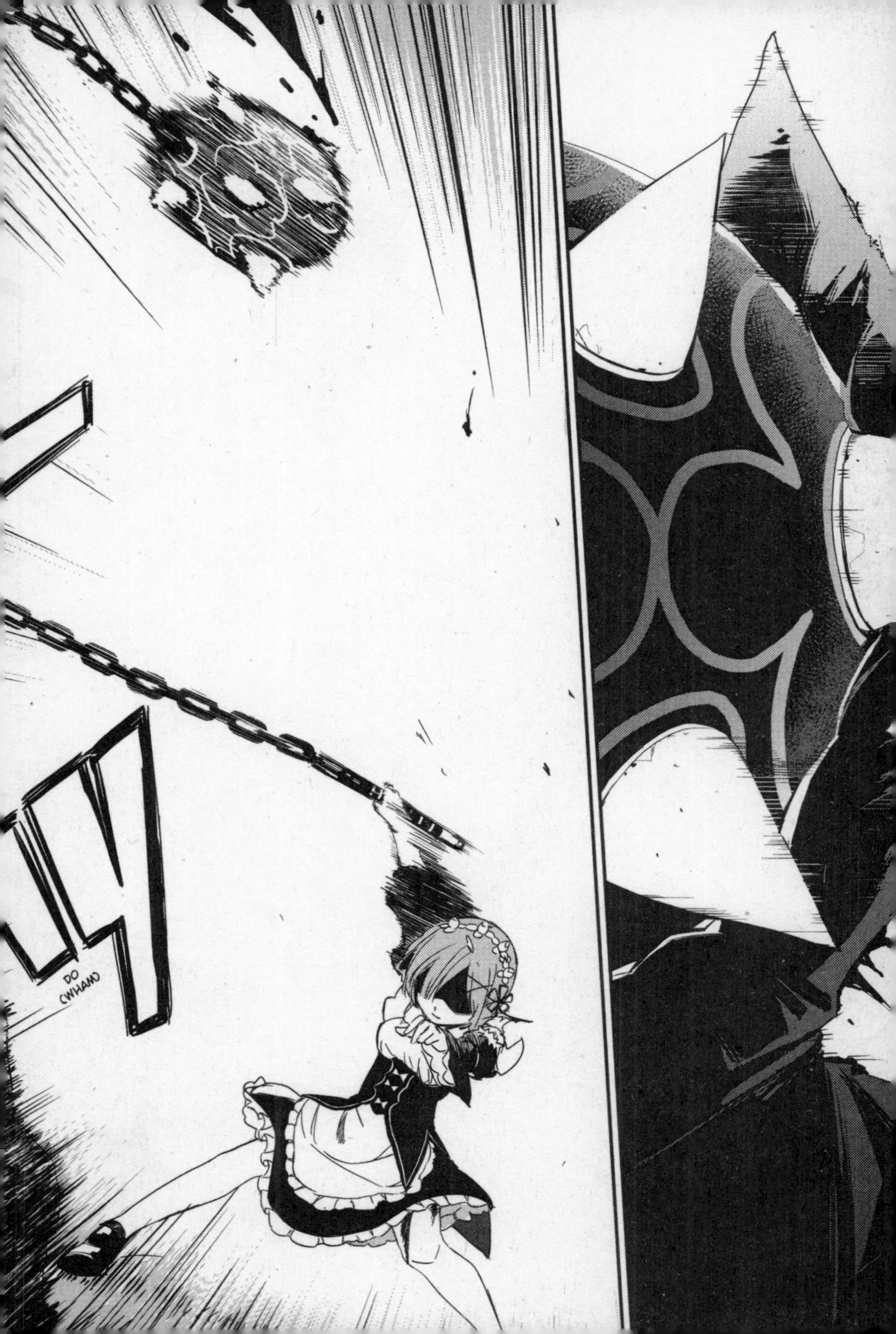
DO
(WHAM)

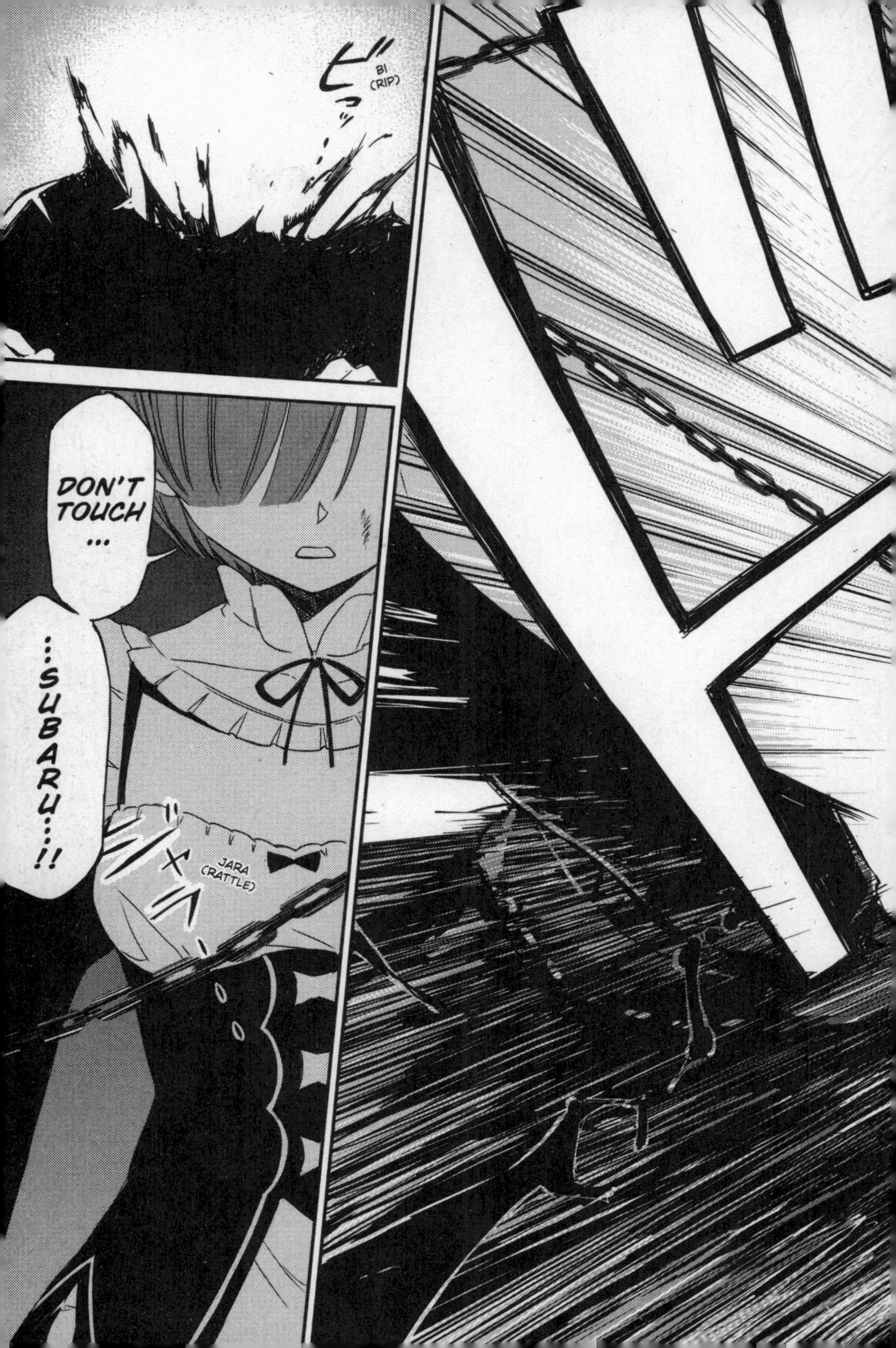
BI (RIP)
DON'T TOUCH ...
...SUBARU...!!
JARA (RATTLE)

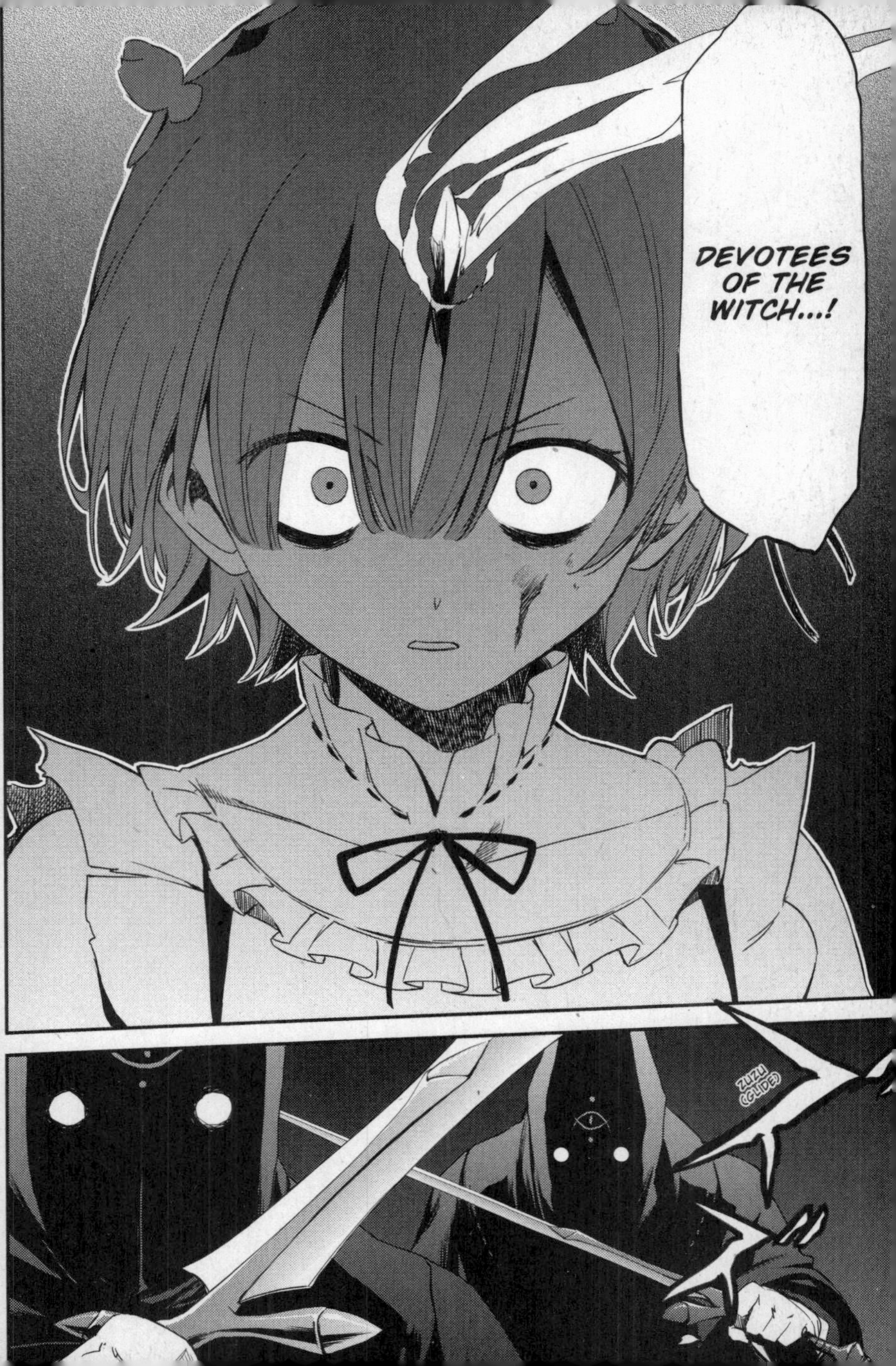
DEVOTEES OF THE WITCH...!
ZUZU (GLIDE)

The only ability Subaru Natsuki gets
when he's summoned to another world is
time travel via his own death. But to save
her, he'll die as many times as it takes.

Re:ZERO

-Starting Life in

Another World-

Re:ZERO -Starting Life in Another World-

Truth of Zero
The only ability Subaru Natsuki gets when he's summoned to another world is time
travel via his own death. But to save her, he'll die as many times as it takes.

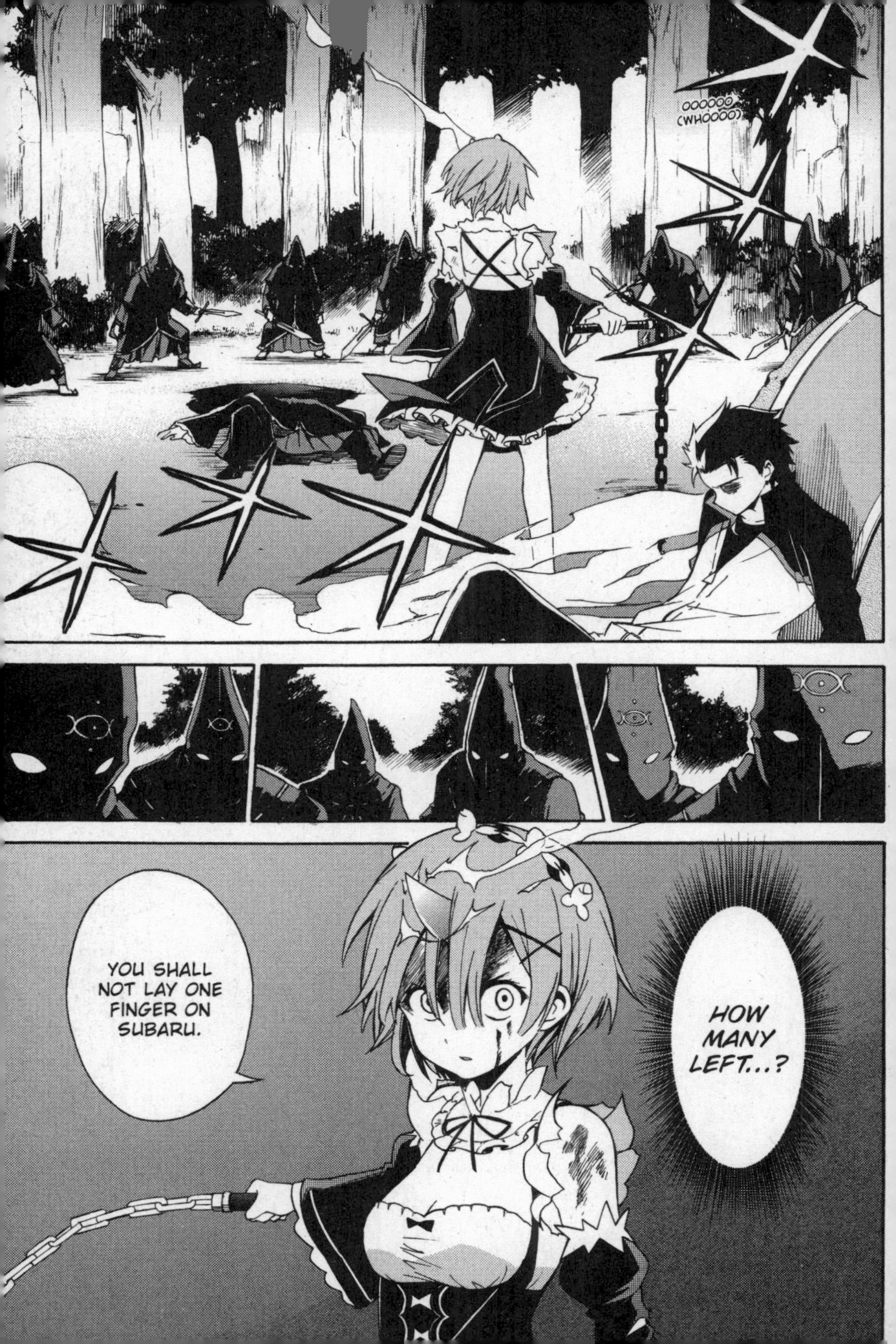
OOOOOO (WHOOOO)
HOW MANY LEFT...?
YOU SHALL NOT LAY ONE FINGER ON SUBARU.

Episode 14 Sloth

Re:ZERO -Starting Life in Another World-
Truth of Zero

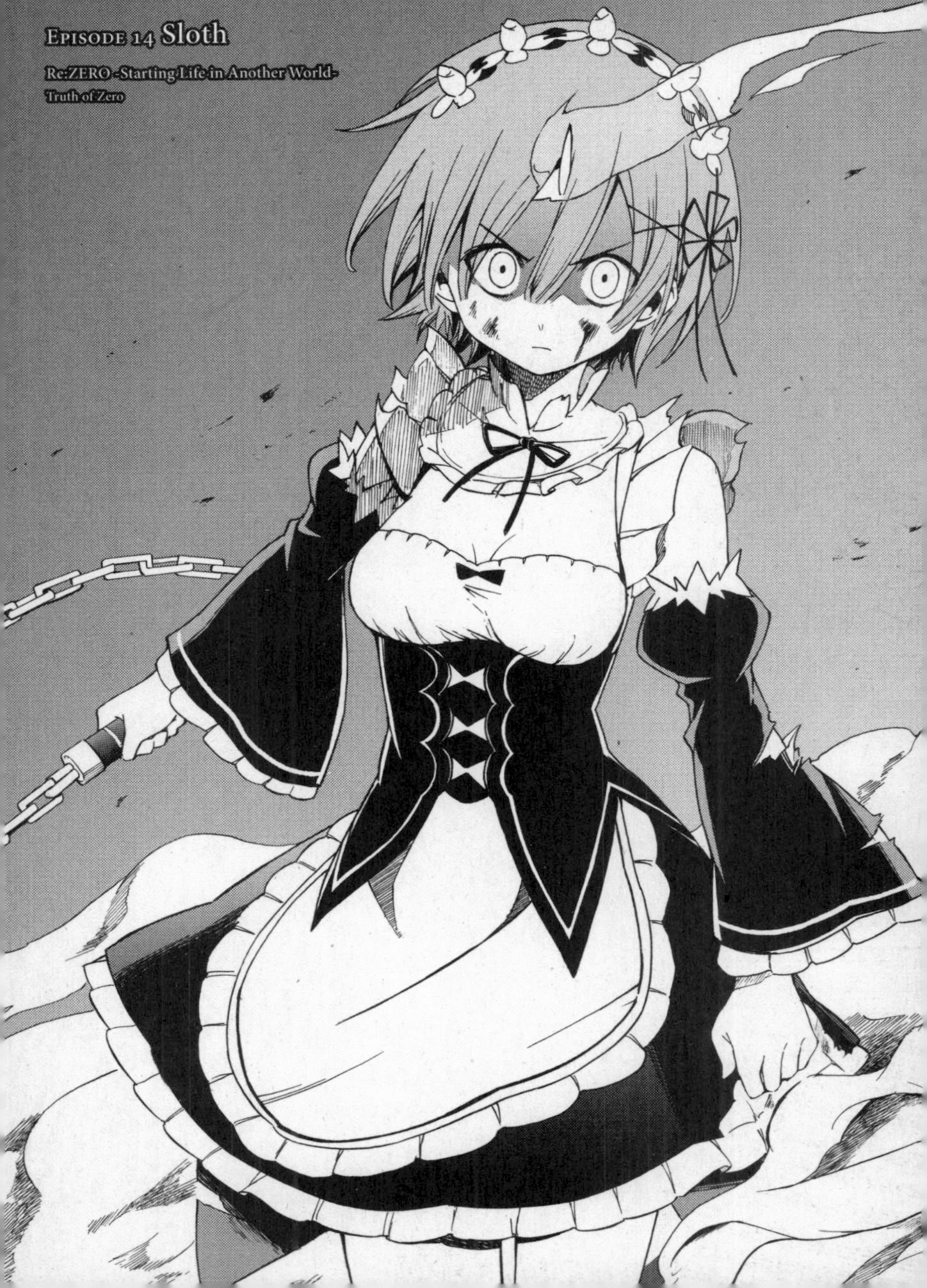

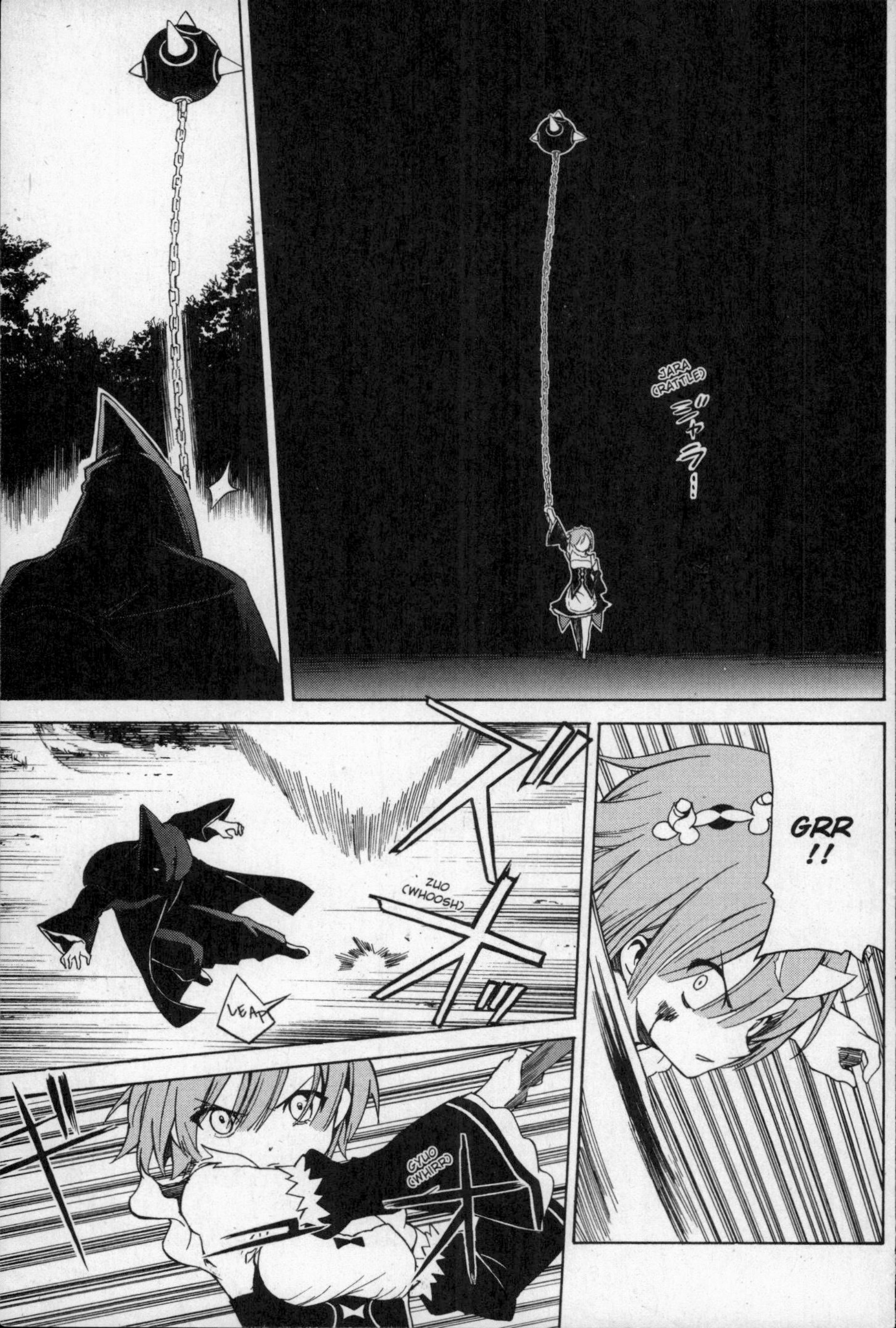
JARA (RATTLE)
ジャラ…
GRR !!
ZUO (WHOOSH)
LEAP
GYUO (WHIRR)

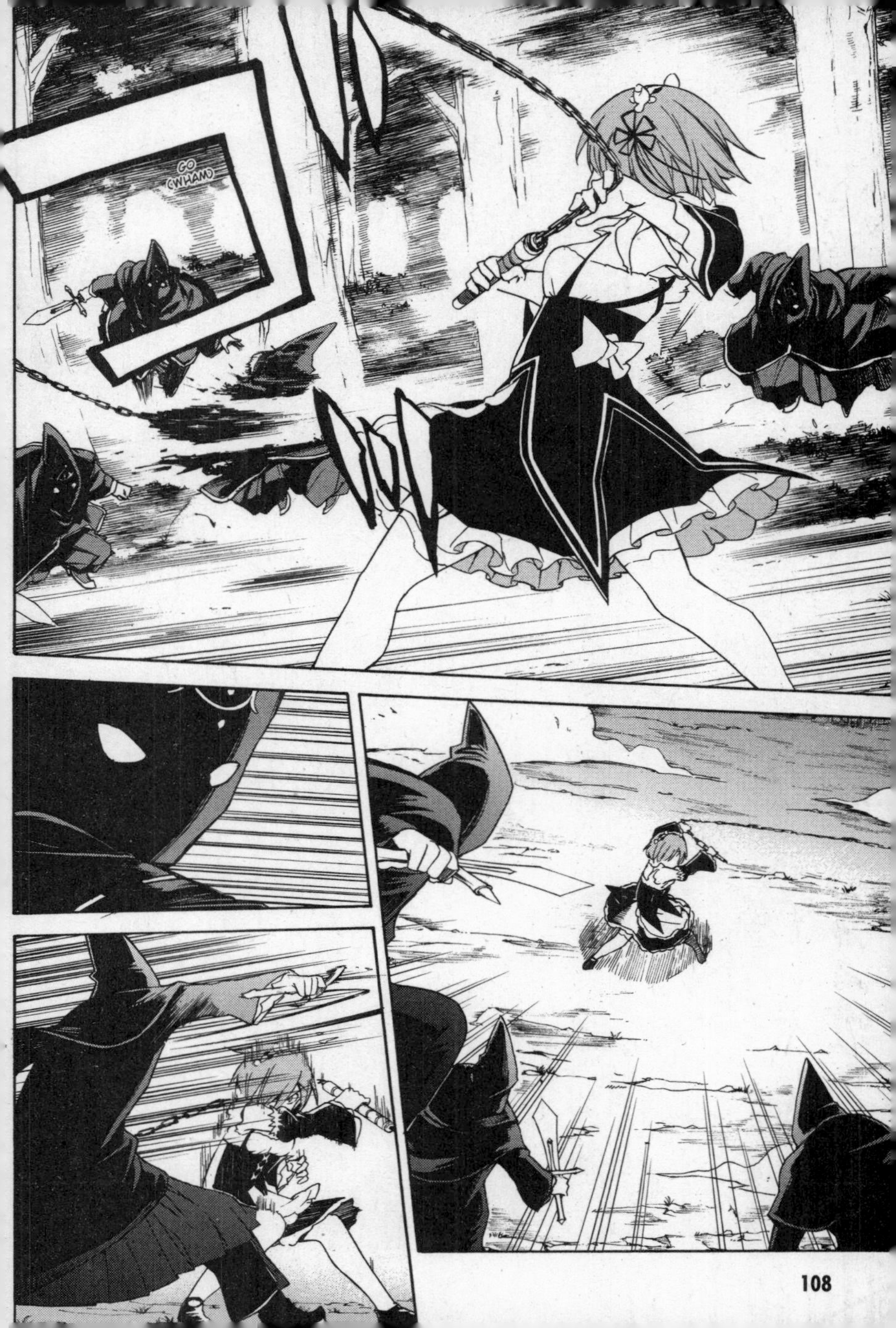
GO
(WHAM)

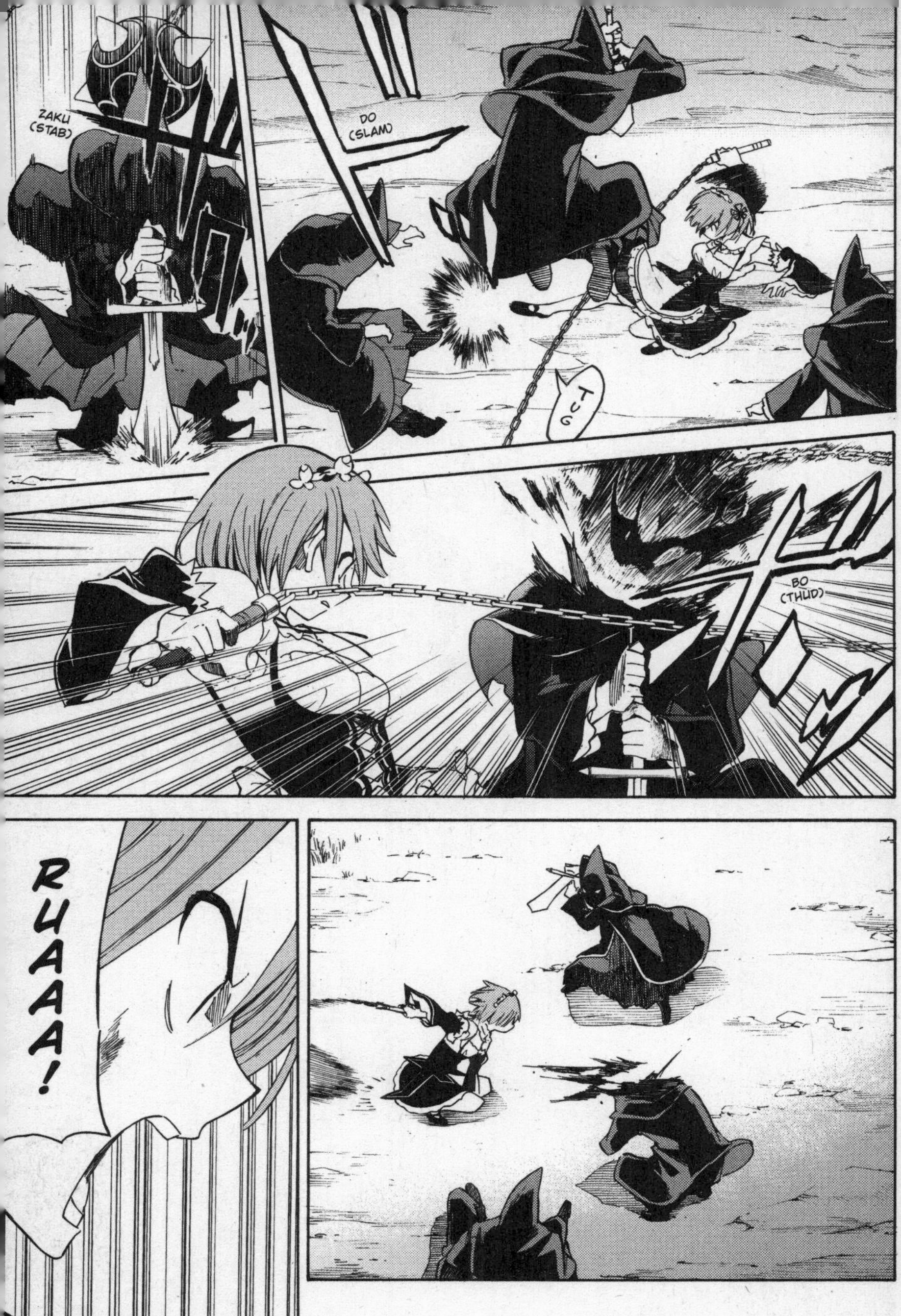
TUG
DO (SLAM)
ZAKU (STAB)
BO (THUD)
RUAAAA!

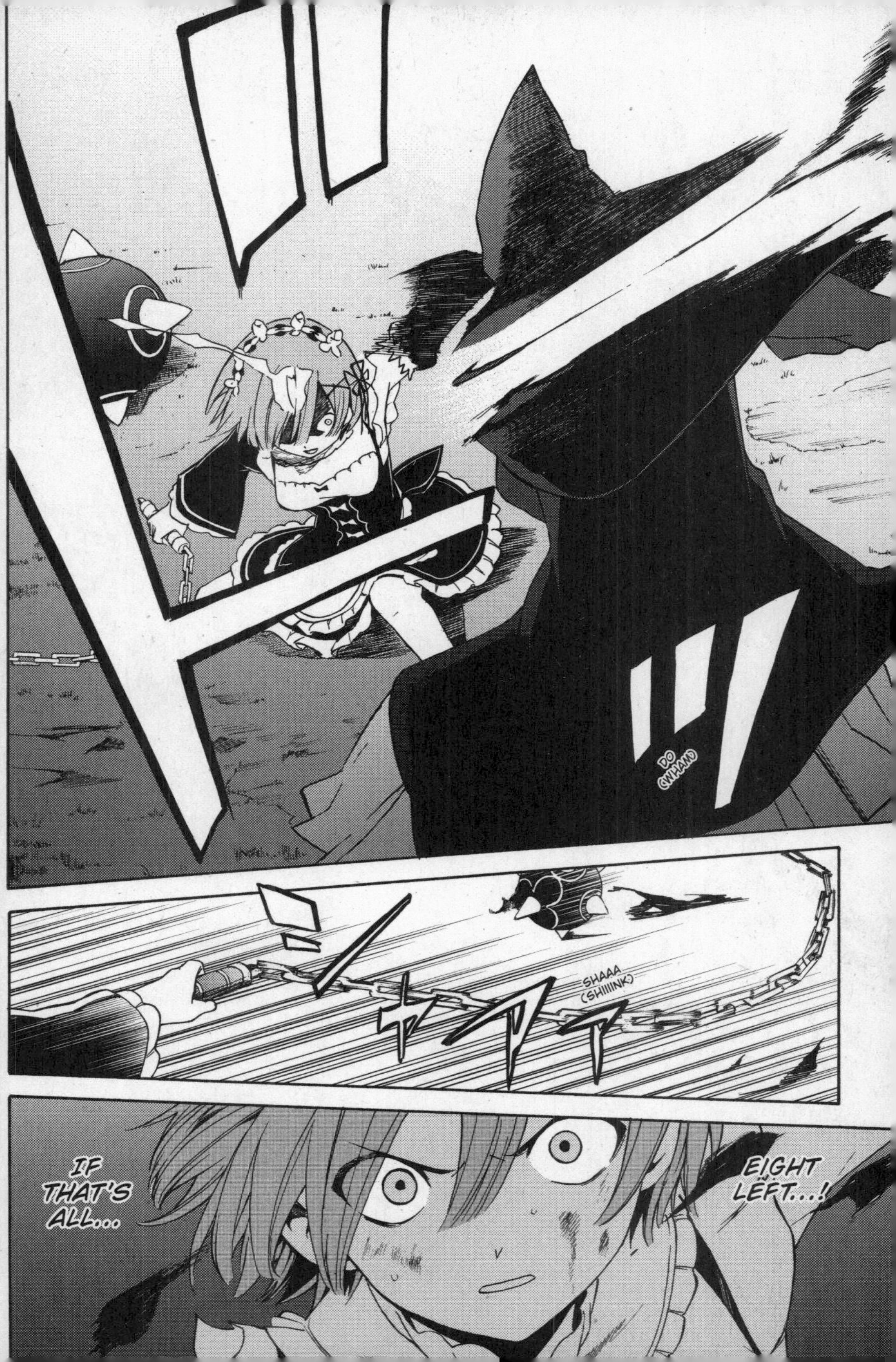
DO (WHAM)
SHAAA (SHIIIINK)
EIGHT LEFT...!
IF THAT'S ALL...

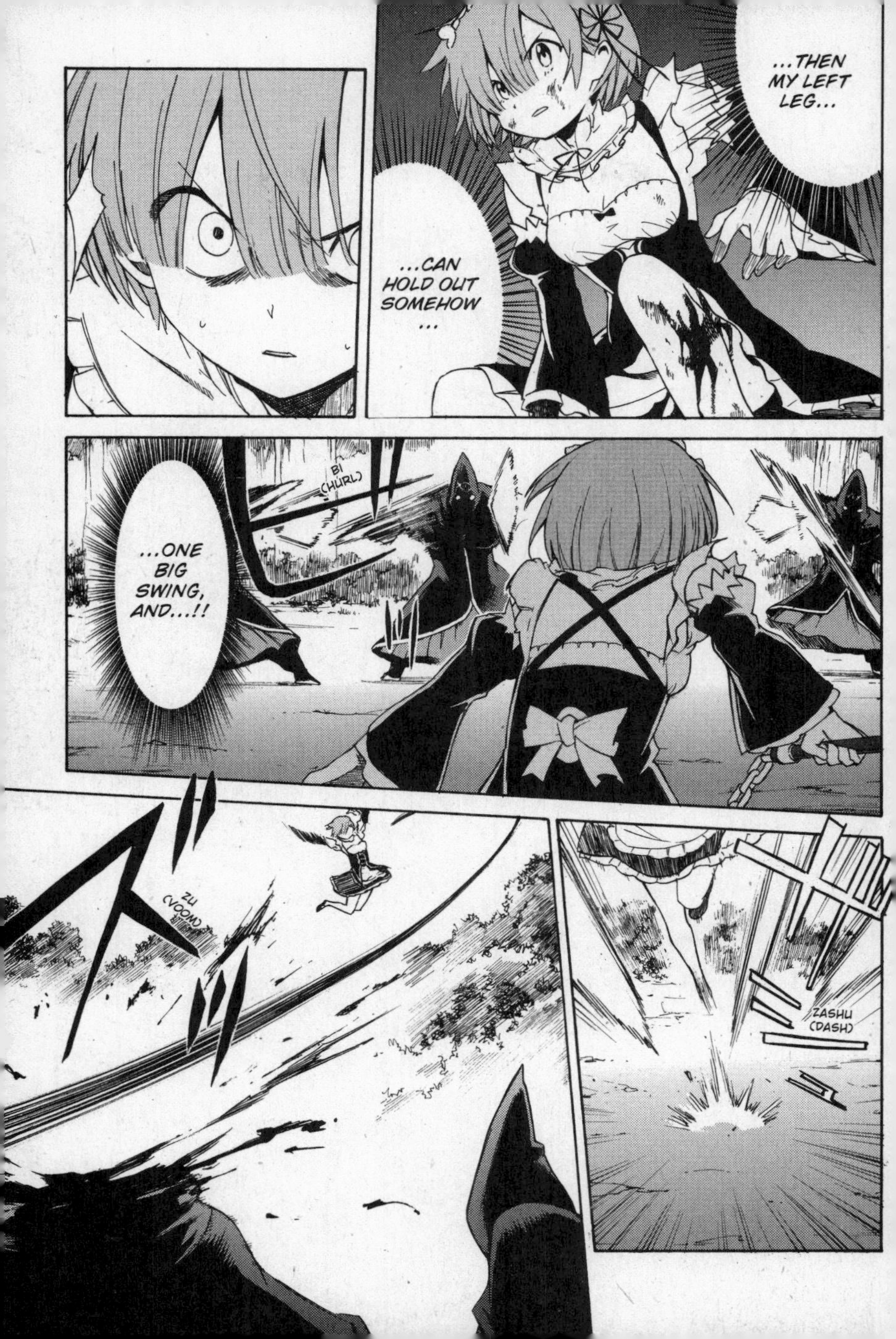
...THEN MY LEFT LEG...
...CAN HOLD OUT SOMEHOW ...
BI (HURL)
...ONE BIG SWING, AND...!!
ZASHU (DASH)
ZU (VOOM)

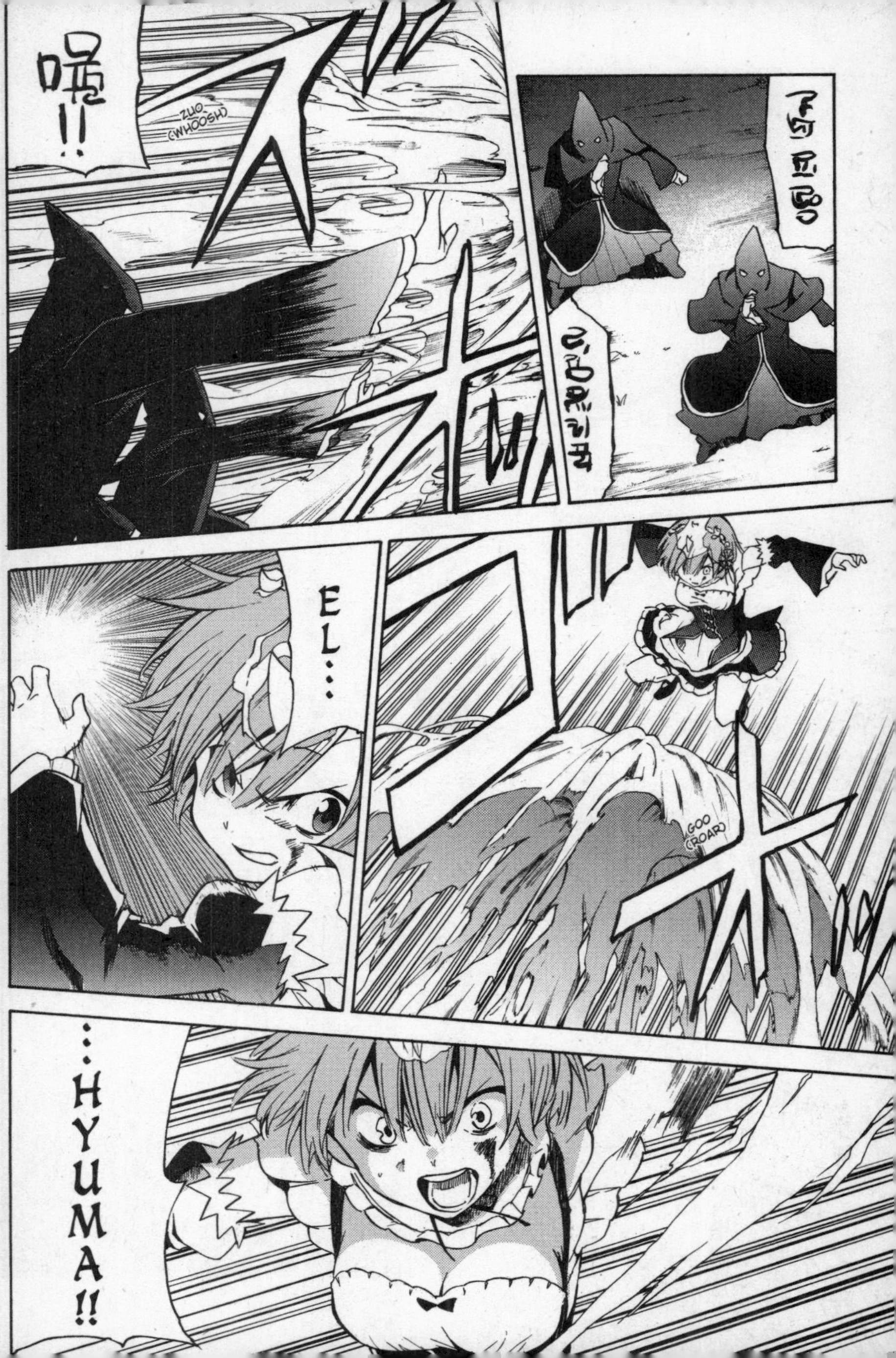
ZUO (WHOOSH)
GOO (ROAR)
EL...
...HYUMA!!

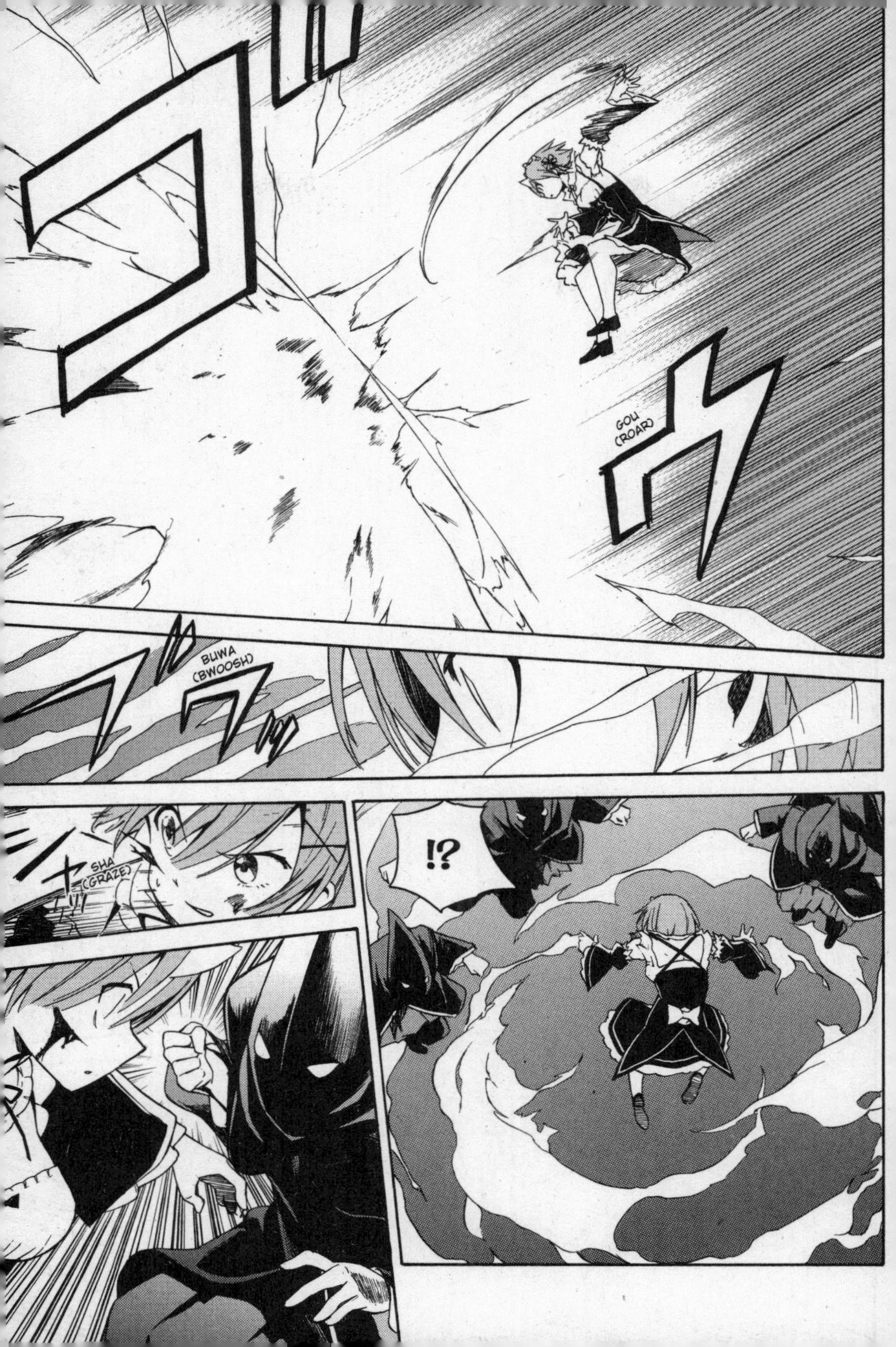
GOU (ROAR)
BUWA (BWOOSH)
!?
SHA (GRAZE)

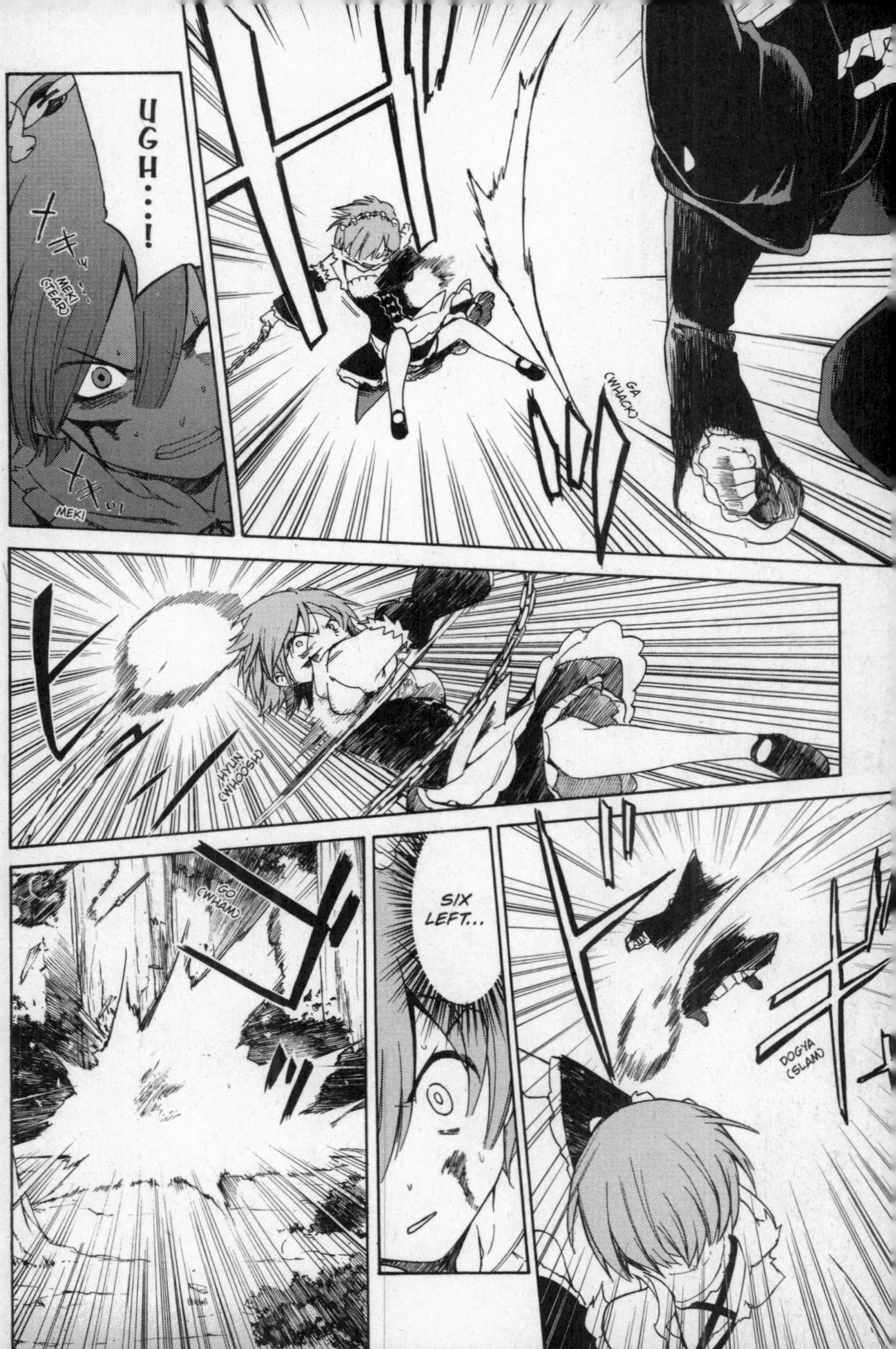
GA (WHACK)
UGH...!
MEKI (TEAR)
MEKI
HYUN (WHOOSH)
DOGYA (SLAM)
SIX LEFT...
GO (WHAM)

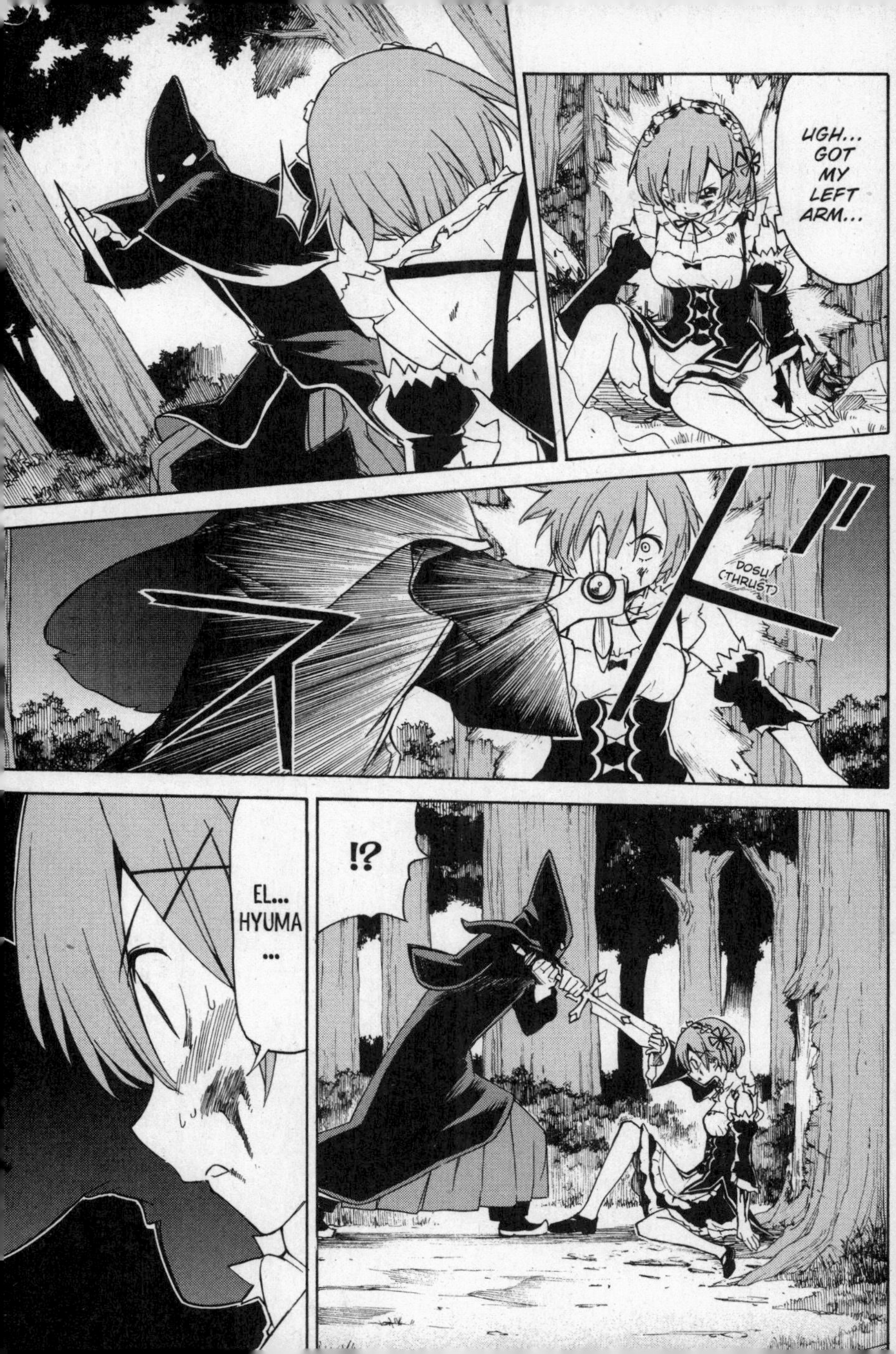
UGH... GOT MY LEFT ARM...
DOSU (THRUST)
!?
EL... HYUMA ...

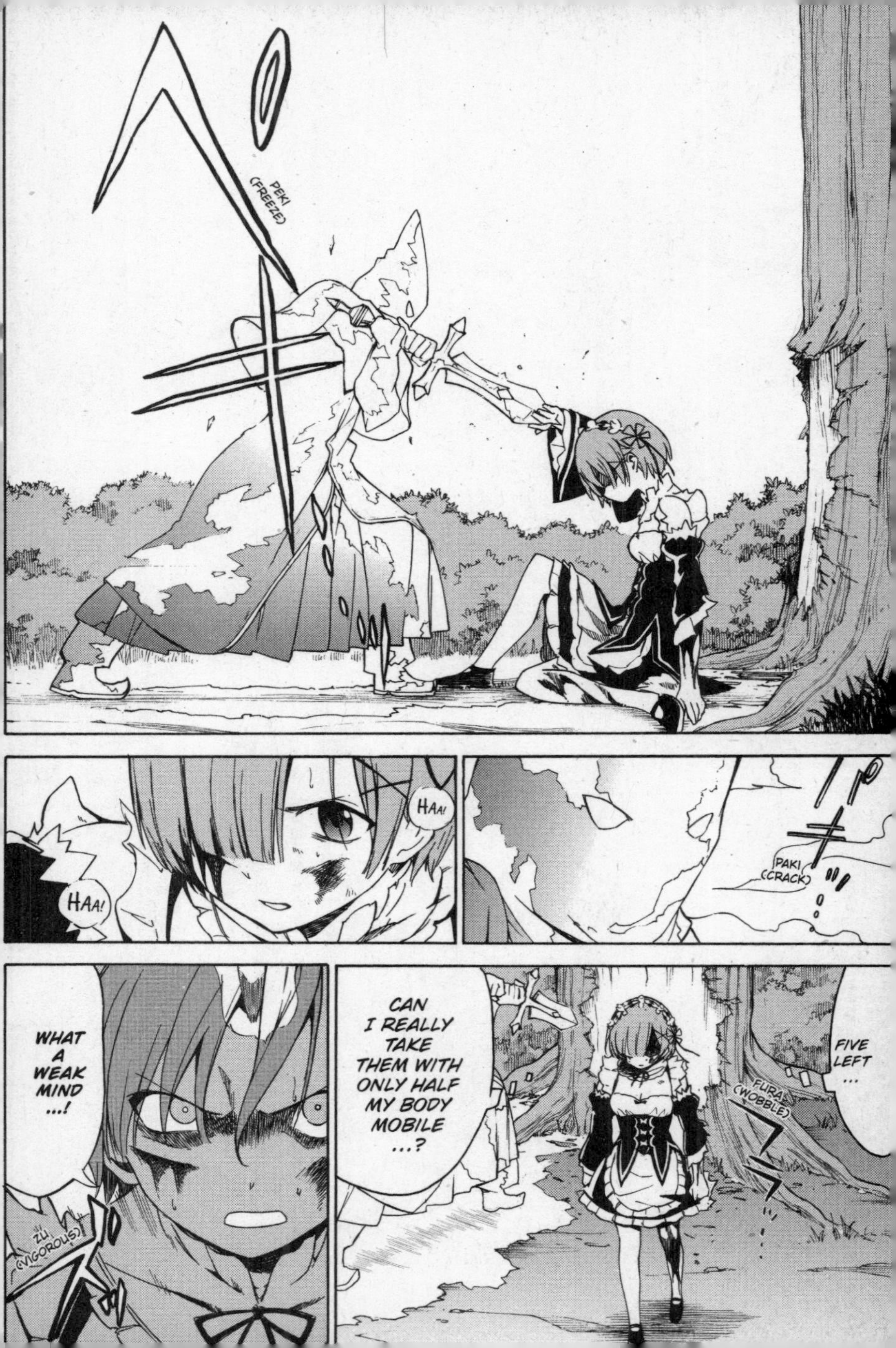
PEKI (FREEZE)
PAKI (CRACK)
HAA!
HAA!
FIVE LEFT...
FURA (WOBBLE)
CAN I REALLY TAKE THEM WITH ONLY HALF MY BODY MOBILE...?
WHAT A WEAK MIND...!
ZU (VIGOROUS)

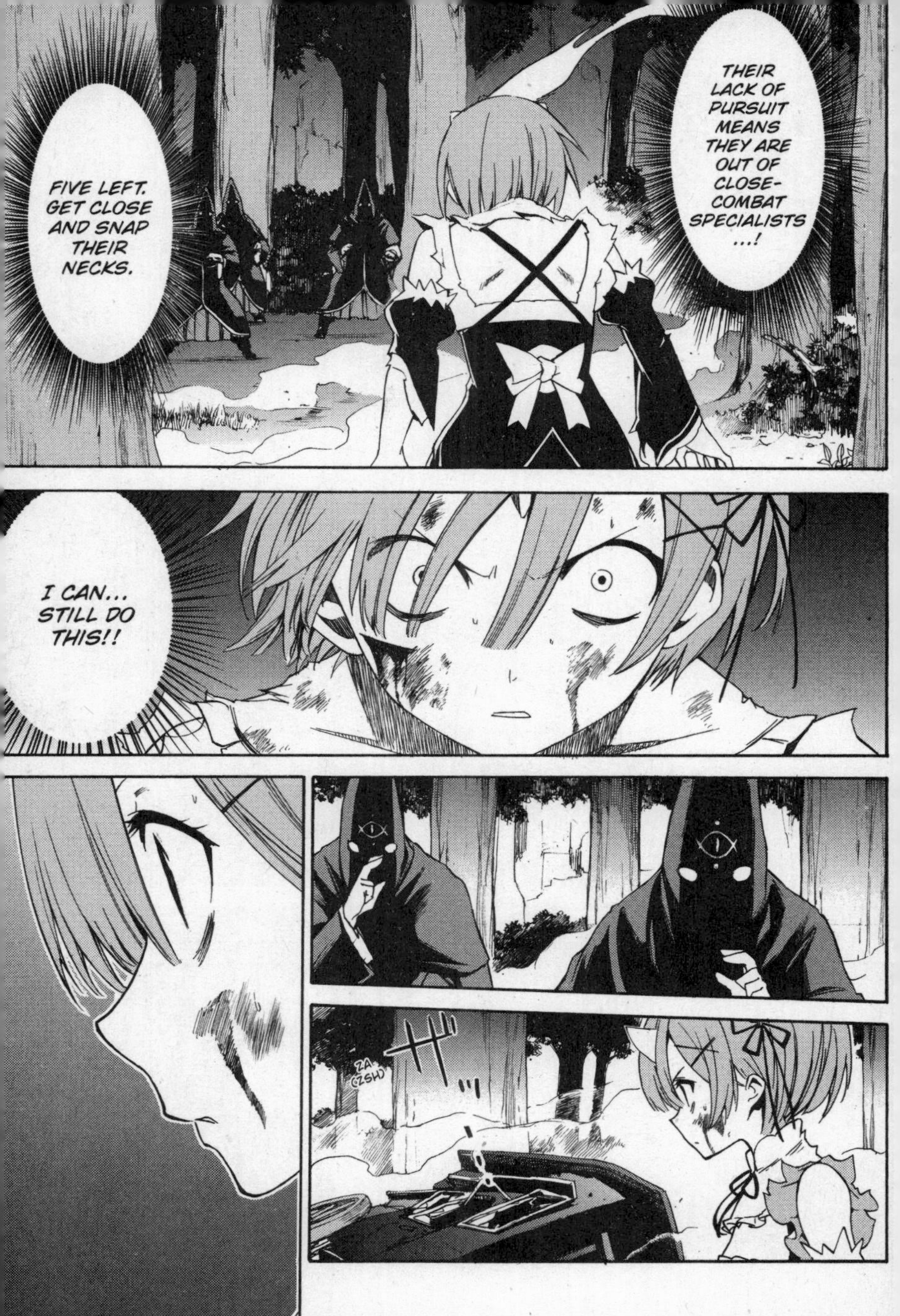
THEIR LACK OF PURSUIT MEANS THEY ARE OUT OF CLOSE-COMBAT SPECIALISTS ...!
FIVE LEFT. GET CLOSE AND SNAP THEIR NECKS.
I CAN... STILL DO THIS!!
ZA (ZSH)

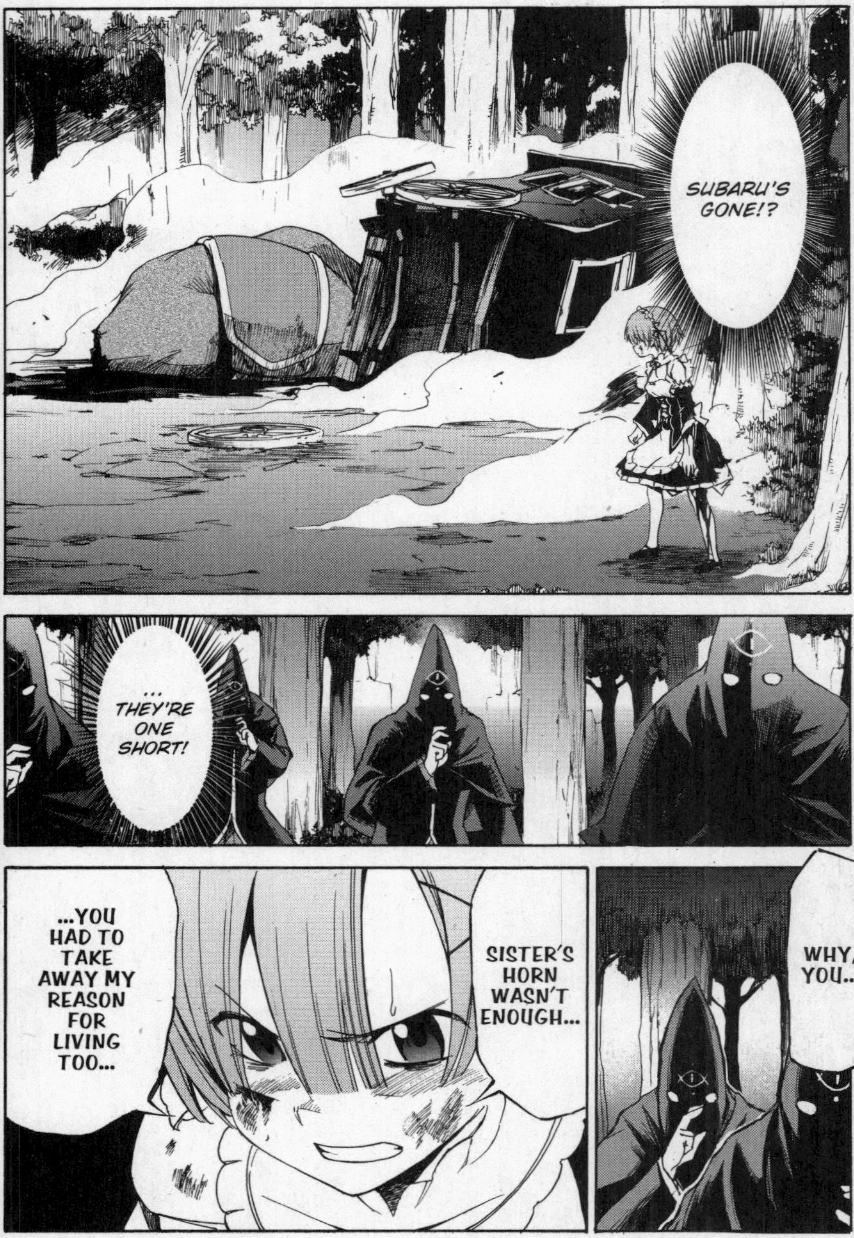
SUBARU'S GONE!?
... THEY'RE ONE SHORT!
WHY, YOU...
SISTER'S HORN WASN'T ENOUGH...
...YOU HAD TO TAKE AWAY MY REASON FOR LIVING TOO...

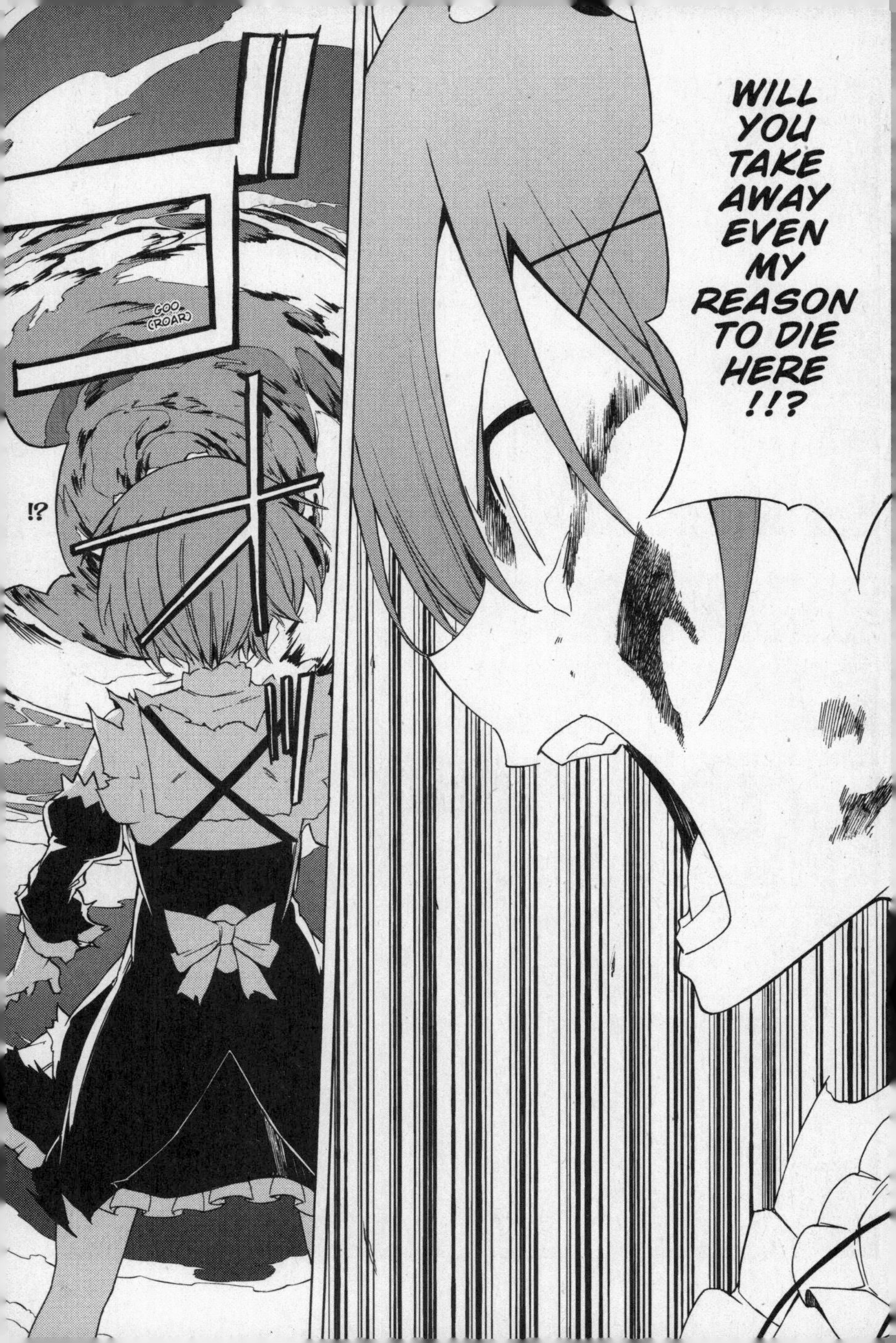
WILL YOU TAKE AWAY EVEN MY REASON TO DIE HERE!!?
GOO (ROAR)
!?

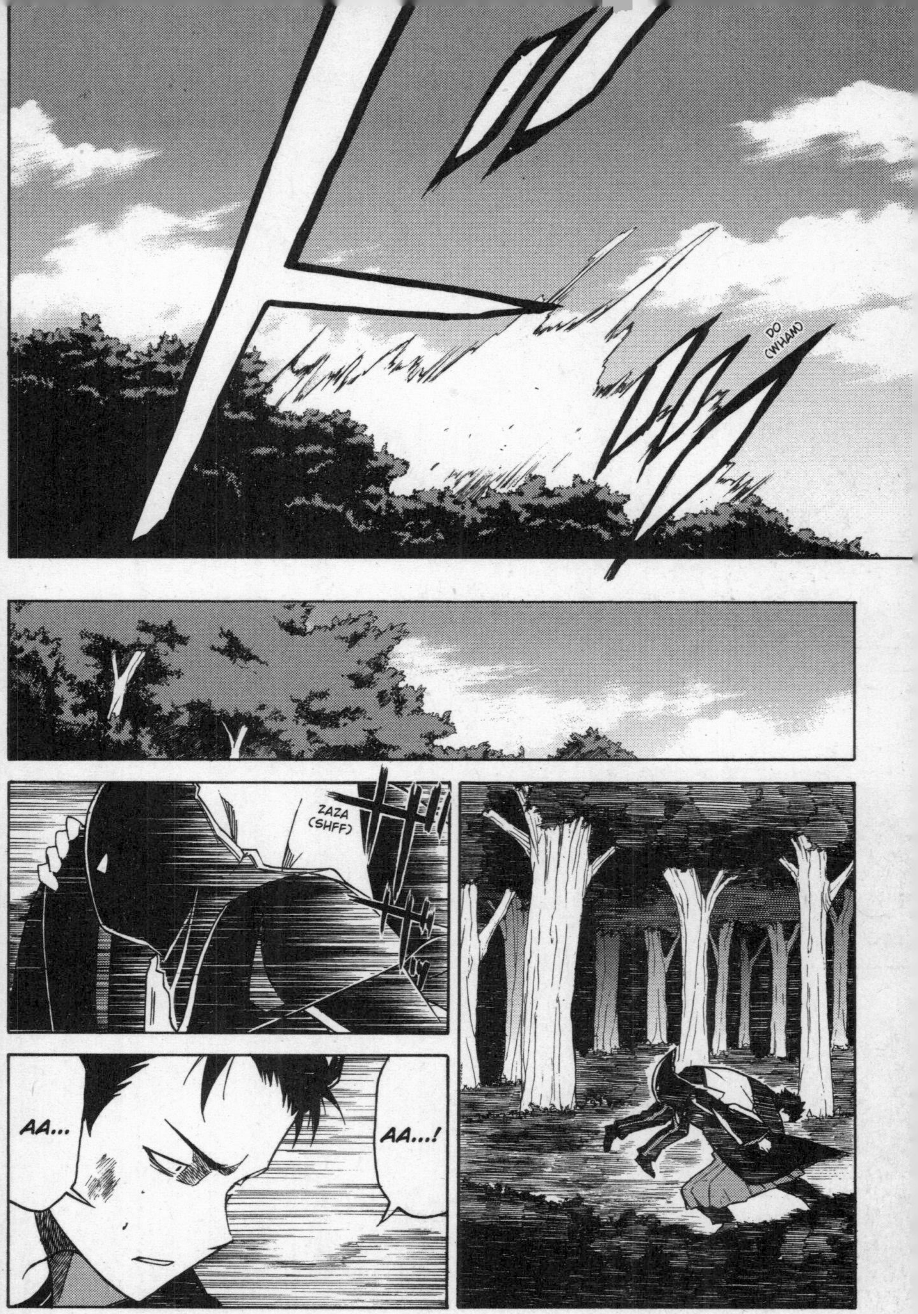
DO (WHAM)
ZAZA (SHFF)
AA...!
AA...

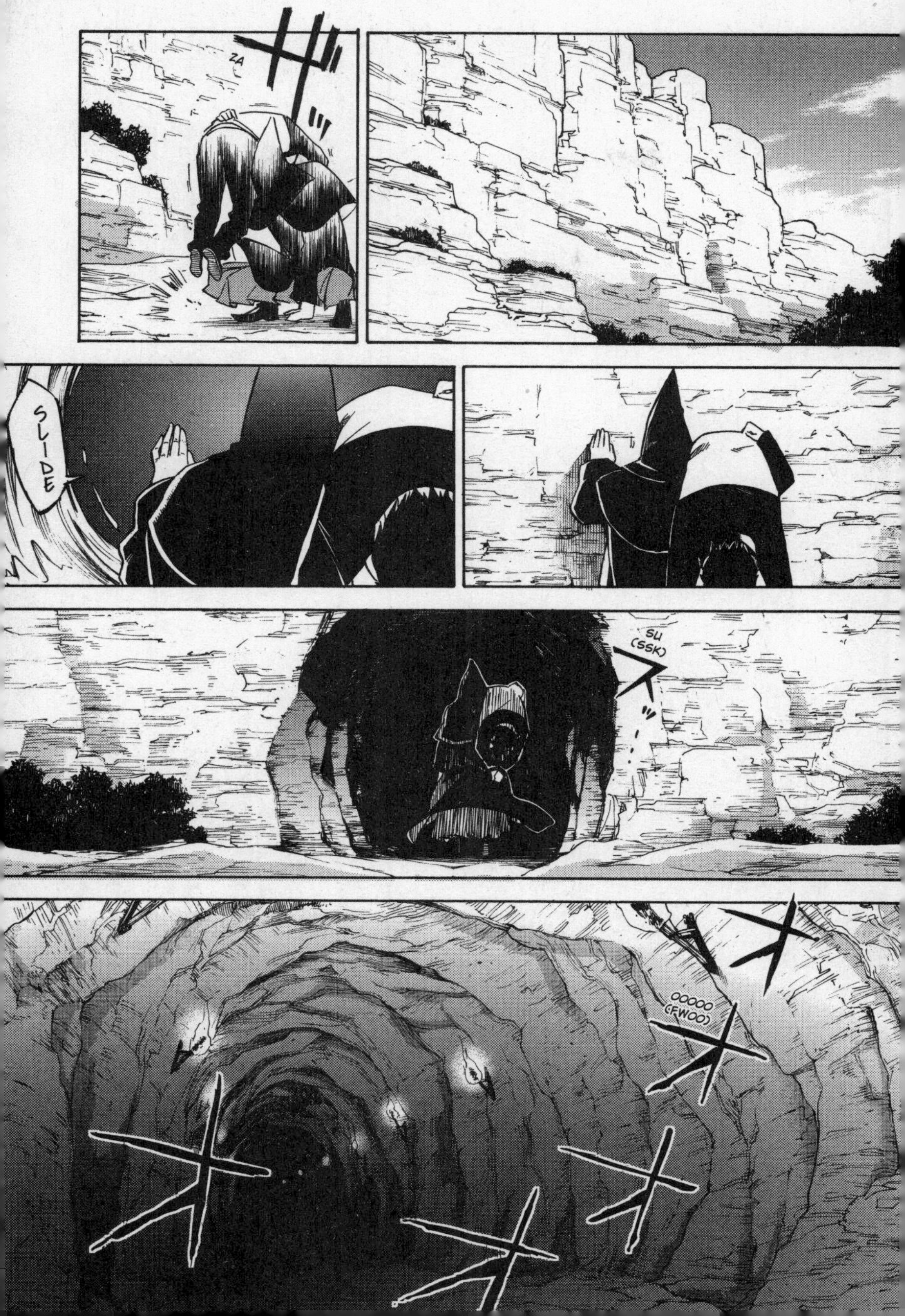
ZA
SLIDE
SU (SSK)
OOOOO (FWOO)

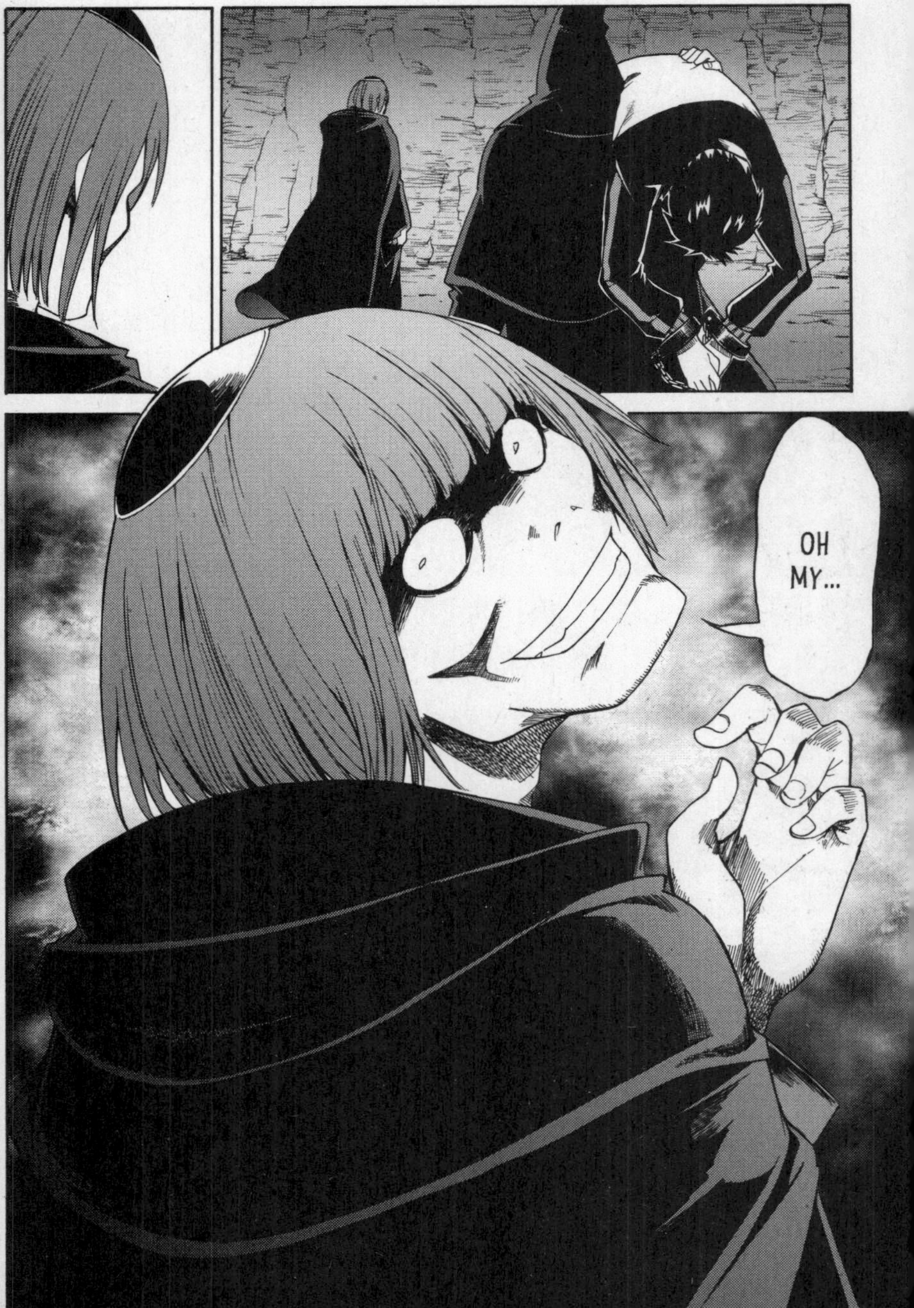
OH MY...

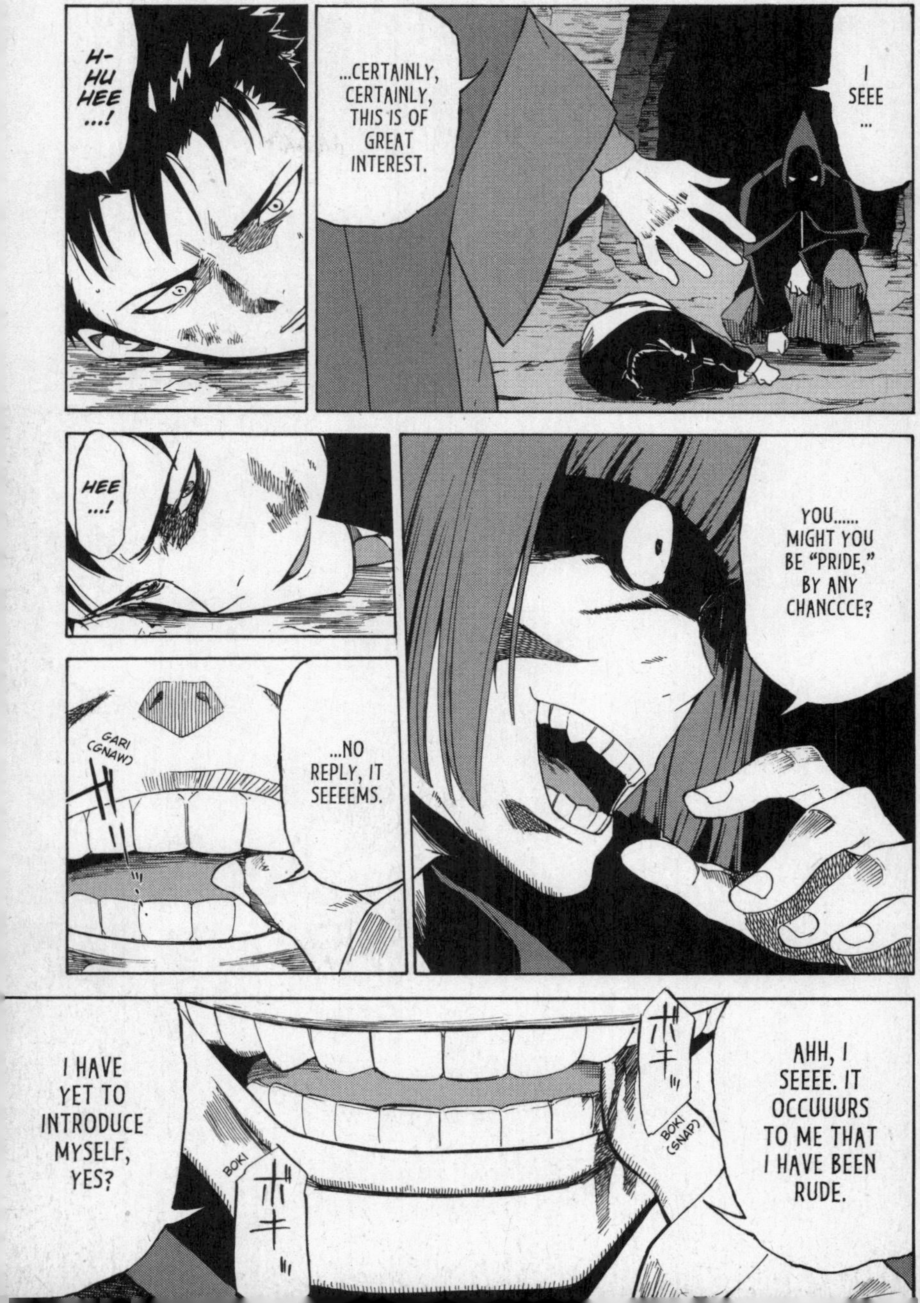
I SEEE ...
...CERTAINLY, CERTAINLY, THIS IS OF GREAT INTEREST.
H-HU HEE ...!
YOU...... MIGHT YOU BE "PRIDE," BY ANY CHANCCCE?
HEE ...!
GARI (GNAW)
...NO REPLY, IT SEEEEMS.
AHH, I SEEEE. IT OCCUUURS TO ME THAT I HAVE BEEN RUDE.
ボキ
BOKI (SNAP)
ボキ
BOKI
I HAVE YET TO INTRODUCE MYSELF, YES?

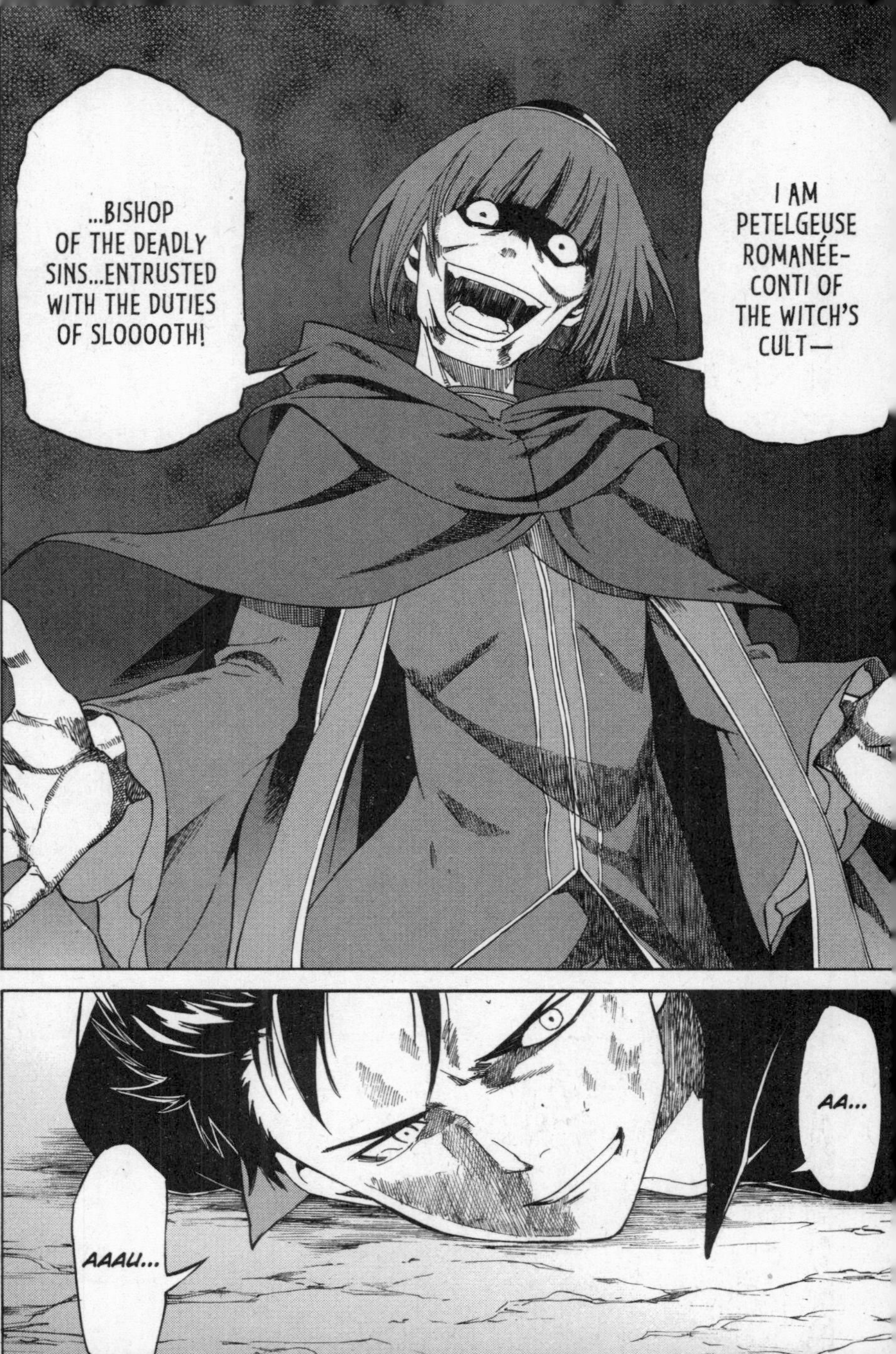
I AM PETELGEUSE ROMANÉE-CONTI OF THE WITCH'S CULT—
...BISHOP OF THE DEADLY SINS...ENTRUSTED WITH THE DUTIES OF SLOOOOTH!
AA...
AAAU...

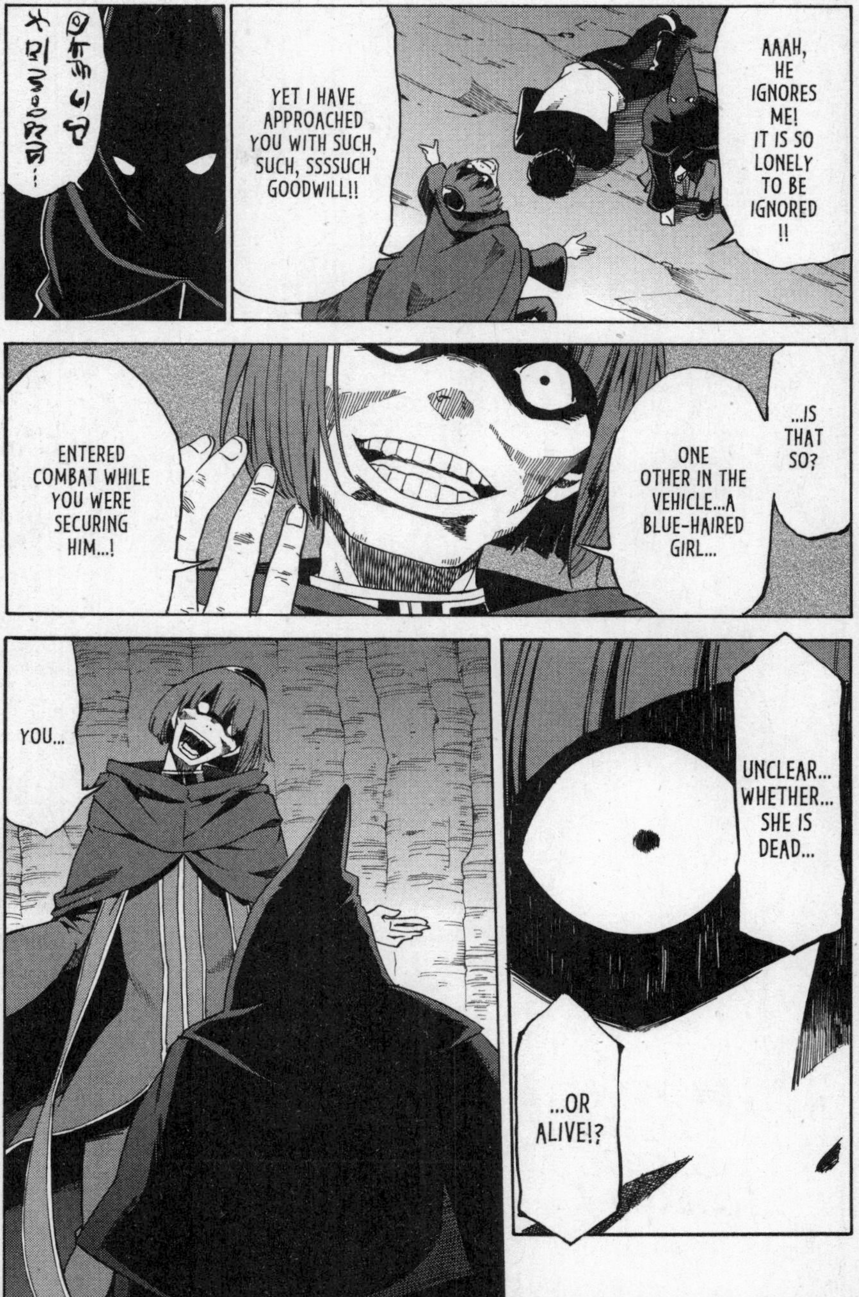
AAAH, HE IGNORES ME! IT IS SO LONELY TO BE IGNORED!!
YET I HAVE APPROACHED YOU WITH SUCH, SUCH, SSSSUCH GOODWILL!!
...IS THAT SO?
ONE OTHER IN THE VEHICLE...A BLUE-HAIRED GIRL...
ENTERED COMBAT WHILE YOU WERE SECURING HIM...!
UNCLEAR... WHETHER... SHE IS DEAD...
...OR ALIVE!?
YOU...

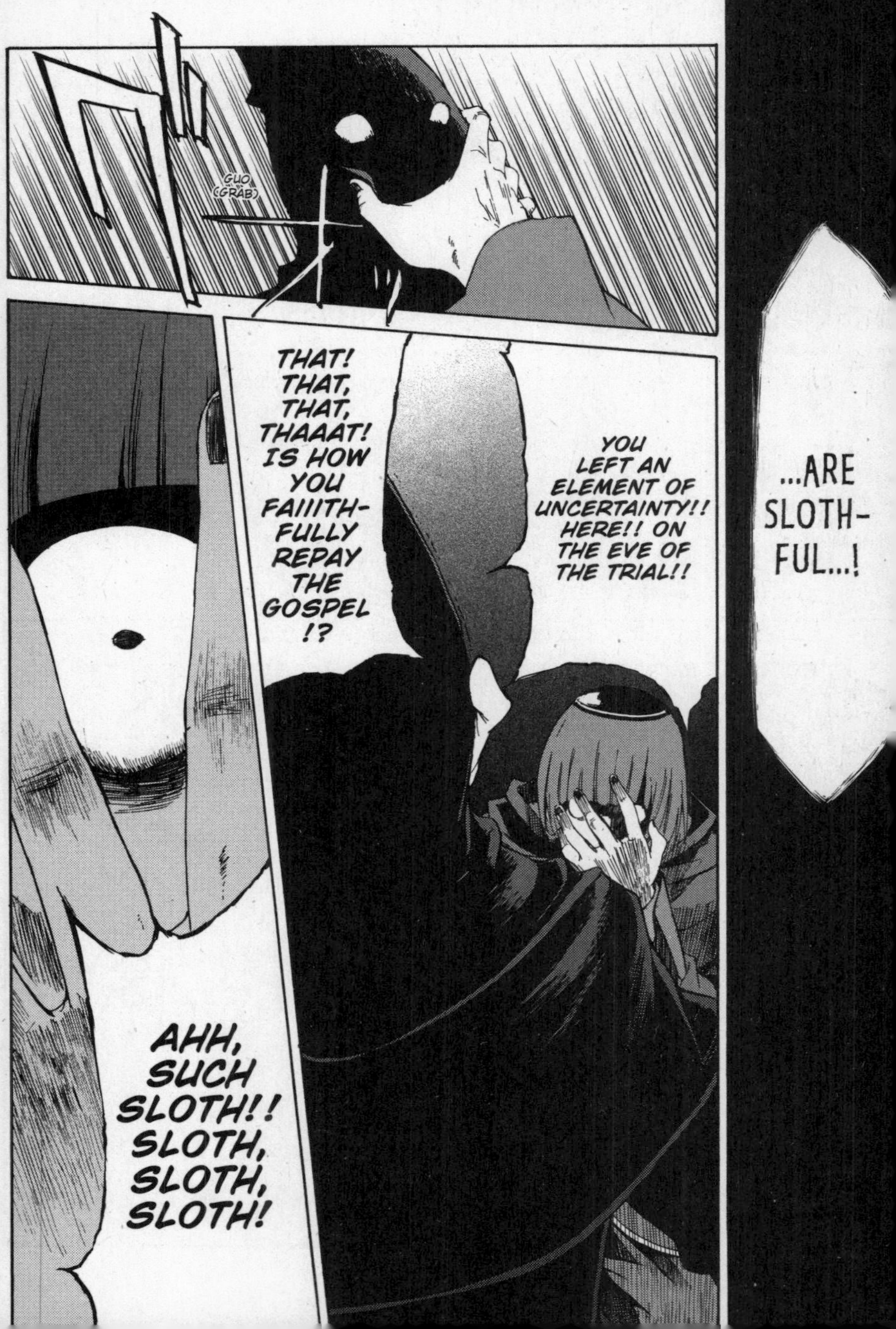
GUO (GRAB)
YOU LEFT AN ELEMENT OF UNCERTAINTY!! HERE!! ON THE EVE OF THE TRIAL!!
THAT! THAT, THAT, THAAAT! IS HOW YOU FAIIIITH-FULLY REPAY THE GOSPEL!?
AHH, SUCH SLOTH!! SLOTH, SLOTH, SLOTH!
...ARE SLOTH-FUL...!

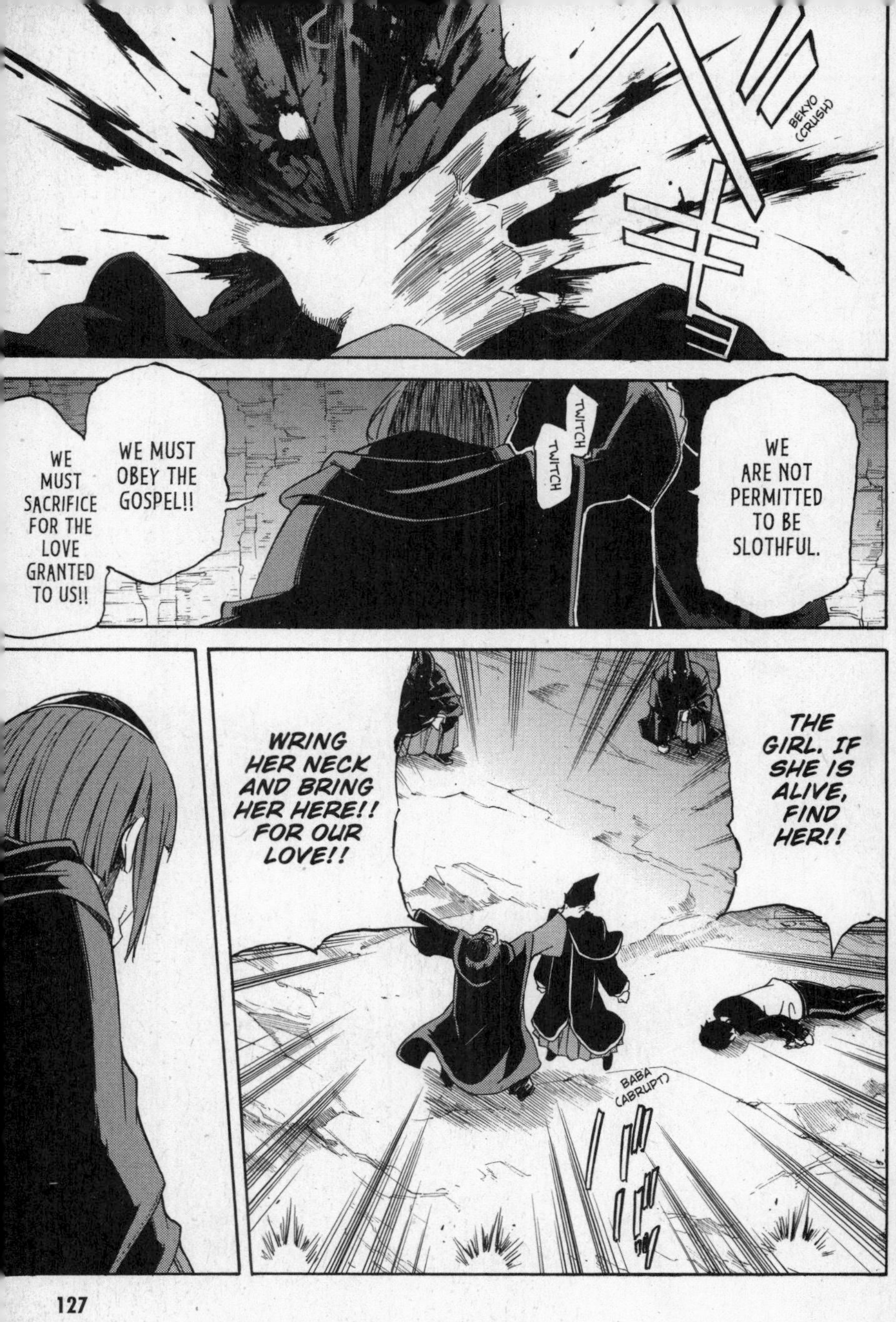
BEKYO (CRUSH)
WE ARE NOT PERMITTED TO BE SLOTHFUL.
TWITCH
TWITCH
WE MUST OBEY THE GOSPEL!!
WE MUST SACRIFICE FOR THE LOVE GRANTED TO US!!
THE GIRL. IF SHE IS ALIVE, FIND HER!!
WRING HER NECK AND BRING HER HERE!! FOR OUR LOVE!!
BABA (ABRUPT)

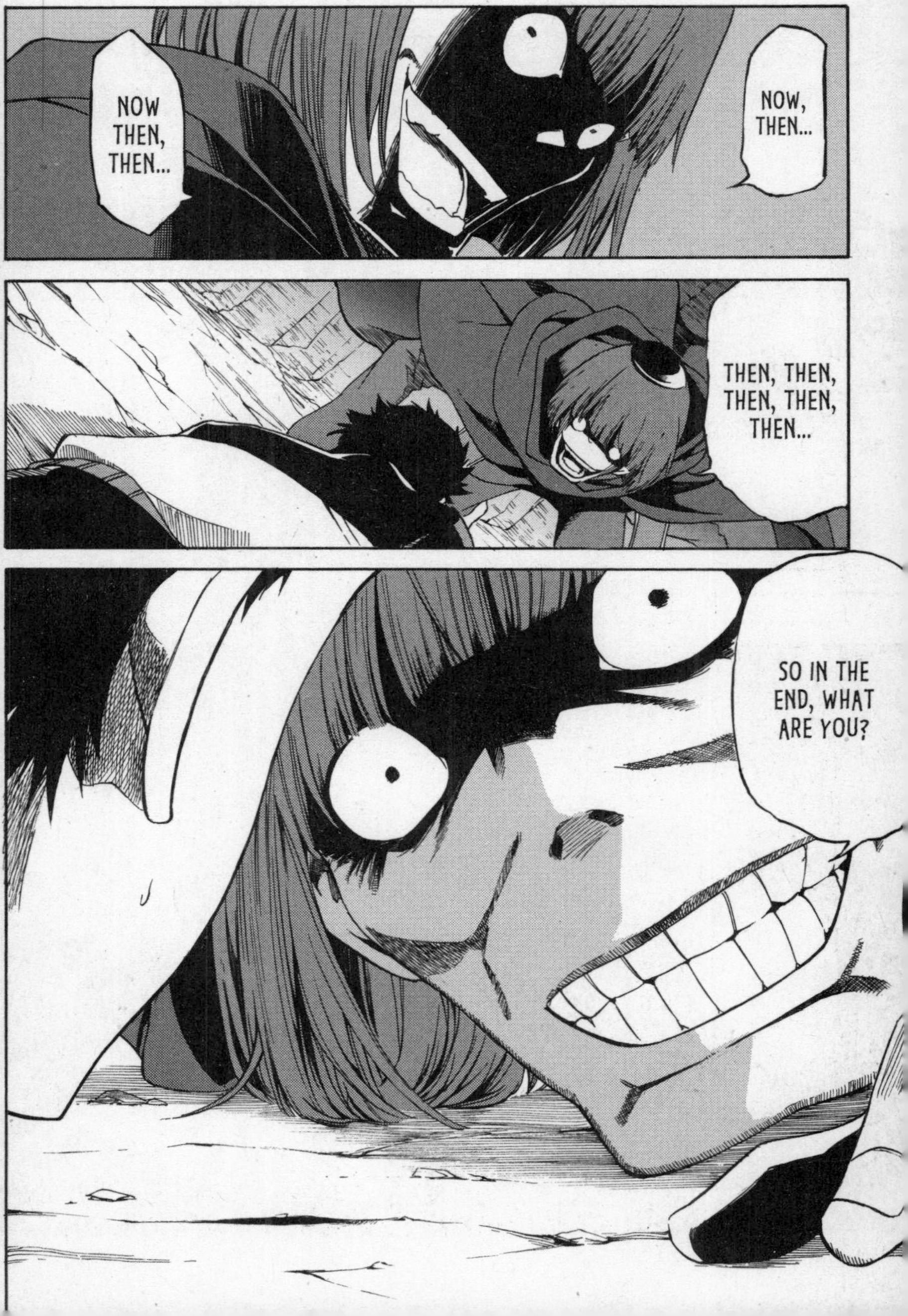
NOW, THEN...
NOW THEN, THEN...
THEN, THEN, THEN, THEN, THEN...
SO IN THE END, WHAT ARE YOU?

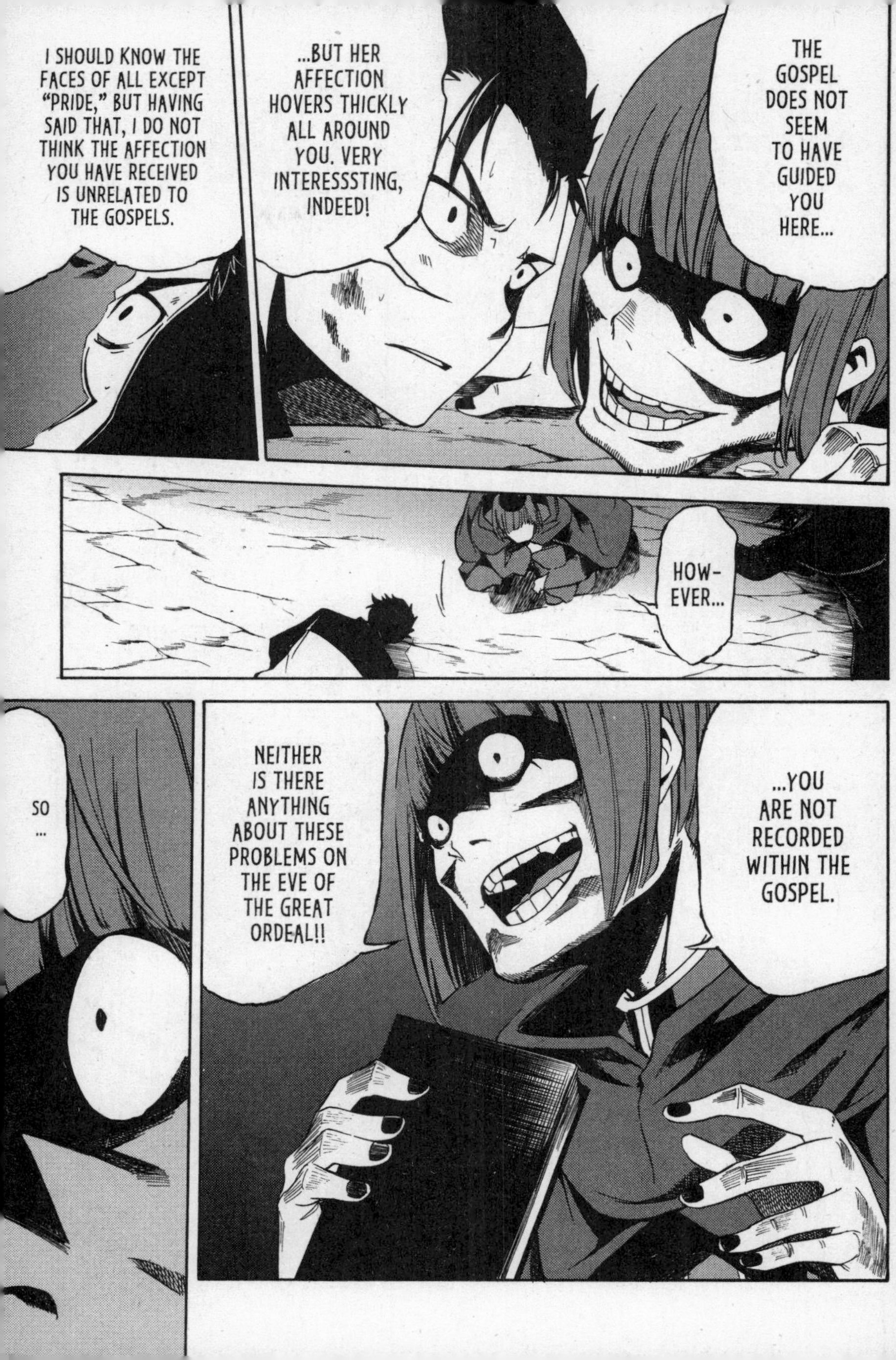
THE GOSPEL DOES NOT SEEM TO HAVE GUIDED YOU HERE...
...BUT HER AFFECTION HOVERS THICKLY ALL AROUND YOU. VERY INTERESSSTING, INDEED!
I SHOULD KNOW THE FACES OF ALL EXCEPT "PRIDE," BUT HAVING SAID THAT, I DO NOT THINK THE AFFECTION YOU HAVE RECEIVED IS UNRELATED TO THE GOSPELS.
HOW-EVER...
...YOU ARE NOT RECORDED WITHIN THE GOSPEL.
NEITHER IS THERE ANYTHING ABOUT THESE PROBLEMS ON THE EVE OF THE GREAT ORDEAL!!
SO ...

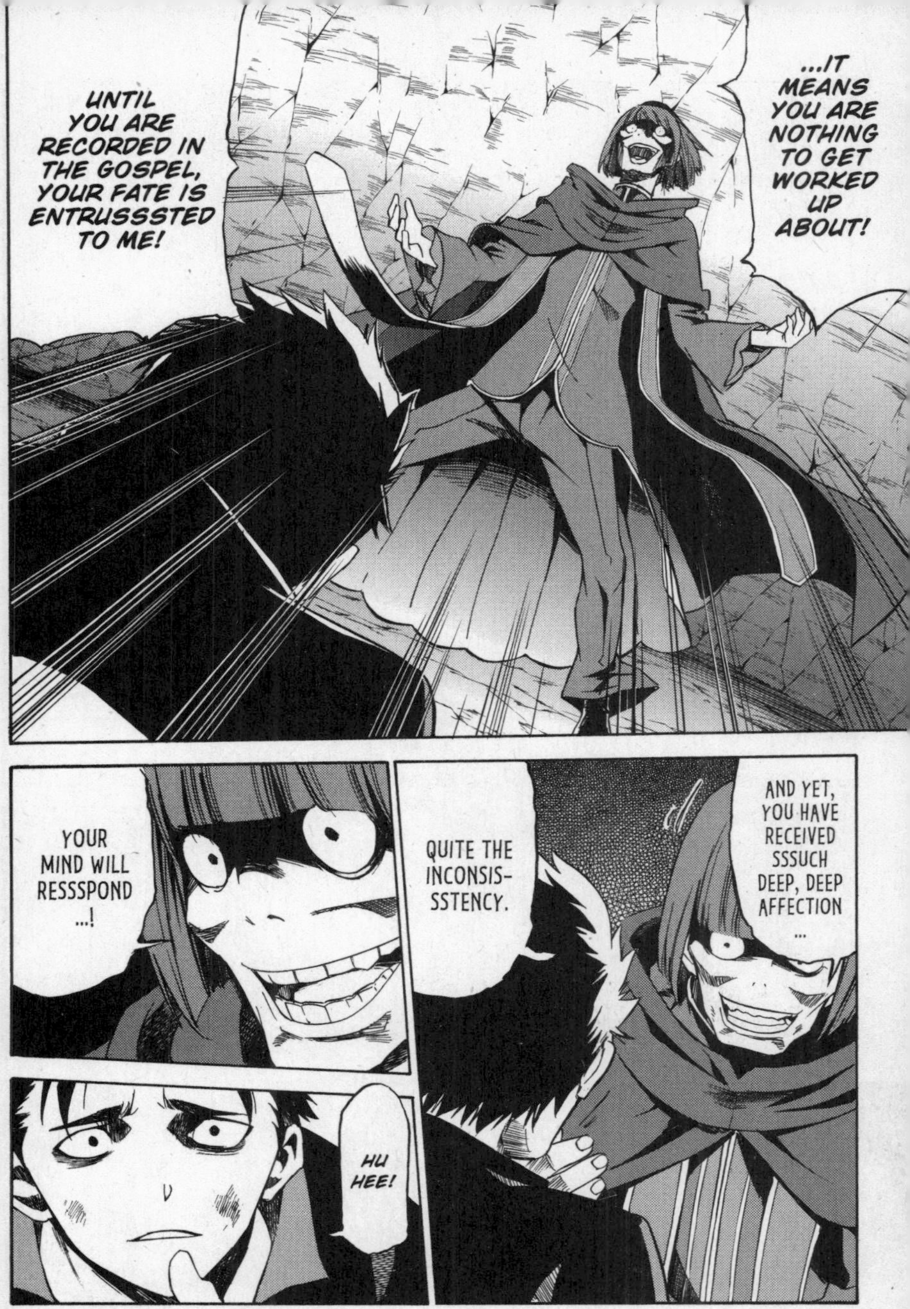
...IT MEANS YOU ARE NOTHING TO GET WORKED UP ABOUT!
UNTIL YOU ARE RECORDED IN THE GOSPEL, YOUR FATE IS ENTRUSSSTED TO ME!
AND YET, YOU HAVE RECEIVED SSSUCH DEEP, DEEP AFFECTION ...
QUITE THE INCONSIS-SSTENCY.
YOUR MIND WILL RESSSPOND ...!
HU HEE!

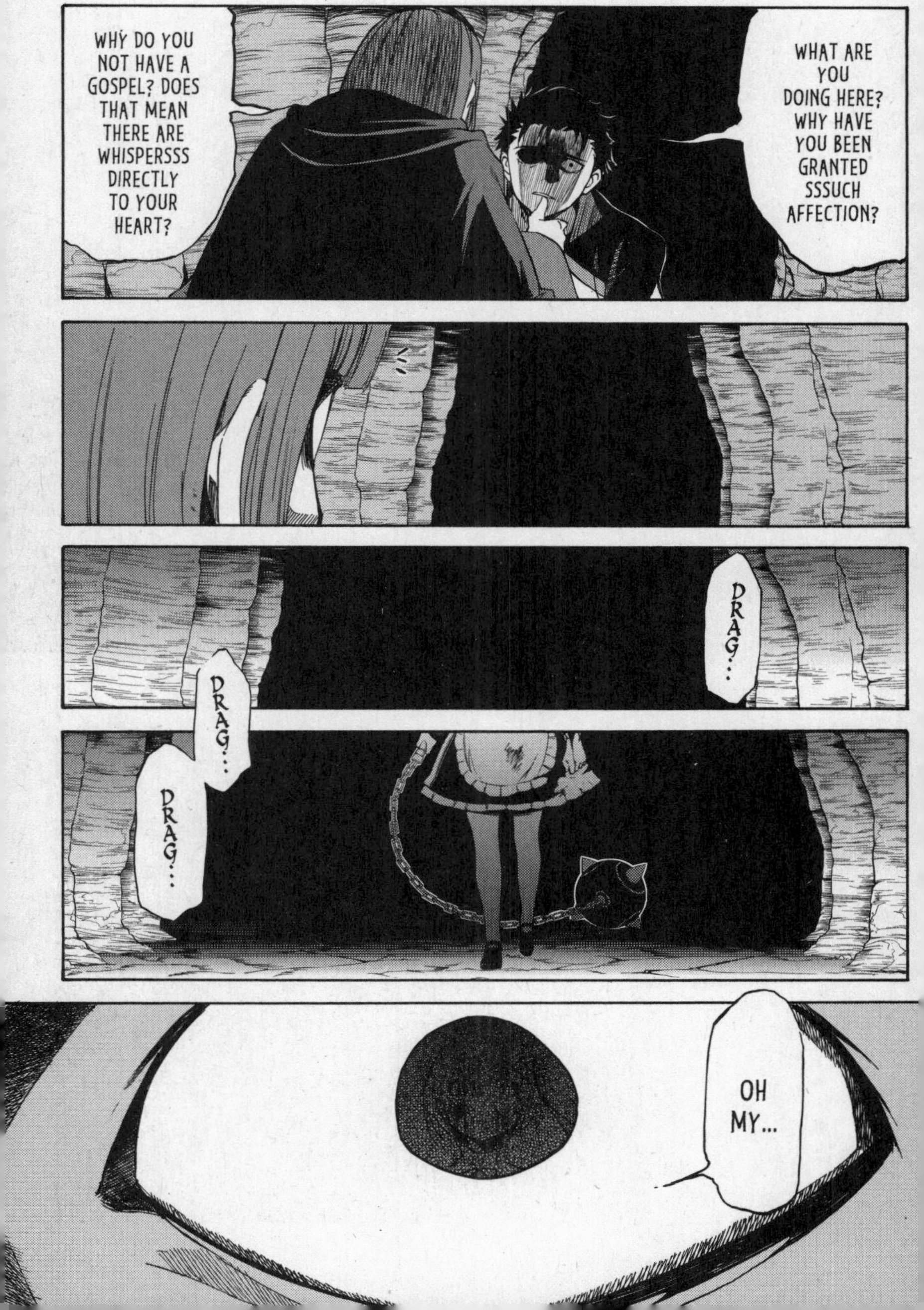
WHAT ARE YOU DOING HERE? WHY HAVE YOU BEEN GRANTED SSSUCH AFFECTION?
WHY DO YOU NOT HAVE A GOSPEL? DOES THAT MEAN THERE ARE WHISPERSSS DIRECTLY TO YOUR HEART?
DRAG...
DRAG...
DRAG...
OH MY...

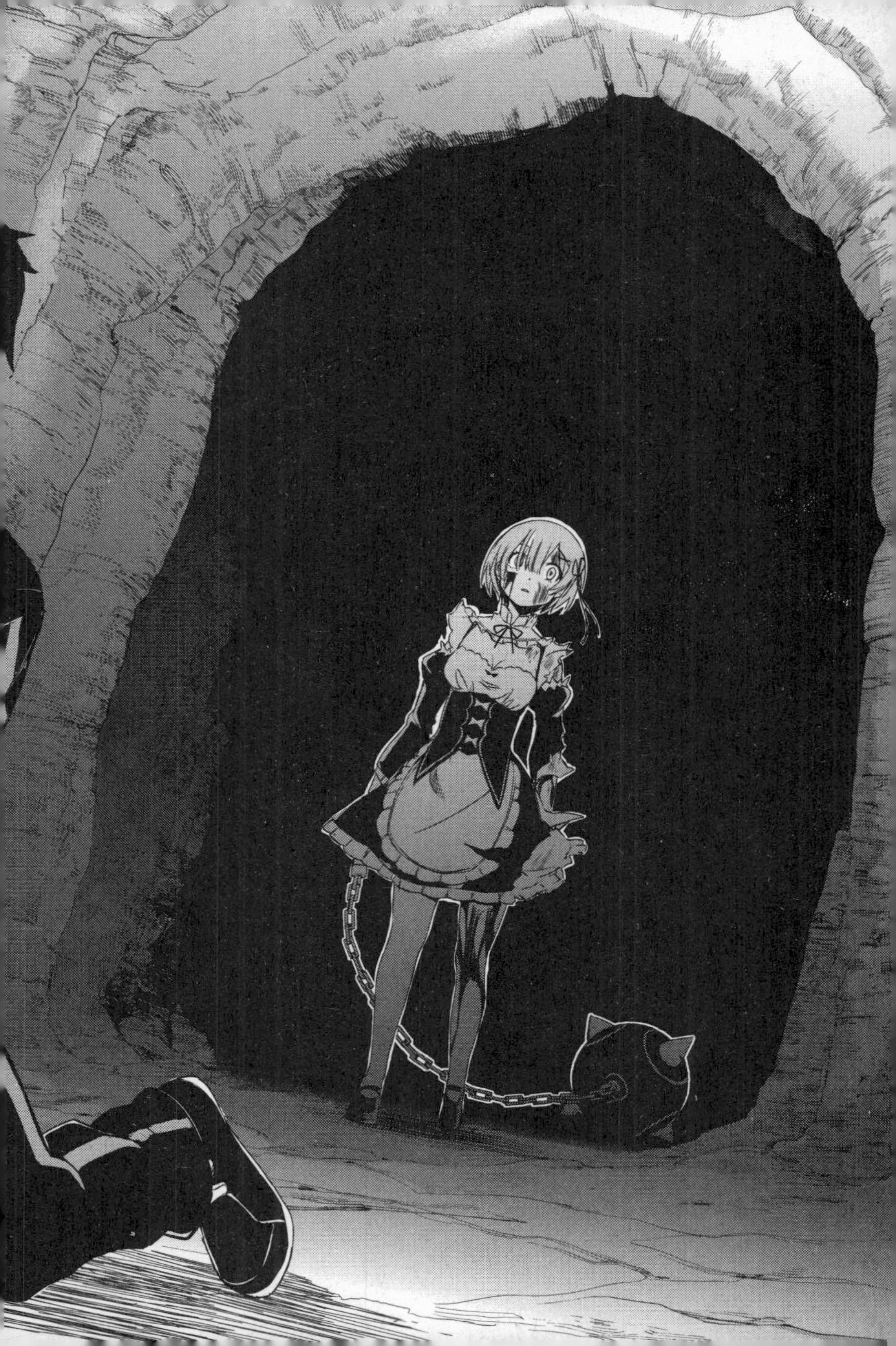

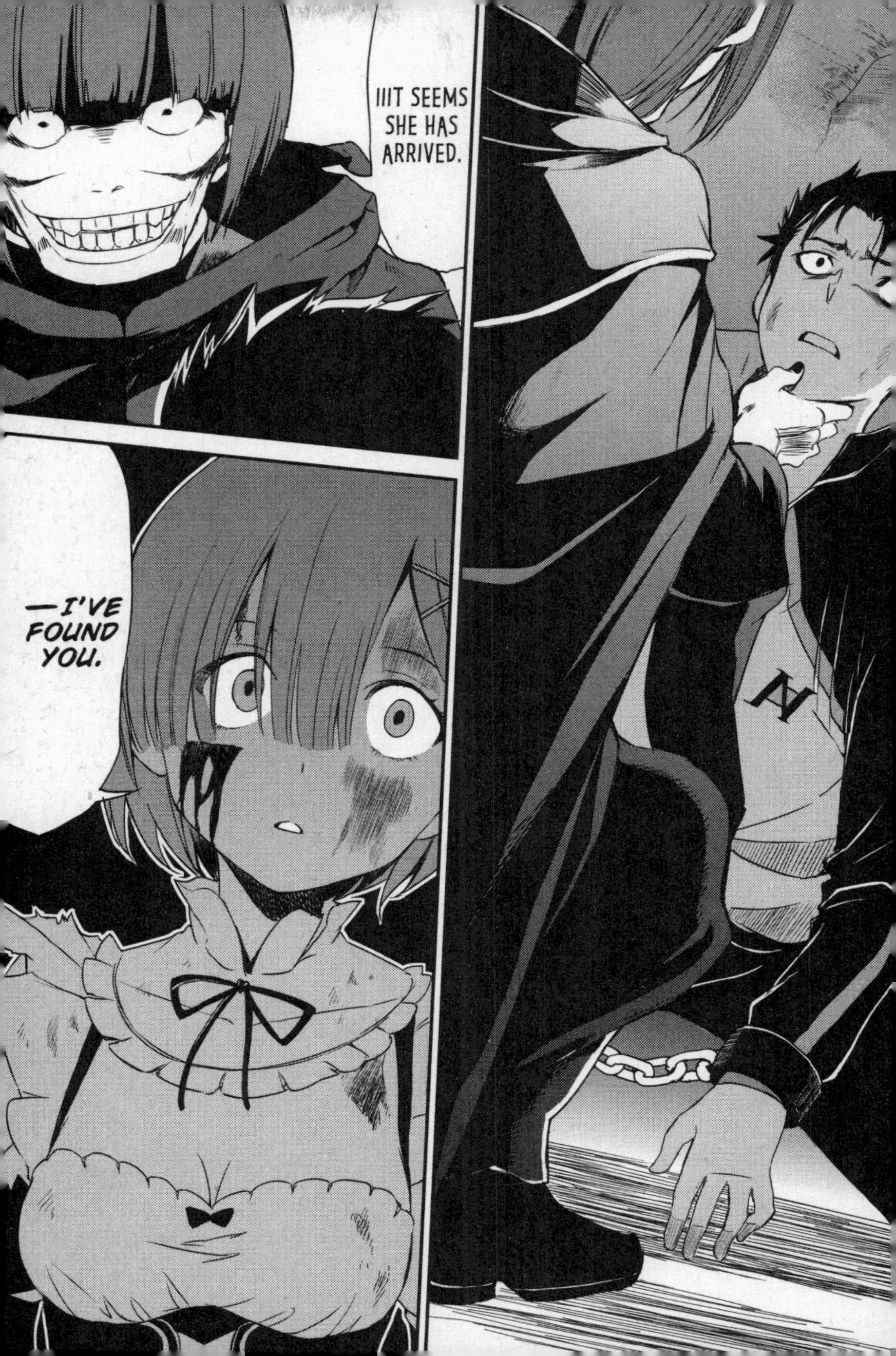
IIIT SEEMS SHE HAS ARRIVED.
—I'VE FOUND YOU.

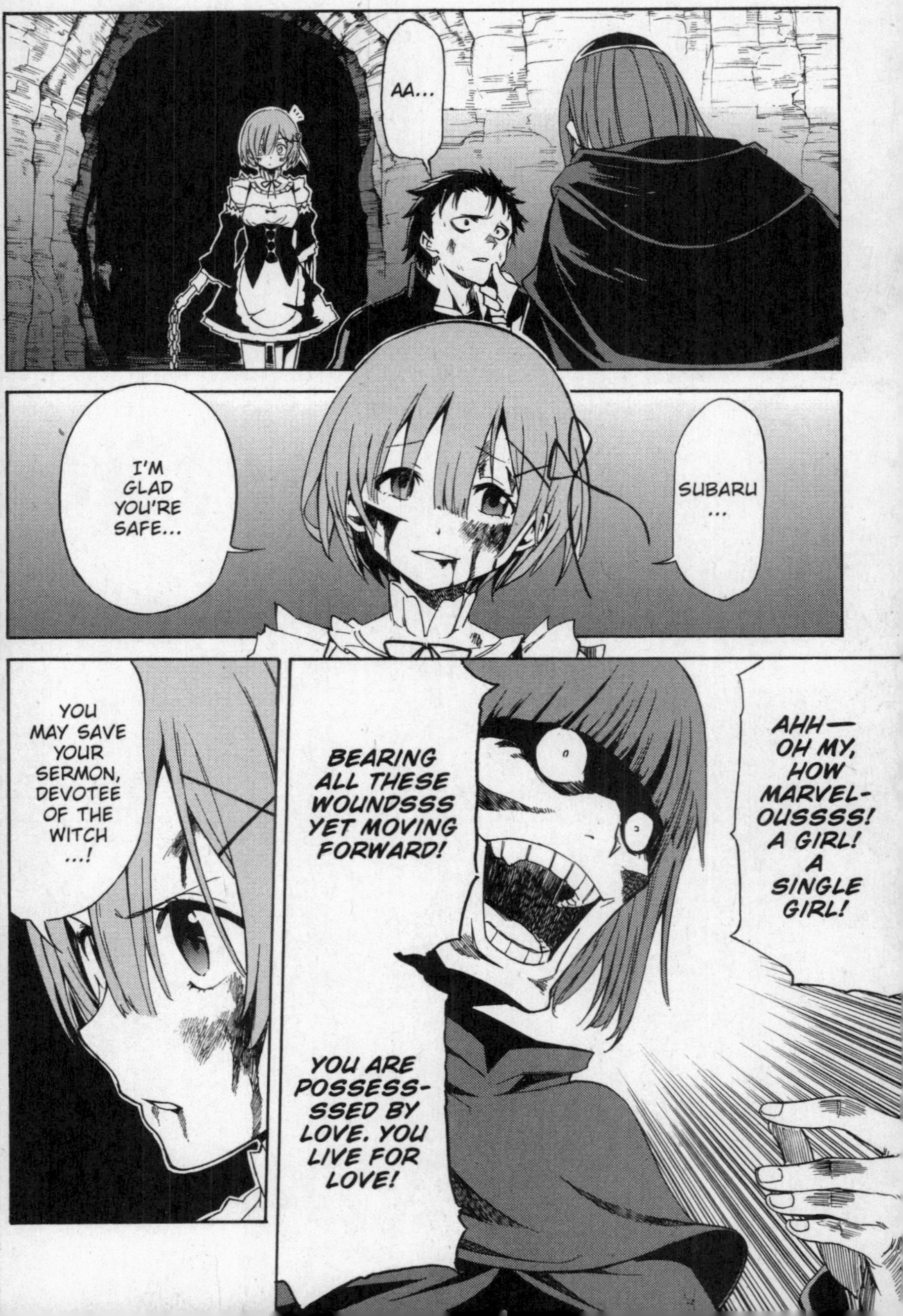
AA...
SUBARU ...
I'M GLAD YOU'RE SAFE...
AHH— OH MY, HOW MARVEL-OUSSSS! A GIRL! A SINGLE GIRL!
BEARING ALL THESE WOUNDSSS YET MOVING FORWARD!
YOU ARE POSSESS-SSED BY LOVE. YOU LIVE FOR LOVE!
YOU MAY SAVE YOUR SERMON, DEVOTEE OF THE WITCH ...!

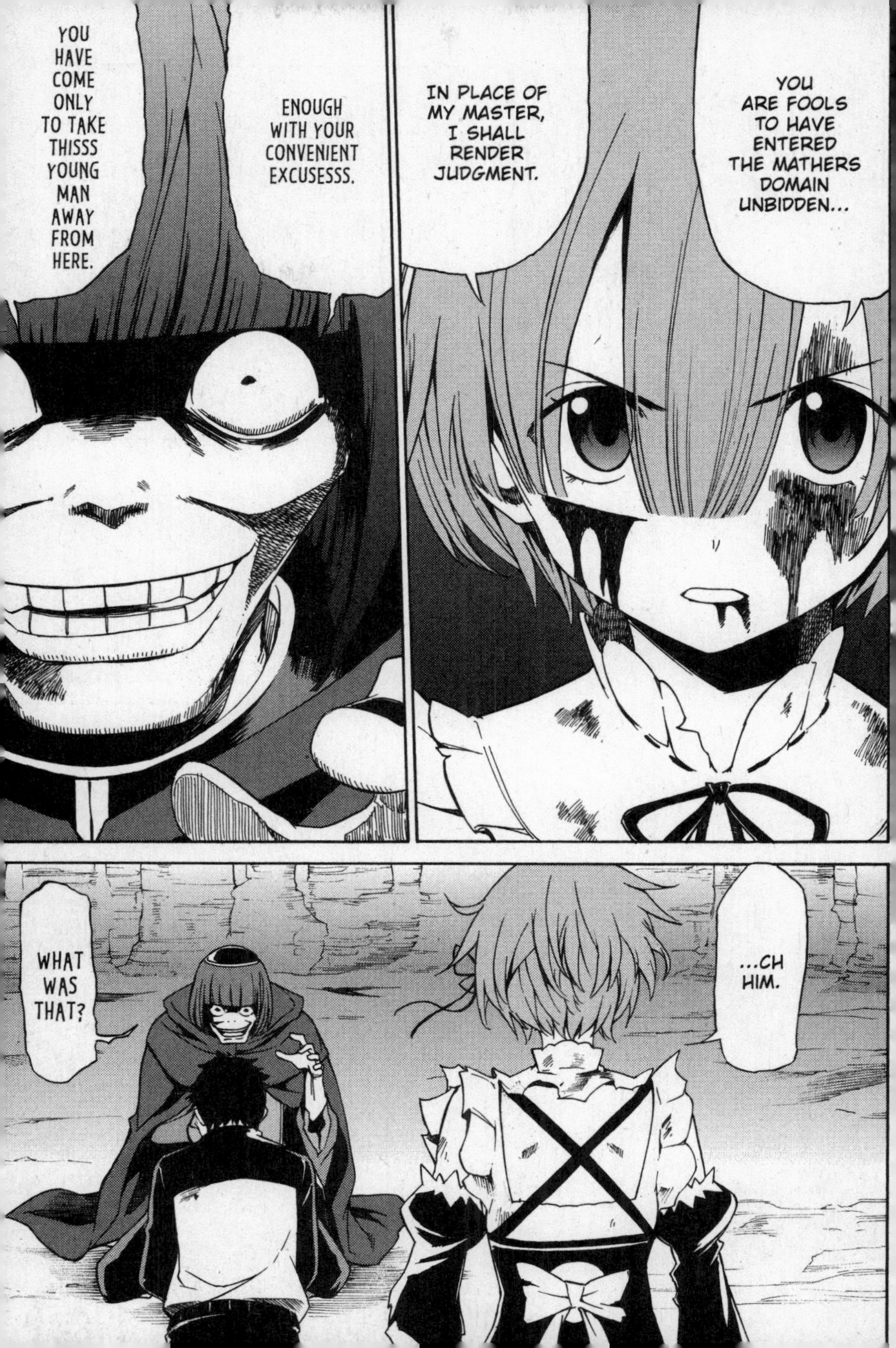
YOU ARE FOOLS TO HAVE ENTERED THE MATHERS DOMAIN UNBIDDEN...
IN PLACE OF MY MASTER, I SHALL RENDER JUDGMENT.
ENOUGH WITH YOUR CONVENIENT EXCUSESSS.
YOU HAVE COME ONLY TO TAKE THISSS YOUNG MAN AWAY FROM HERE.
...CH HIM.
WHAT WAS THAT?

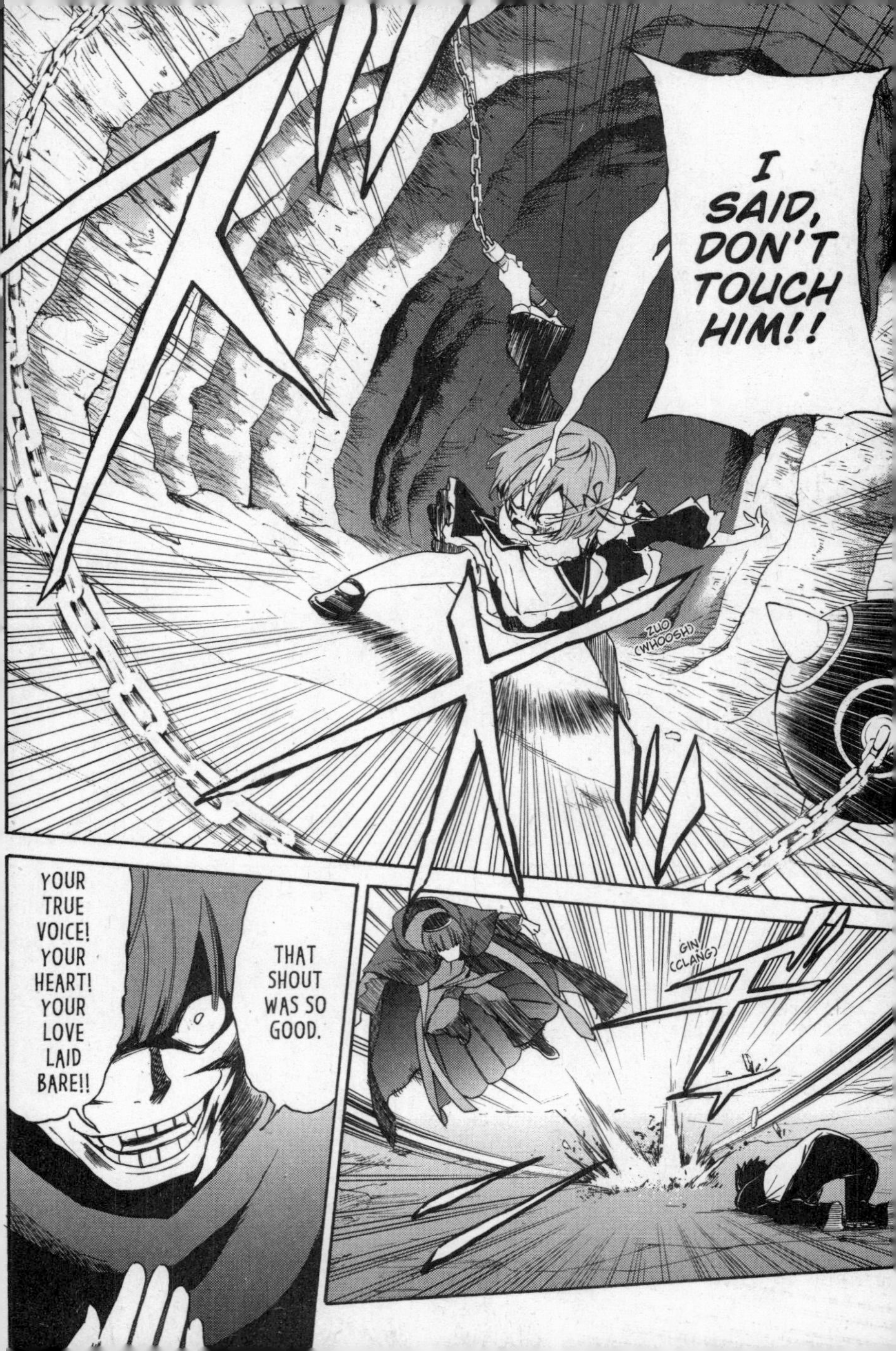
I SAID, DON'T TOUCH HIM!!
ZUO (WHOOSH)
GIN (CLANG)
THAT SHOUT WAS SO GOOD.
YOUR TRUE VOICE! YOUR HEART! YOUR LOVE LAID BARE!!

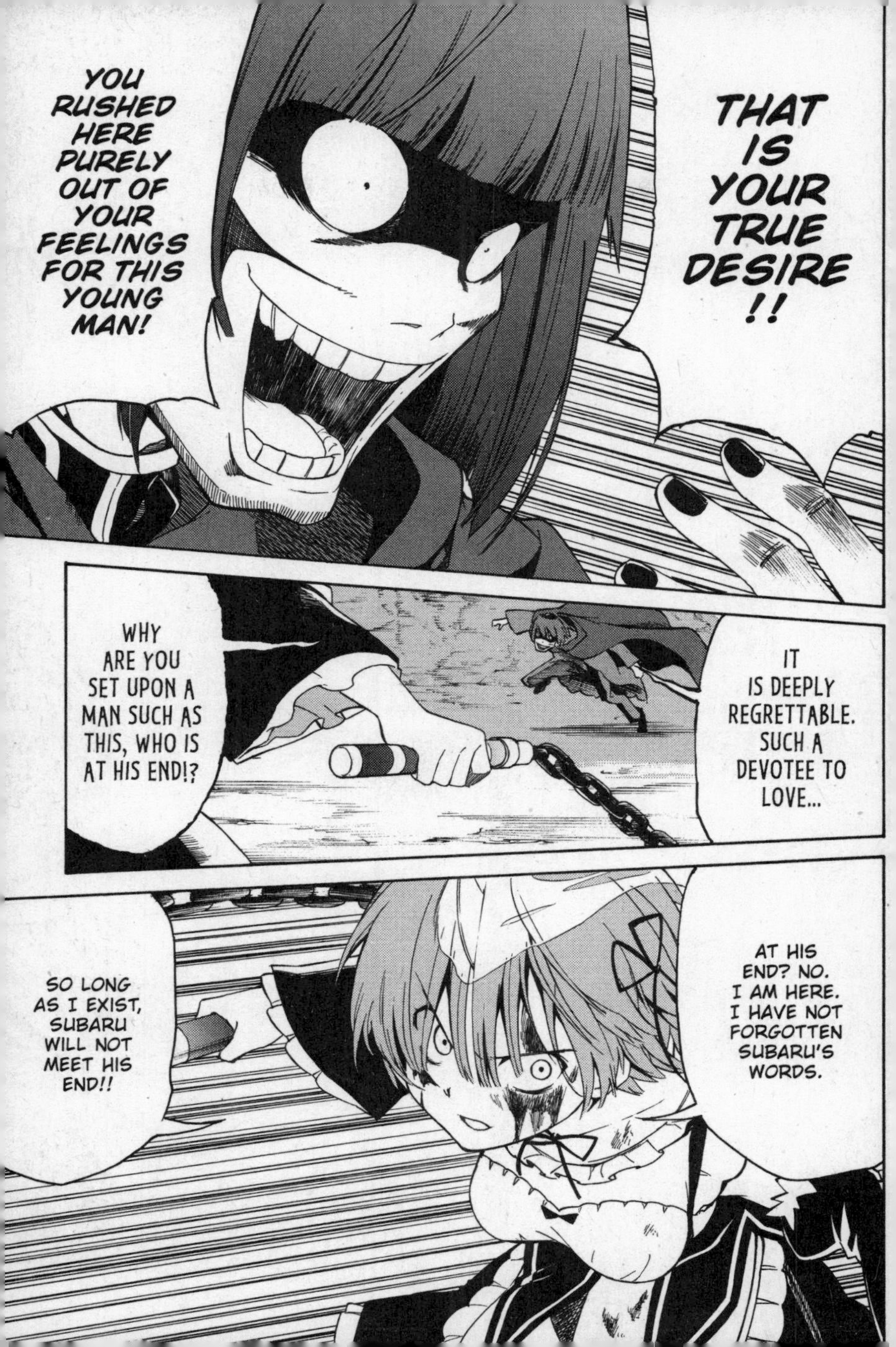
THAT IS YOUR TRUE DESIRE!!
YOU RUSHED HERE PURELY OUT OF YOUR FEELINGS FOR THIS YOUNG MAN!
IT IS DEEPLY REGRETTABLE. SUCH A DEVOTEE TO LOVE...
WHY ARE YOU SET UPON A MAN SUCH AS THIS, WHO IS AT HIS END!?
AT HIS END? NO. I AM HERE. I HAVE NOT FORGOTTEN SUBARU'S WORDS.
SO LONG AS I EXIST, SUBARU WILL NOT MEET HIS END!!

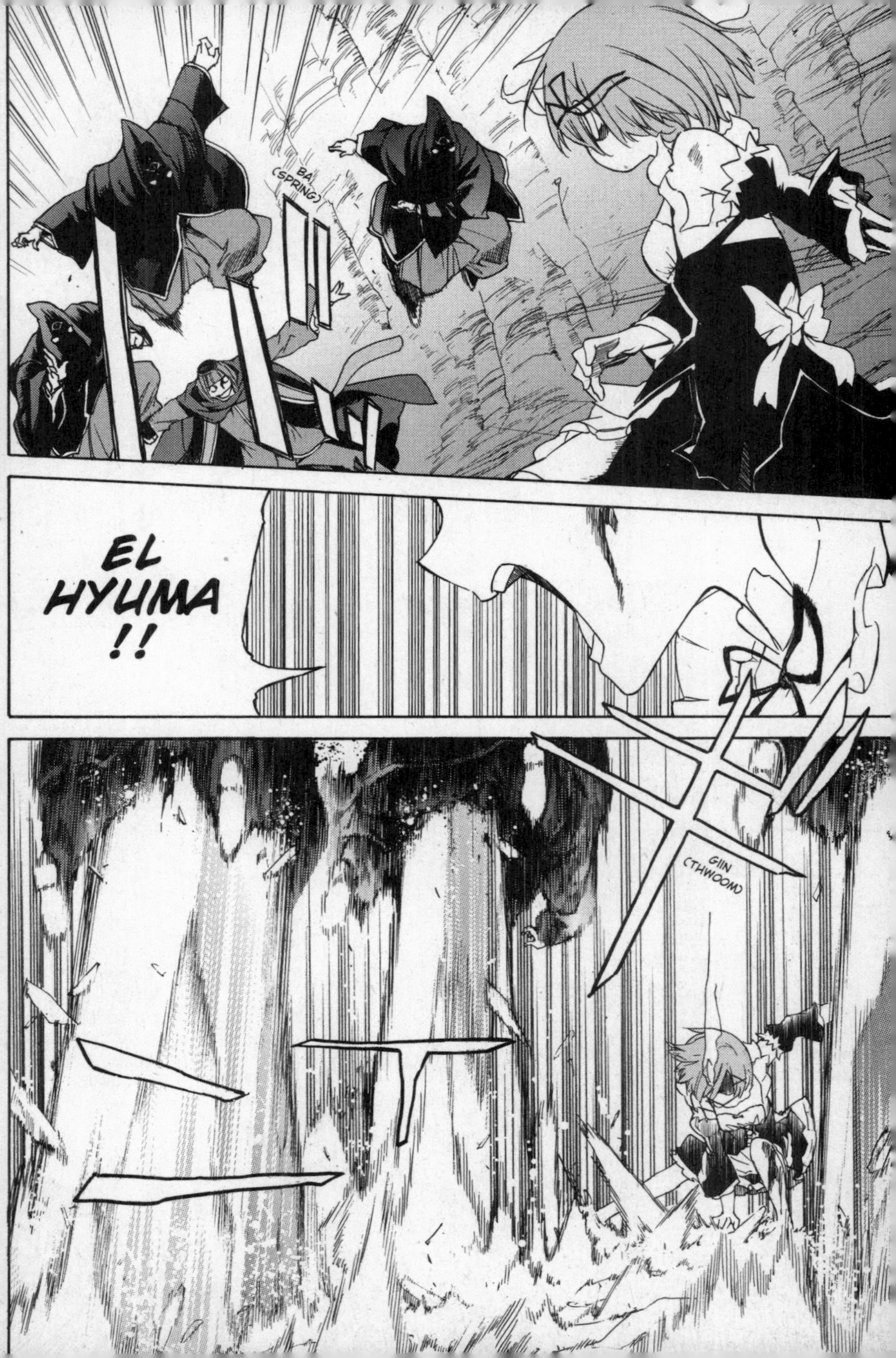
BA (SPRING)
EL HYUMA !!
GIIN (THWOOM)

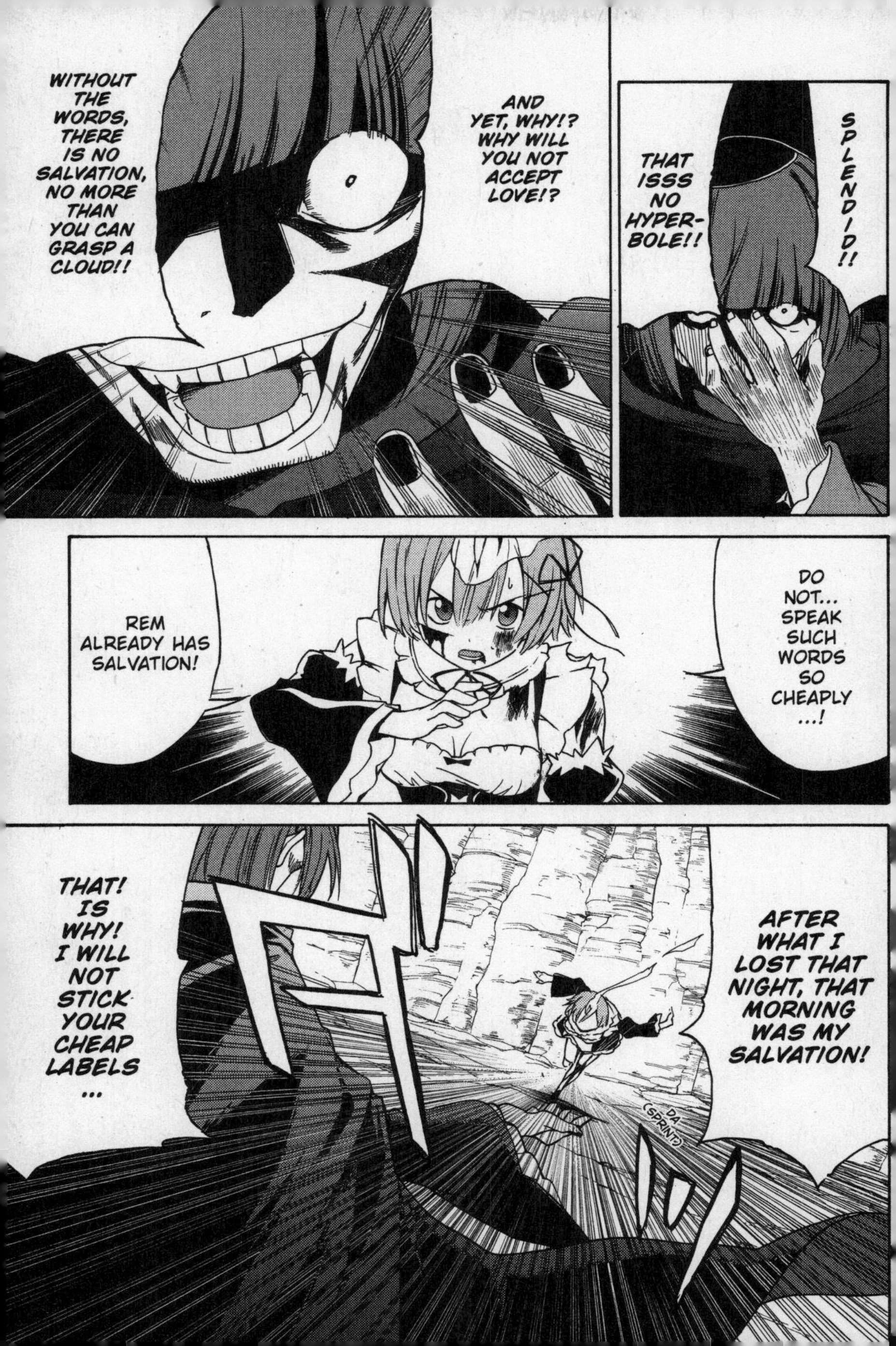
SPLENDID!!
THAT ISSS NO HYPERBOLE!!
AND YET, WHY!? WHY WILL YOU NOT ACCEPT LOVE!?
WITHOUT THE WORDS, THERE IS NO SALVATION, NO MORE THAN YOU CAN GRASP A CLOUD!!
DO NOT... SPEAK SUCH WORDS SO CHEAPLY ...!
REM ALREADY HAS SALVATION!
AFTER WHAT I LOST THAT NIGHT, THAT MORNING WAS MY SALVATION!
DA (SPRINT)
THAT! IS WHY! I WILL NOT STICK YOUR CHEAP LABELS ...

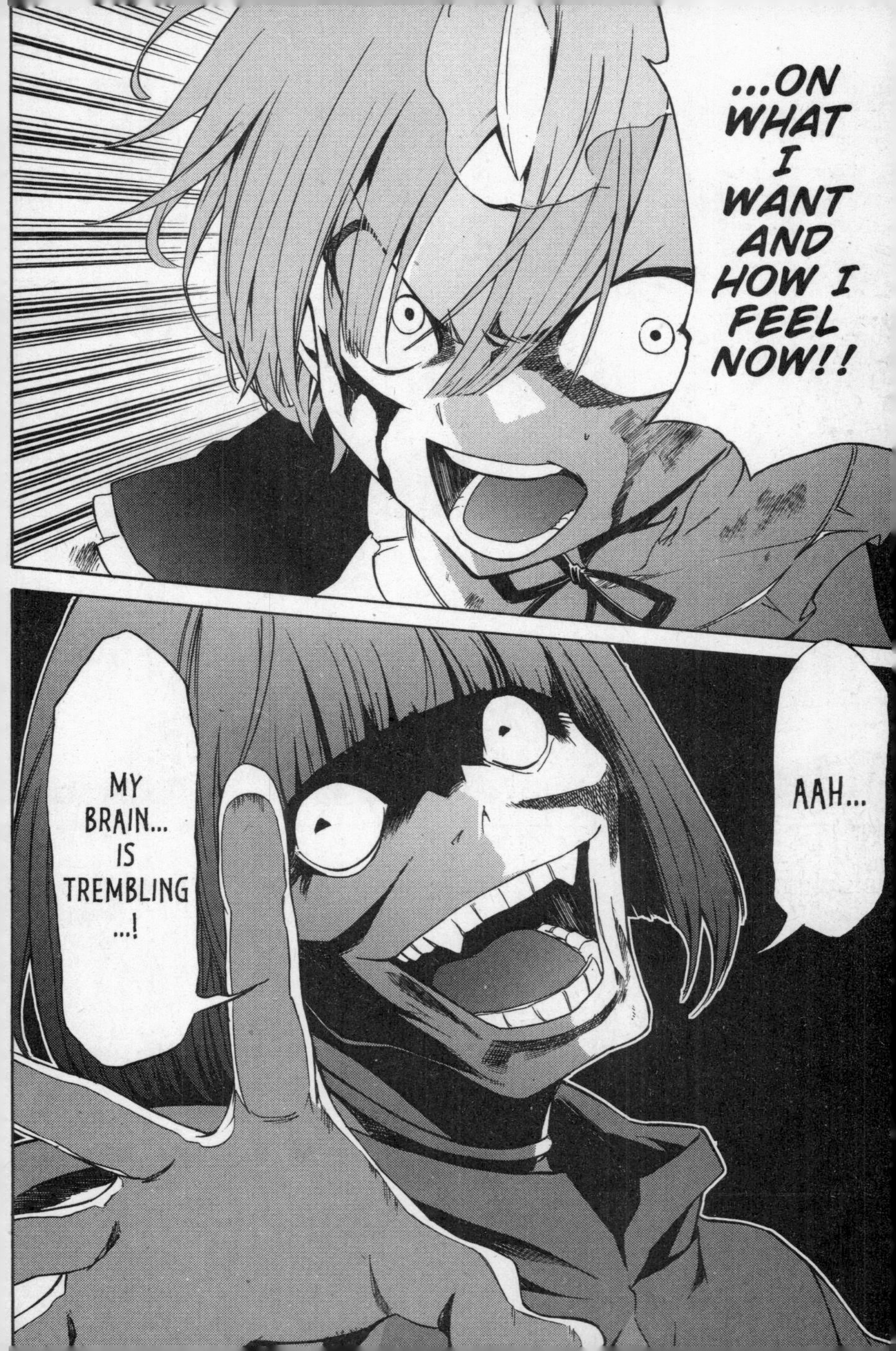
...ON WHAT I WANT AND HOW I FEEL NOW!!
AAH...
MY BRAIN... IS TREMBLING ...!

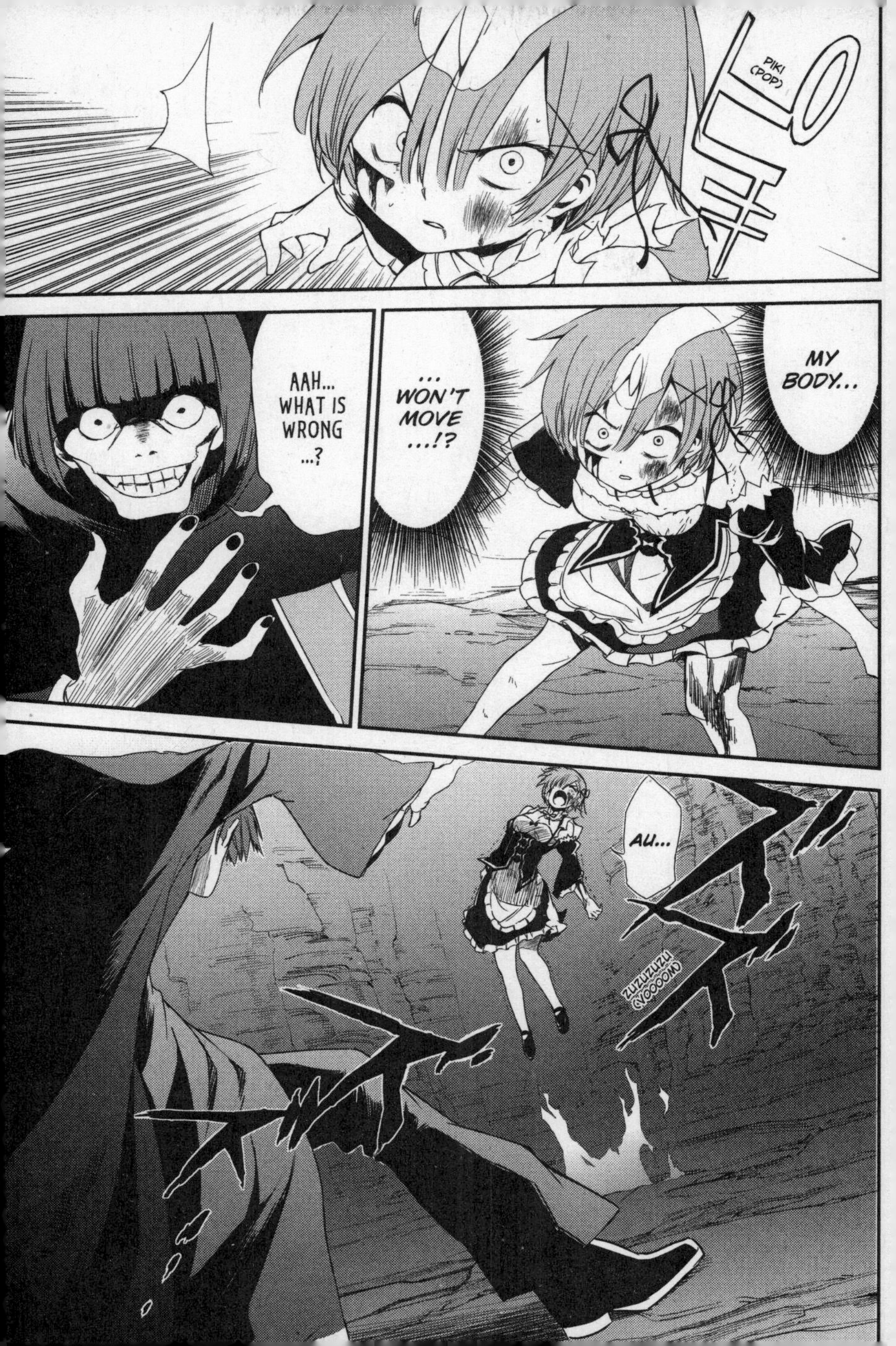
PIKI (POP)
MY BODY...
...WON'T MOVE ...!?
AAH... WHAT IS WRONG ...?
AU...
ZUZUZUZU (VOOOOM)

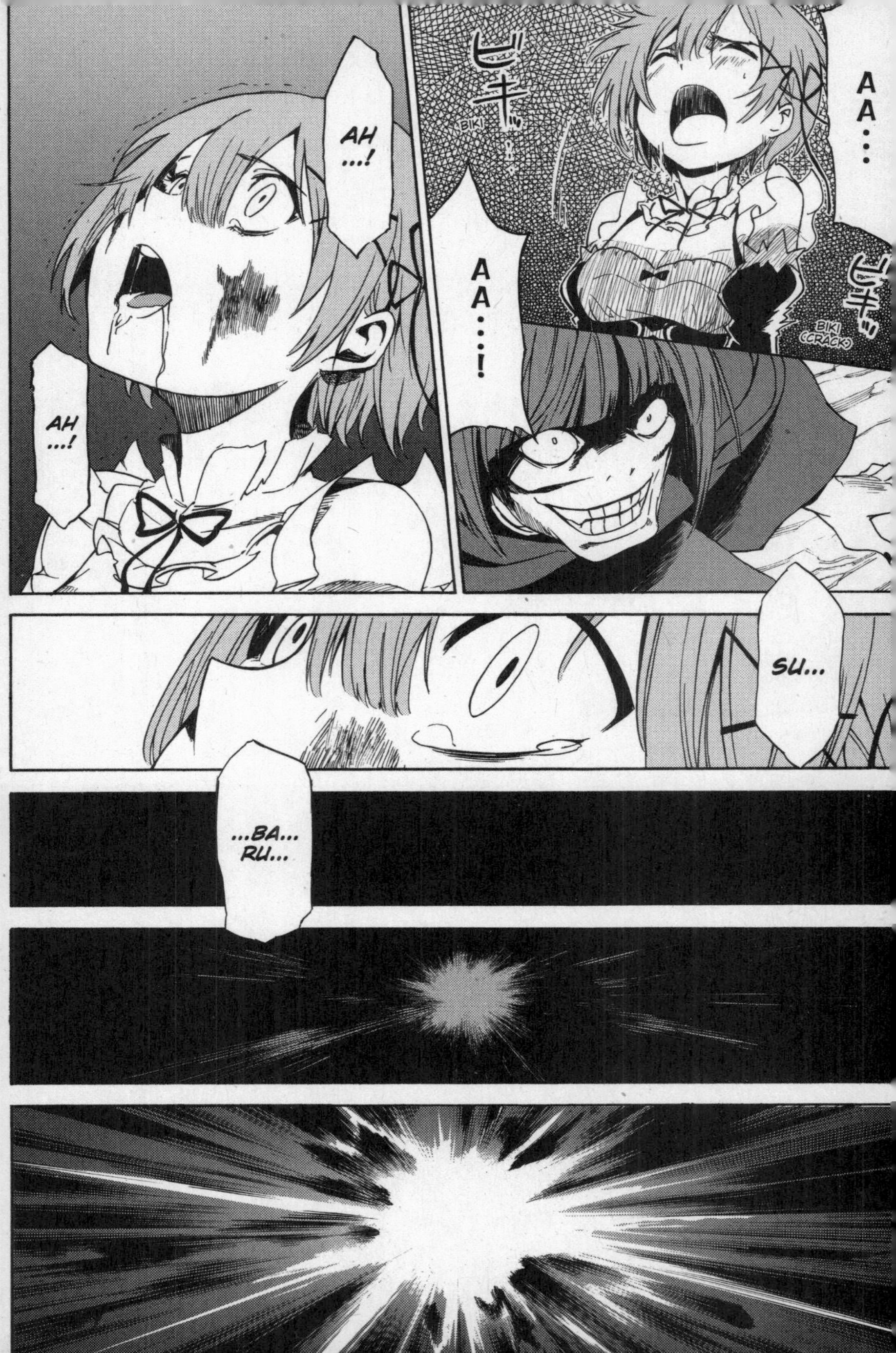
BIKI
AA...
BIKI (CRACK)
AA...!
AH ...!
AH ...!
SU...
...BA... RU...

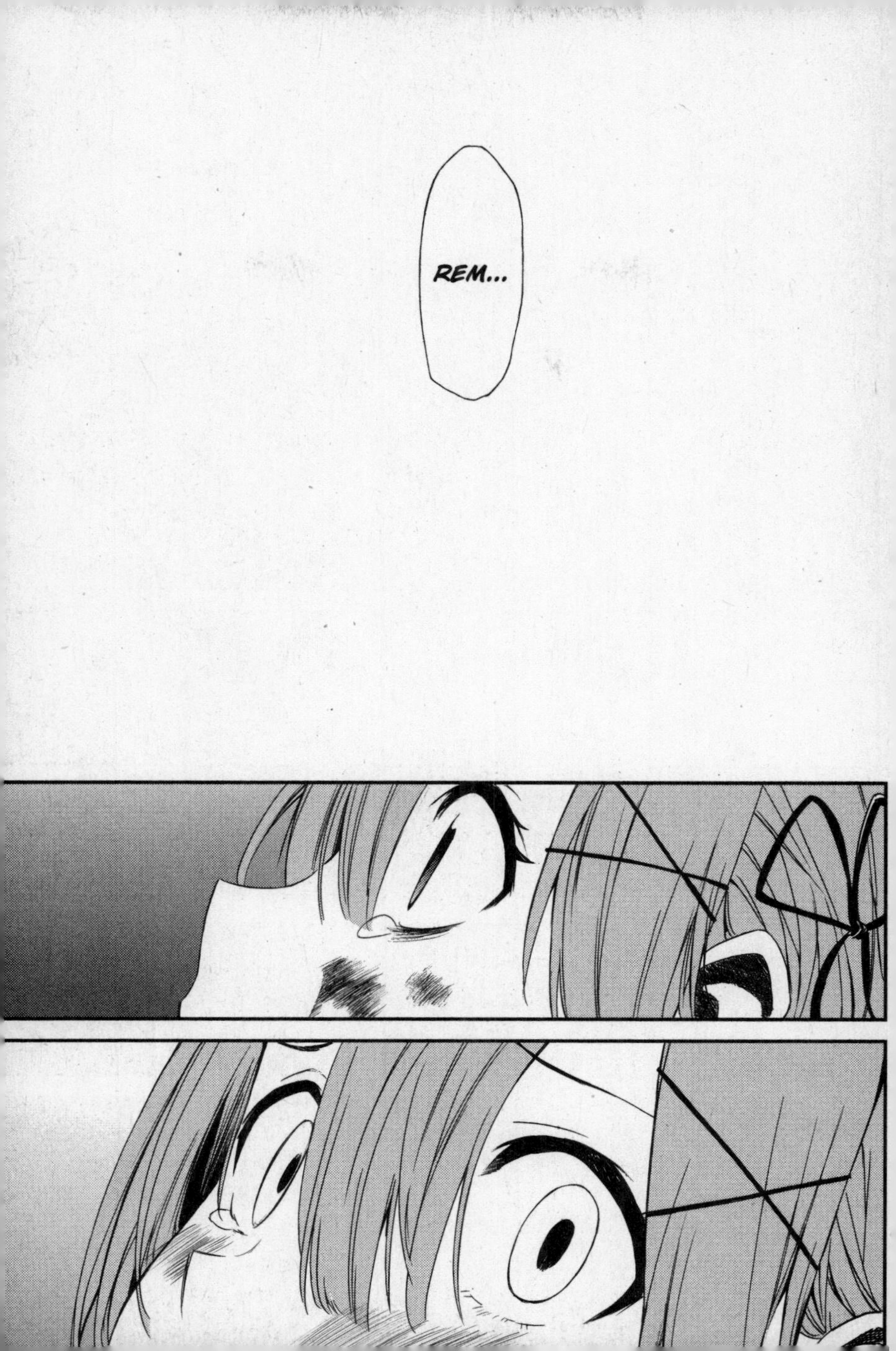
REM...

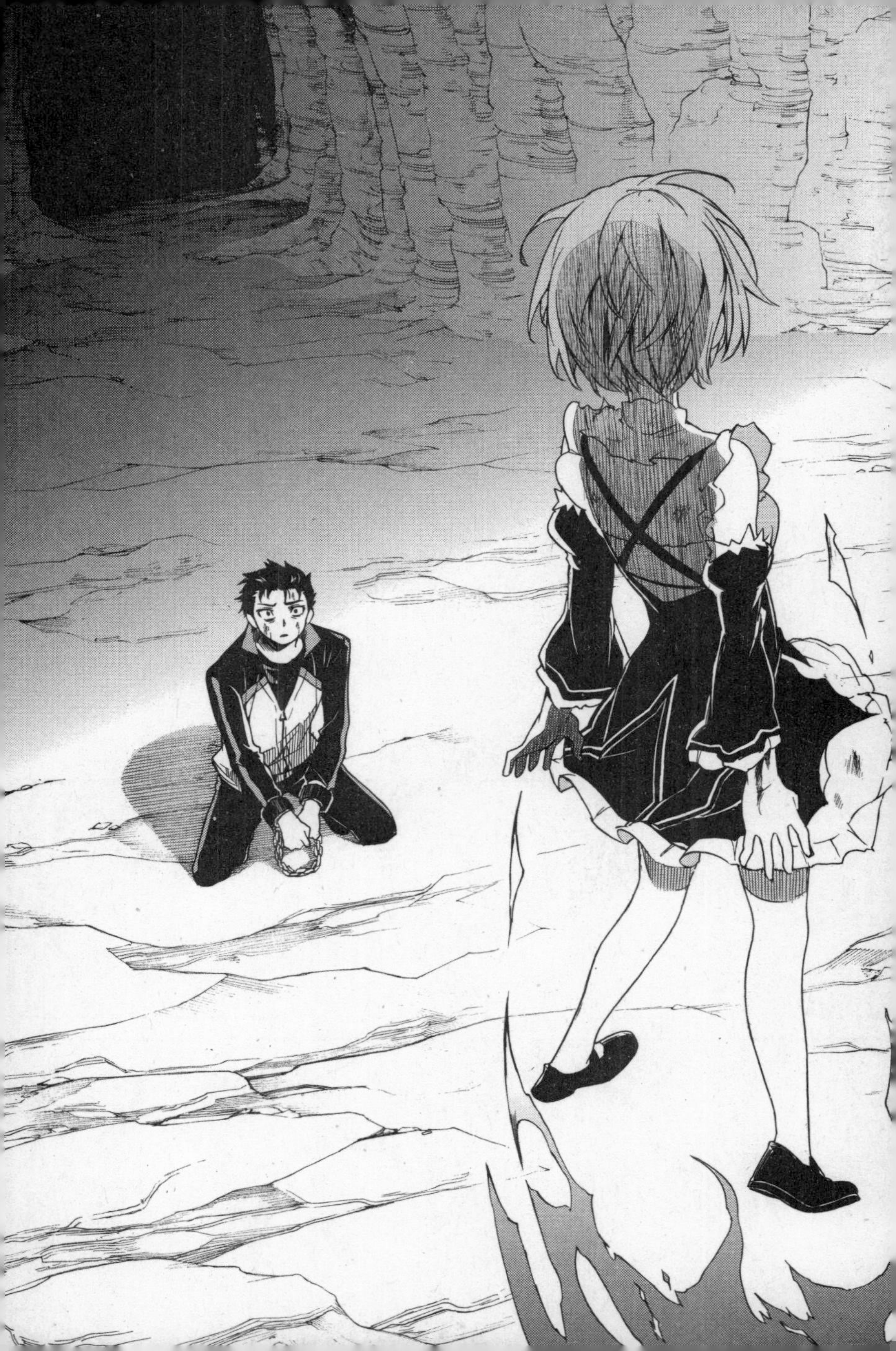

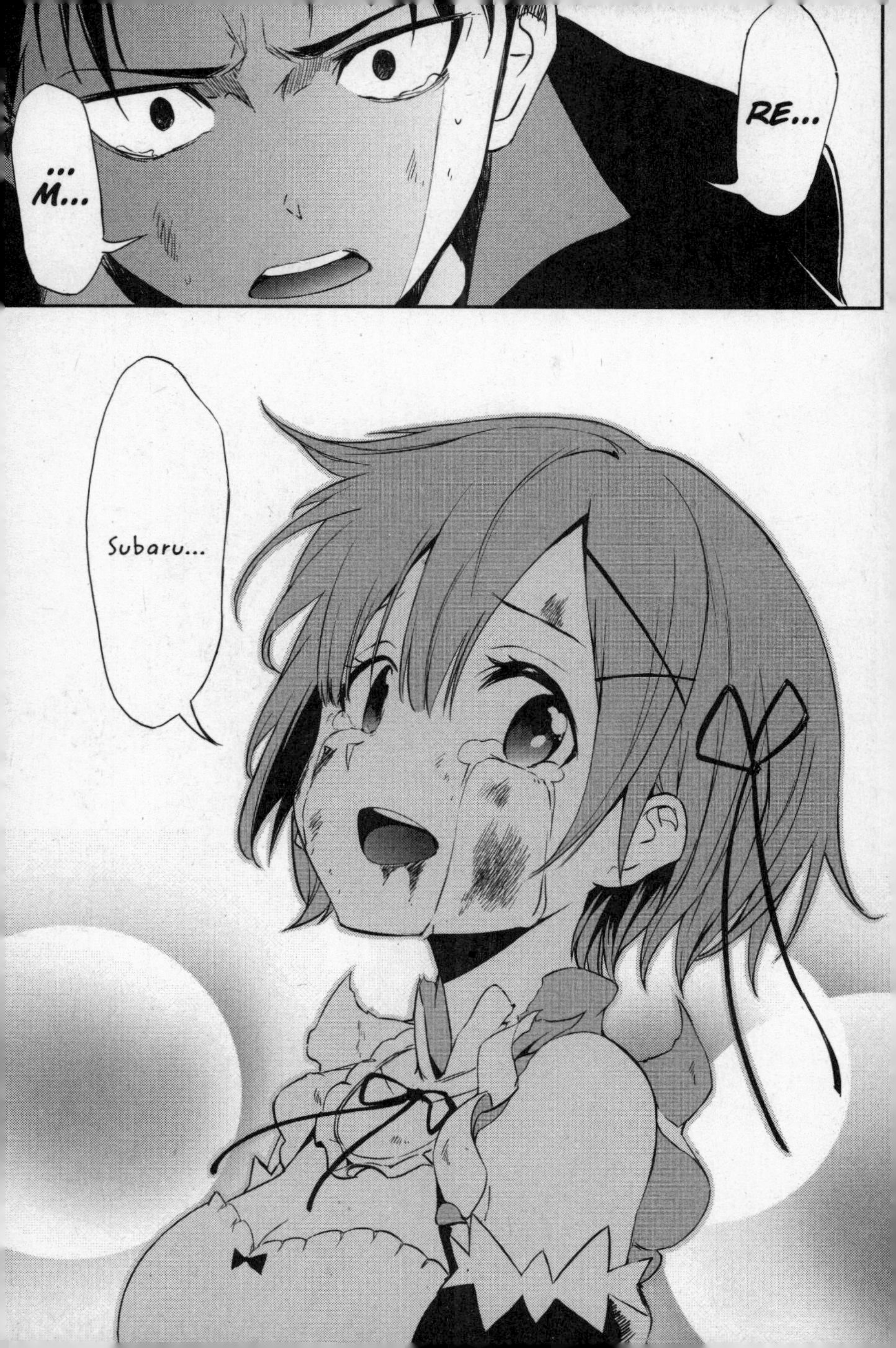
RE...
...M...
Subaru...

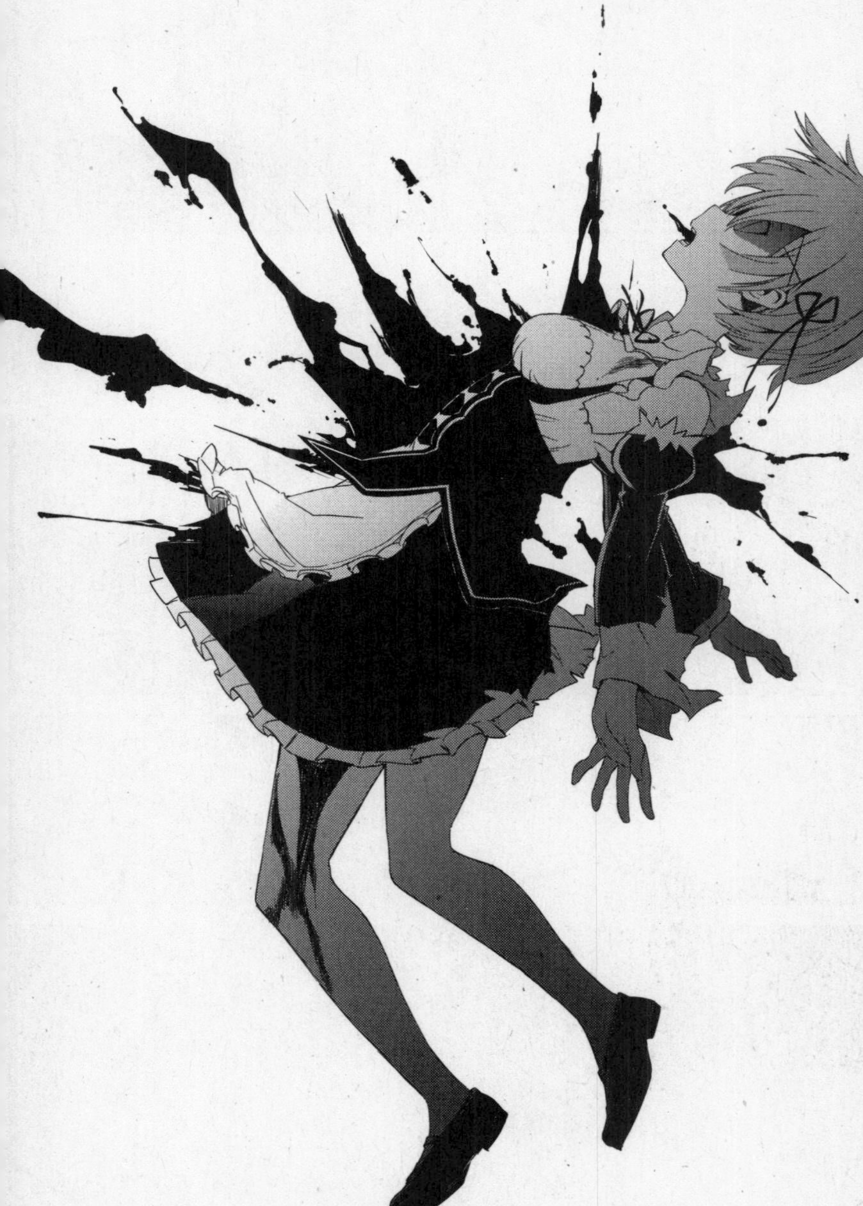

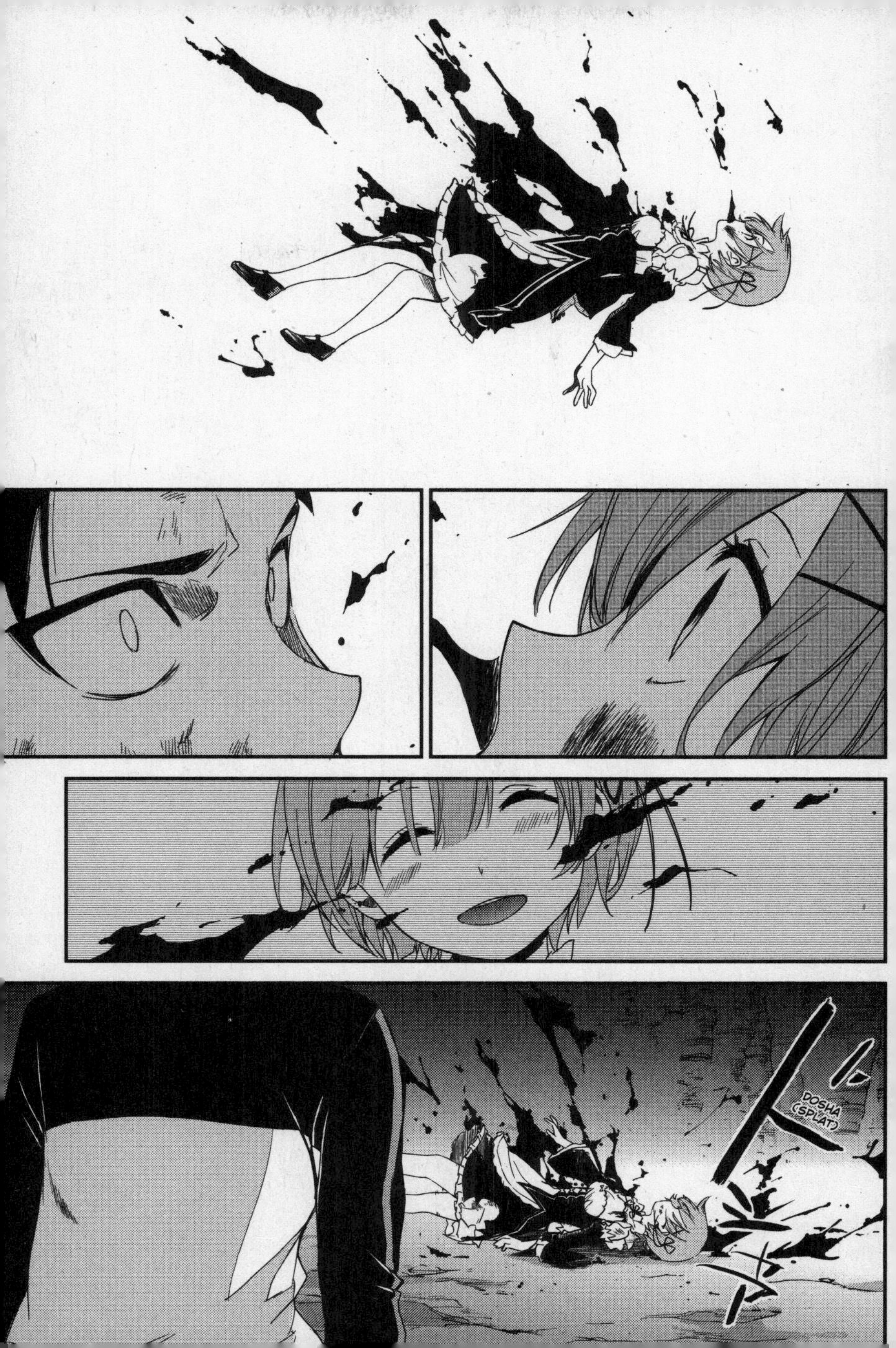
DOSHA
(SPLAT)

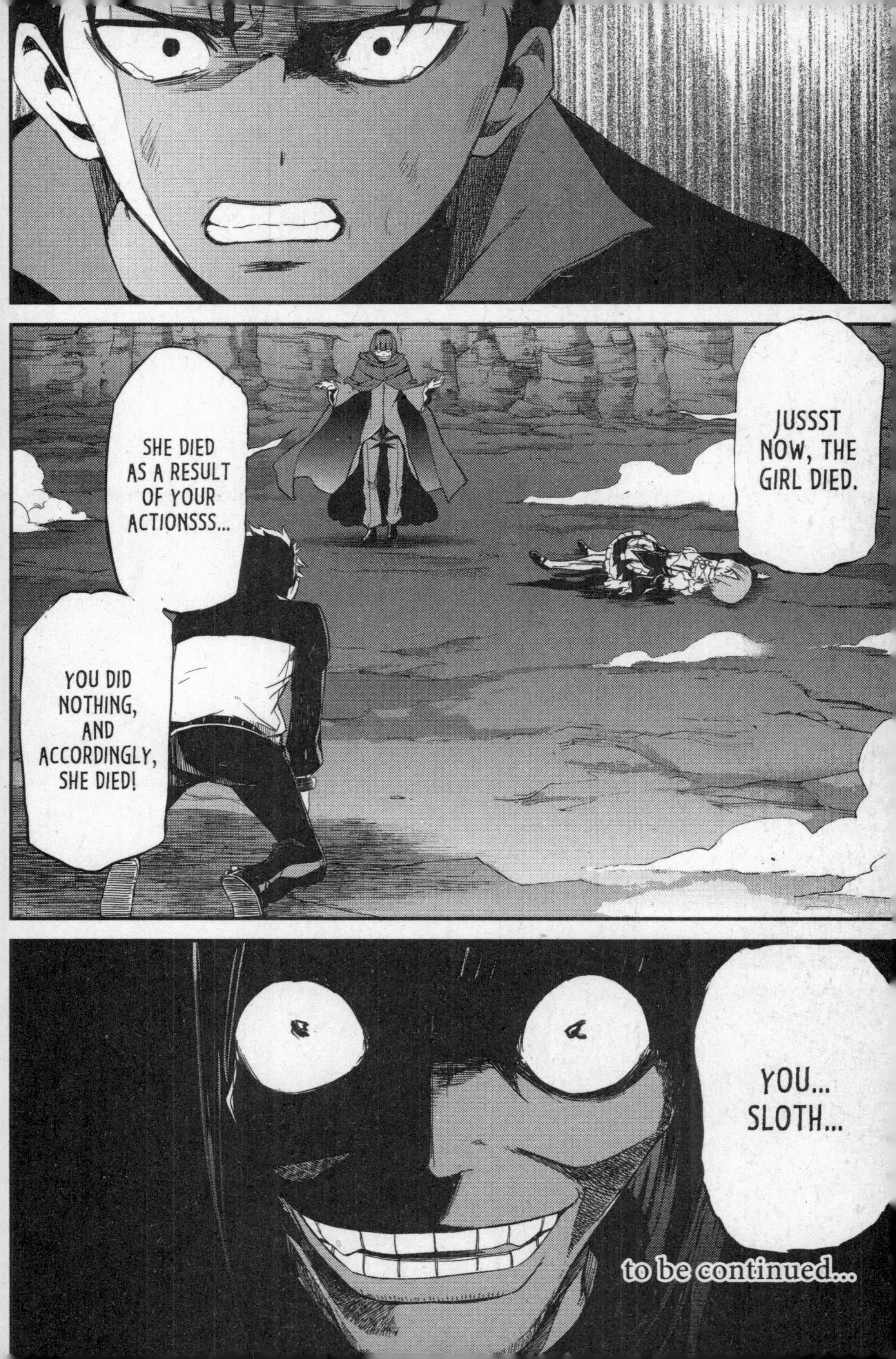
JUSSST NOW, THE GIRL DIED.
SHE DIED AS A RESULT OF YOUR ACTIONSSS...
YOU DID NOTHING, AND ACCORDINGLY, SHE DIED!
YOU... SLOTH...
to be continued...

Re:ZERO -Starting Life in Another World-

Truth of Zero

The only ability Subaru Natsuki gets when he's summoned to another world is time travel via his own death. But to save her, he'll die as many times as it takes.

The only ability Subaru Natsuki gets when he's
summoned to another world is time travel via his own
death. But to save her, he'll die as many times as it takes.

Truth of Zero

Re:ZERO -Starting
Life in Another World-

Illustration by Shinichirou Otsuka (Character Designer)

Re:ZERO -Starting Life in Another World-

Supporting Comments from the Author of the Original Work, Tappei Nagatsuki

Daichi Matsuse-sensei, congratulations on Volume 3 of this *Re:ZERO* comic going on sale. Thank you very much!

Many would call Chapter 3 and beyond the main act of *Re:ZERO*, but I believe the contents of this very third volume are why they call it as such. Seeing this volume made me think all over again of how truly grateful I am that Matsuse-sensei handled this story, one requiring drawings that are powerful in multiple senses.

Given the structure of the tale, I am grateful as always for how you included a bounty of scenes, including those that didn't make it into the anime, enriching the work beyond the boundaries of my own writing.

To be honest, this third chapter has many scenes that are difficult to watch and to draw. With considerable artistic strength, Matsuse-sensei depicted Subaru running amok, a very heroic Rem, so cool and so adorable...and the same goes for when he appeared on the stage.

With Subaru's "enemy" emerging and much hardship yet awaiting him, *Re:ZERO* heads toward the "main act" of the main act, and as a reader, I will enjoy Matsuse-sensei's artistic strength even more!

Let's all enjoy Matsuse-sensei's version of life in another world in the "main act" that began with this third volume!

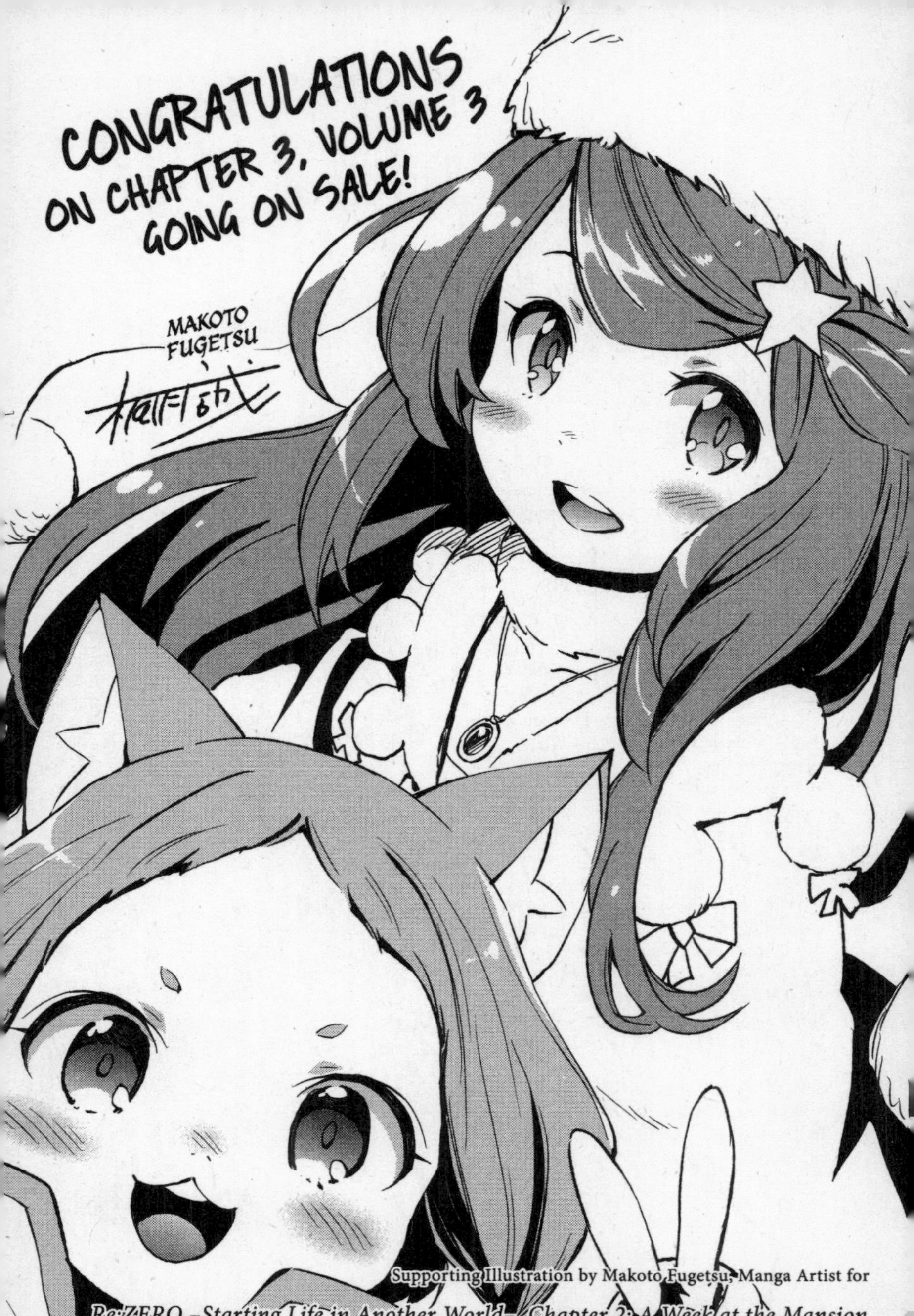
CONGRATULATIONS ON CHAPTER 3, VOLUME 3 GOING ON SALE!
MAKOTO FUGETSU

Supporting Illustration by Makoto Fugetsu, Manga Artist for

Re:ZERO -Starting Life in Another World-, Chapter 2: A Week at the Mansion

Re:ZERO -Starting Life in Another World-
Chapter 3: Truth of Zero

Artist Comments

AFTERWORD

FINALLY, THE COMIC VERSION OF THE THIRD CHAPTER HAS COME THIS FAR. FOR SUBARU, THIS IS A SERIES OF HARDSHIPS, BUT I'M SURE HE'LL OVERCOME THEM!
TO ALL OF YOU READERS WHO HAVE READ THIS FAR: THANK YOU VERY MUCH.

WELL THEN, SEE YOU NEXT VOLUME!

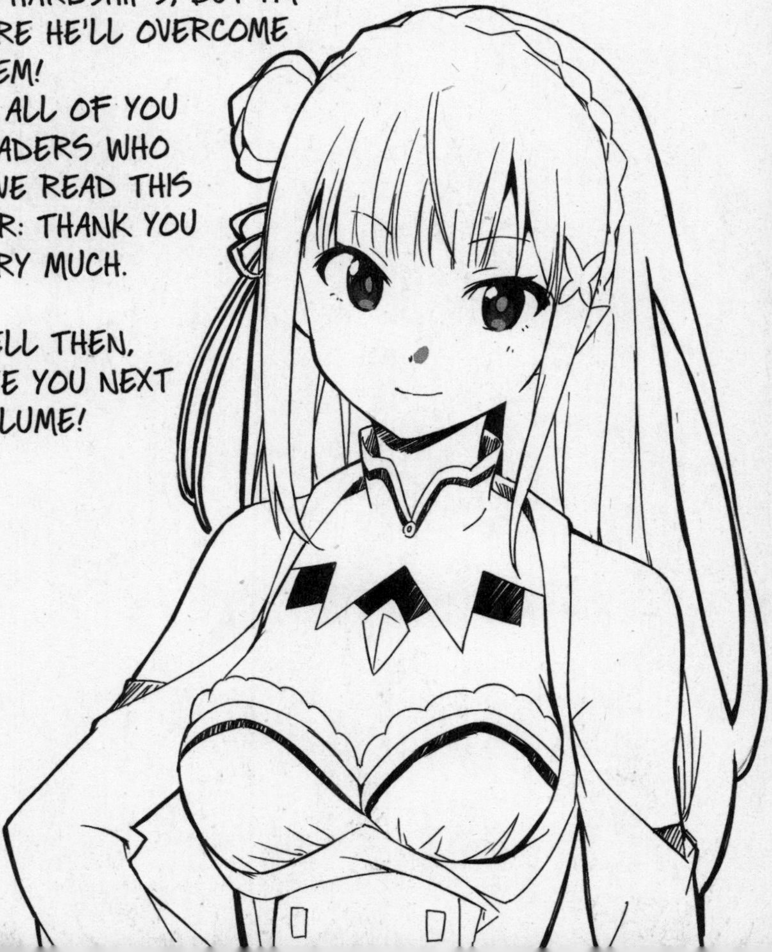

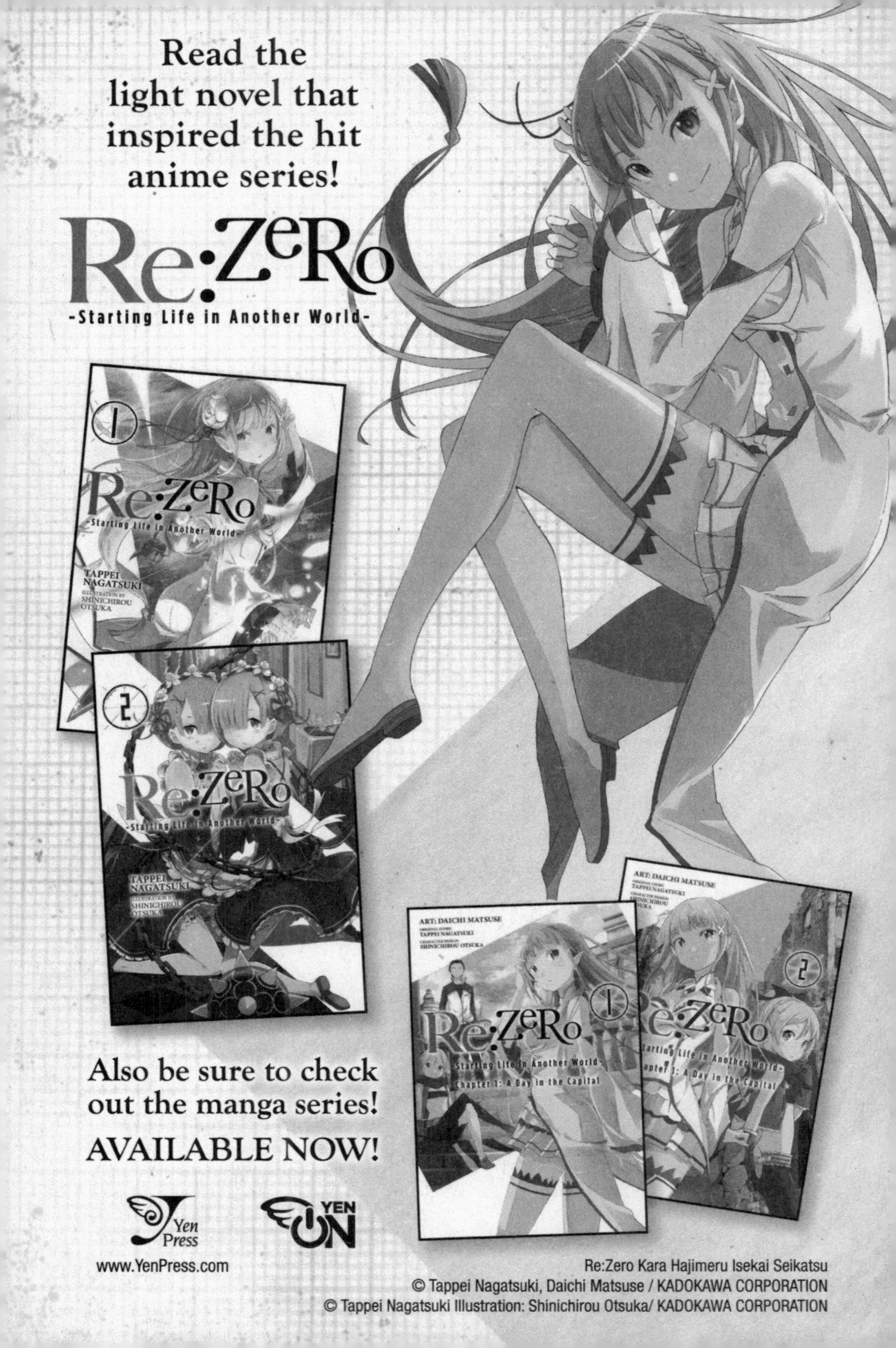
Read the light novel that inspired the hit anime series!
Re:ZeRo
-Starting Life in Another World-
Also be sure to check out the manga series!
AVAILABLE NOW!
Yen Press
YEN ON
www.YenPress.com
Re:Zero Kara Hajimeru Isekai Seikatsu
© Tappei Nagatsuki, Daichi Matsuse / KADOKAWA CORPORATION
© Tappei Nagatsuki Illustration: Shinichirou Otsuka/ KADOKAWA CORPORATION

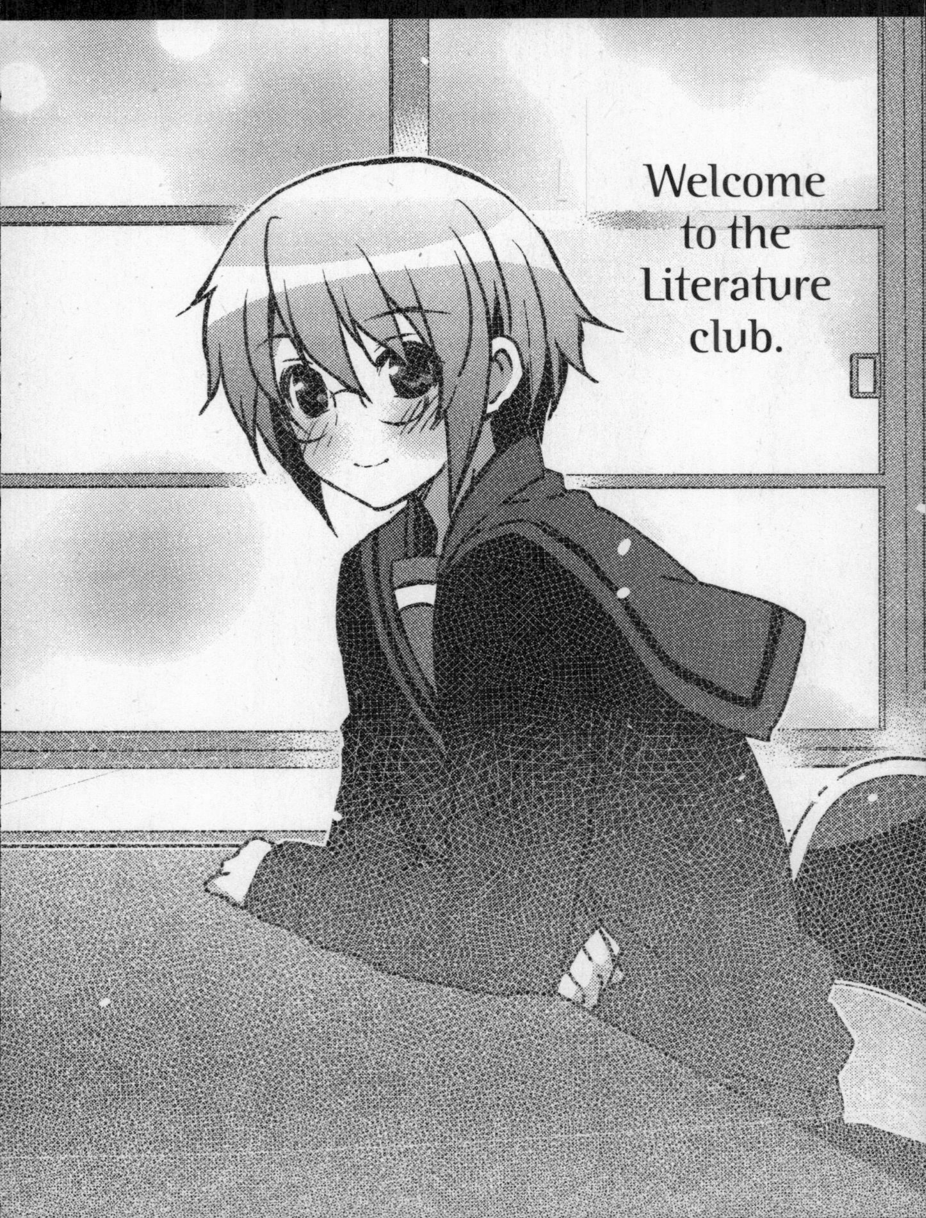
Welcome to the Literature club.

THE BEAT OF THE
SOUL CONTINUES...

VOL. 1 - 5 AVAILABLE NOW!

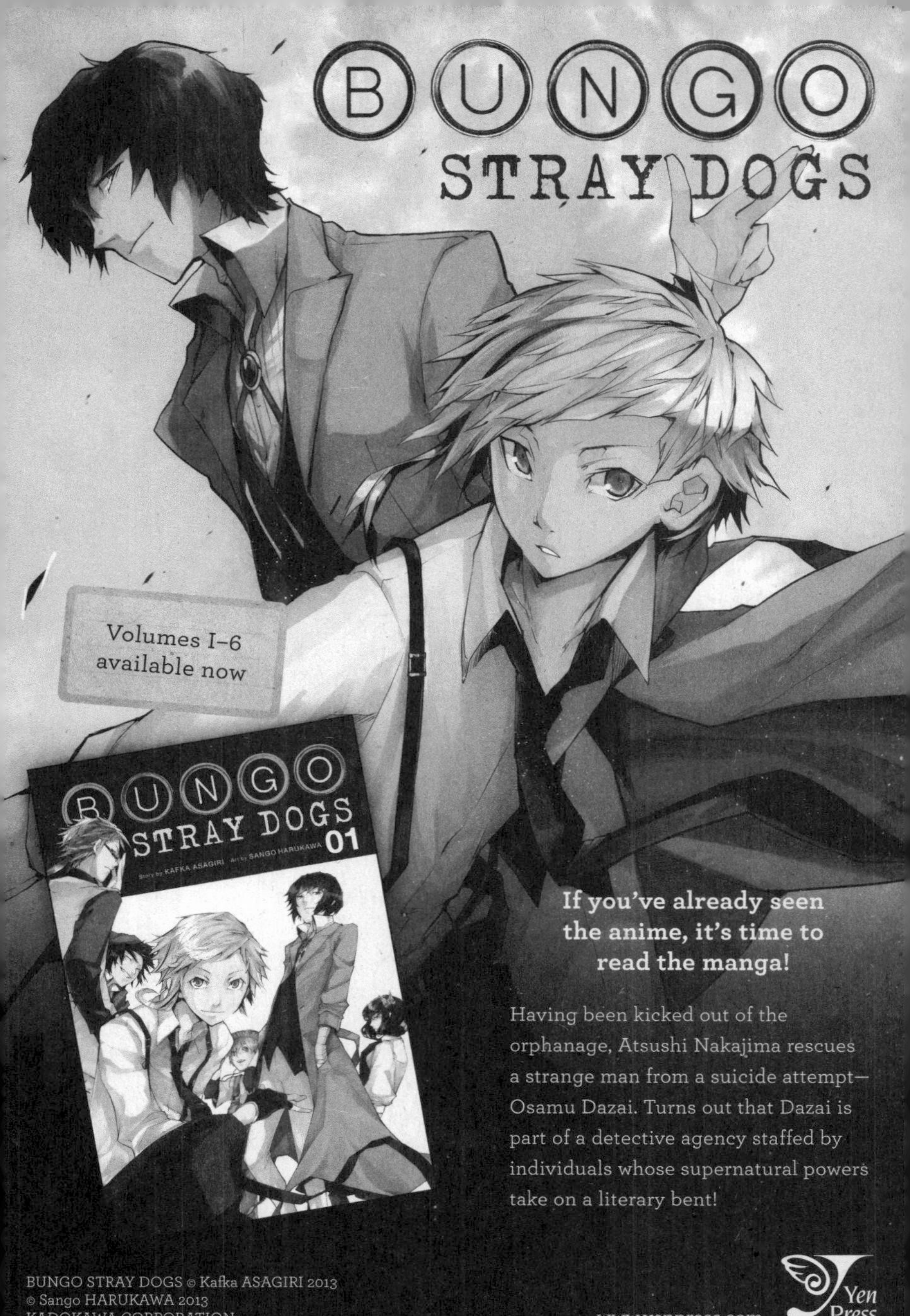

BUNGO STRAY DOGS
Volumes 1–6 available now
BUNGO STRAY DOGS 01
If you've already seen the anime, it's time to read the manga!
Having been kicked out of the orphanage, Atsushi Nakajima rescues a strange man from a suicide attempt—Osamu Dazai. Turns out that Dazai is part of a detective agency staffed by individuals whose supernatural powers take on a literary bent!
BUNGO STRAY DOGS © Kafka ASAGIRI 2013
© Sango HARUKAWA 2013
KADOKAWA CORPORATION
www.yenpress.com
Yen Press

RE:ZERO -STARTING LIFE IN ANOTHER WORLD- ③

Chapter 3: Truth of Zero

Art: **Daichi Matsuse**
Original Story: **Tappei Nagatsuki**
Character Design: **Shinichirou Otsuka**

Translation: Jeremiah Bourque
Lettering: Anthony Quintessenza

RE:ZERO KARA HAJIMERU ISEKAI SEIKATSU DAISANSHO
Truth of Zero Vol. 3
© Daichi Matsuse 2016
© Tappei Nagatsuki 2016
Licensed by KADOKAWA CORPORATION
First published in Japan in 2016 by KADOKAWA CORPORATION, Tokyo. English translation rights arranged with KADOKAWA CORPORATION, Tokyo through TUTTLE-MORI AGENCY, Inc.

Yen Press
1290 Avenue of the Americas
New York, NY 10104

Visit us at yenpress.com
facebook.com/yenpress
twitter.com/yenpress
yenpress.tumblr.com
instagram.com/yenpress

First Yen Press Edition: April 2018

Yen Press is an imprint of Yen Press, LLC.
The Yen Press name and logo are trademarks of Yen Press, LLC.

Library of Congress Control Number: 2016936537

ISBNs: 978-0-316-55951-5 (paperback)
978-0-316-55952-2 (ebook)

10 9 8 7 6 5 4 3 2 1

WOR

Printed in the United States of America